# AGAINST PURITY

# AGAINST PURITY

## LIVING ETHICALLY IN COMPROMISED TIMES

ALEXIS SHOTWELL

UNIVERSITY OF MINNESOTA PRESS

MINNEAPOLIS • LONDON

Chapter 1 was previously published as "Unforgetting as a Collective Tactic," in
*White Self-Criticality beyond Anti-racism: How Does It Feel to Be a White Problem?*,
ed. George Yancy, 57–68 (Lanham, Md.: Lexington Books, 2014).

Chapter 2 was previously published as "'Women Don't Get AIDS,
They Just Die From It': Memory, Classification, and the Campaign to Change
the Definition of AIDS," in *Hypatia* 29, no. 2 (Spring 2014): 509–25.

Chapter 5 was previously published as "Open Normativities: Gender, Disability, and
Collective Political Change," in *Signs: Journal of Women in Culture and Society* 37, no. 4
(2012): 989–1014. Copyright 2012 by the University of Chicago. All rights reserved.

Published by the University of Minnesota Press
111 Third Avenue South, Suite 290
Minneapolis, MN 55401-2520
http://www.upress.umn.edu

Printed in the United States of America on acid-free paper

The University of Minnesota is an equal-opportunity educator and employer.

22 21 20 19 18 17 16          10 9 8 7 6 5 4 3 2 1

Library of Congress Cataloging-in-Publication Data

Names: Shotwell, Alexis, author.
Title: Against purity : living ethically in compromised times / Alexis Shotwell.
Description: Minneapolis : University of Minnesota Press, 2016. |
Includes bibliographical references and index.
Identifiers: LCCN 2016008376 (print) | ISBN 978-0-8166-9862-2 (hc) |
ISBN 978-0-8166-9864-6 (pb)
Subjects: LCSH: Purity (Ethics) | Purity (Philosophy) | Conduct of life. |
Civilization, Modern—21st century.
Classification: LCC BJ1533.P97 S56 2016 (print) | DDC 170—dc23
LC record available at https://lccn.loc.gov/2016008376

# Contents

# Complexity and Complicity
## An Introduction to Constitutive Impurity

O n the plane back from a conference titled "Anthropocene: Arts of Living on a Damaged Planet"—a generative conference at my alma mater
organized by Anna Tsing, a conference that made me remember why I love
going to conferences—I washed my hands in the tiny, smelly, normal airplane bathroom. Then I took a picture of the soap, which was fancy soap for
an airplane bathroom: *philosophy* brand, part of its "pure grace" line. It narrated, all lowercase (lowercase font is to "remind us to live life with curiosity,
wisdom, and abundant joy," as their website notes): "philosophy: with clean
hands we find our grace. we realize the slate can be as clean as we allow it
to be." On the plane from San Francisco to Ottawa, using something like
5.8 tons of greenhouse gasses for my personal trip, which I had not carbon
offset, although the airline offered this option to me when I was buying my
ticket, I had been feeling bad about using a plastic cup to have some ginger
ale—but I had had some ginger ale because airline travel is irritating, flying
itself is so evil that what weight does a single plastic cup hold, and I wanted
some sugar and bubbles. I had been reflecting about what it meant to travel
across the continent to a state experiencing a profound drought, using fossil
fuels in order to talk with other scholars, many of whom had come from
further away—Europe and Australia in particular—about what it means to
inaugurate a term to name the time we are living in that identifies humans
as responsible for harmful planetary transformation partially through our
use of fossil fuels. I had doubts about what "clean hands" could mean in this
context, and also how long they'd last after I finished rinsing the pure grace
soap from my hands and touched literally anything.

There have been many conferences now about the Anthropocene—what it is, what it means to name it—and many more people writing and thinking about it. Mostly the people I've heard talking about the Anthropocene (or Capitalocene) are aiming to mobilize a transformation in our planetary political economy. Mostly, the markers used to measure this transformation measure the effects of human behavior on the world we live in, and often these effects are externalities to economic calculations, carried as body burdens by living creatures or experienced as the entangled effects that alter or kill beings and ecosystems. Coral reefs change and die in relation to acidifying oceans, soil carries loads of lead or heavy metals from mining or automobile exhaust, new forms of rock are made out of plastic, plastiglomerates (Corcoran, Moore, and Jazvac 2014), or we acquire the radioisotope signatures of past nuclear bomb use, and we might mark these as dividing lines marking the beginning of the age we're in. Simon Lewis and Mark Maslin suggest colonialism as an origin point, offering 1610 as a dividing line between the Holocene (the recent era that we may be leaving) and the Anthropocene. As Dana Luciano summarizes, that date

> was chosen because it was the lowest point in a decades-long decrease in atmospheric carbon dioxide, measurable by traces found in Artic ice cores. The change in the atmosphere, Lewis and Maslin deduced, was caused by the death of over 50 million indigenous residents of the Americas in the first century after European contact, the result of "exposure to diseases carried by Europeans, plus war, enslavement and famine." . . . Lewis and Maslin's proposal is compelling because it is, as far as I know, the first proposal for an Anthropocene "golden spike" to recognize genocide as part of the cause of epochal division. (Luciano 2015)

However we mark its start, thinking about the Anthropocene makes it difficult to feel that pure grace is available through hand soap used in carbon-intensive travel across borders laid down on genocidally colonized land.

I don't want to harp too much on philosophy—the "well being beauty brand"—but it is a little as though the person writing their marketing copy is writing directly for me in my concern about the evocations of purity and cleanliness, so let's look at one other product: *purity made simple: one-step facial cleanser*. Here is the company's copy:

philosophy: purity is natural. we come into this world with all the right in-
stincts. we are innocent and, therefore, perceive things as they should be,
rather than how they are. our conscience is clear, our hands clean and the world
at large is truly beautiful. it is at this time we feel most blessed. to begin feeling young again, we must begin with the most basic step of all, the daily ritual
of cleansing. ("Purity Made Simple | One-Step Facial Cleanser | Philosophy
Cleansers" 2015)

I turn to this product in part because the hand soap from my plane trip
isn't listed on the *philosophy* website, and I want to talk about ingredients.
But also this copy constellates brilliantly an ethos I believe we could—if
it were measurable in geologic time—use to mark the beginning of the
Anthropocene: roughly, the moment that humans worry that we have lost
a natural state of purity or decide that purity is something we ought to
pursue and defend. This ethos is the idea that we can access or recover a
time and state before or without pollution, without impurity, before the
fall from innocence, when the world at large *is truly beautiful.* This is a
time of youth, blessing, but also, interestingly, a natural state that precludes
or resists education—we *perceive things as they should be, rather than how
they are.* A piece of this ethos is perhaps also the sense that we can buy a
product that brings this natural state of purity back, though particularly in
certain left scenes, ideological purity seems to behave as a one-step facial
cleanser.

To dig into this, let's look at the ingredients in the "multitasking" (it
cleanses, tones, *and* moisturizes!) face wash, *purity made simple*:

water (aqua), sodium lauroamphoacetate, sodium trideceth sulfate, limnan-
thes alba (meadowfoam) seed oil, coco-glucoside, cocos nucifera (coconut)
alcohol, peg-120 methyl glucose dioleate, aniba rosaeodora (rosewood) wood
oil, geranium maculatum oil, guaiac (guaiacum officinale) extract, cymbo-
pogon martini oil, rosa damascena extract, amyris balsamifera bark oil, santa-
lum album (sandalwood) oil, salvia officinalis (sage) oil, cinnamomum cassia
leaf oil, anthemis nobilis flower oil, daucus carota sativa (carrot) seed oil, piper
nigrum (pepper) seed extract, polysorbate 20, glycerin, carbomer, triethanol-
amine, methylparaben, propylparaben, citric acid, imidazolidinyl urea, yellow
5 (ci 19140).

Most of these ingredients are not actually so bad—other soaps in the *philosophy* line, for example, use sodium laureth sulfate, here replaced by sodium trideceth sulfate. Both are surfactants, helping to make soap foamy, and emulsifying oils. Sodium laureth sulfate has gotten a bad rap, partly because even industry classifies it as a harsh soap, and partially because it is frequently contaminated by 1,4-dioxane, which does seem to be a carcinogen; sodium trideceth sulfate doesn't raise any particular flags in the usual databases of cosmetics toxicity. More worrying, perhaps, are the methyl- and propylparabens, both of which have studies indicating associated endocrine disruption and possible reproductive-system effects. Imidazolidinyl urea, often derived from urine, is a formaldehyde-releaser, which works as an antimicrobial agent by forming formaldehyde in our long shelf-life cosmetics without having to list formaldehyde on the ingredients list. Most of us are familiar with the smell of formaldehyde if we dissected frogs in high school biology classes. It is classified as a "known" or "potential human carcinogen." I'm focusing on the ingredients with chemical-ish names, but of course there is no particular reason to assume that the "natural" oils are so wonderful— the entire world is chemical, after all. If philosophy, as a brand, can teach us anything, it is that in this world purity is never made simple. Aspirations to purity are, perhaps, usually exactly what this cleansing-toning-moisturizing face wash offers: misleading ad copy on one level and secret carcinogens as a cell boundary-crossing material reality on another.

The delineation of theoretical purity, purity of classification, is always imbricated with the forever-failing attempt to delineate material purity—of race, ability, sexuality, or, increasingly, illness. The imbrication of failure with attempt, as I'll discuss, is a feature of classification itself. More significantly, the world always exceeds our conception of it. Despite this, we can still pursue changed worlds. Living well might feel impossible, and certainly living purely is impossible. The slate has never been clean, and we can't wipe off the surface to start fresh—there's no "fresh" to start. Endocrine-disrupting soap doesn't offer a purity made simple because there isn't one. All there is, while things perpetually fall apart, is the possibility of acting from where we are. Being against purity means that there is no primordial state we might wish to get back to, no Eden we have desecrated, no pretoxic body we might uncover through enough chia seeds and kombucha. There is not a preracial state we could access, erasing histories of slavery, forced labor on railroads, colonialism, genocide, and their concomitant responsibilities and requirements.

There is no food we can eat, clothing we can buy, or energy we can use without deepening our ties to complex webs of suffering. So, what happens if we start from there?

This book champions the usefulness of thinking about complicity and compromise as a starting point for action. Often there is an implicit or explicit idea that in order to live authentically or ethically we ought to avoid potentially reprehensible results in our actions. Since it is not possible to avoid complicity, we do better to start from an assumption that everyone is implicated in situations we (at least in some way) repudiate. We are compromised and we have made compromises, and this will continue to be the way we craft the worlds to come, whatever they might turn out to be. So, I interpellate myself into Donna Haraway's modest yet difficult framing of situatedness as a place to start. Speaking about knowledge, she writes:

> So, I think my problem and "our" problem is how to have *simultaneously* an account of radical historical contingency for all knowledge claims and knowing subjects, a critical practice for recognizing our own "semiotic technologies" for making meanings, *and* a no-nonsense commitment to faithful accounts of a "real" world, one that can be partially shared and friendly to earth-wide projects of finite freedom, adequate material abundance, modest meaning in suffering, and limited happiness. (Haraway 1991, 187)

Thinking about politics, my problem in this book, and "our" problem in this world, is how to have *simultaneously an account of radical historical contingency* of the conditions under which we take ethical and political action, critical practices for accounting for our own situatedness in histories that have shaped the conditions of possibility for our actions, and a *no-nonsense commitment* to the kind of real, possible world Haraway describes. That world is partially shared, offers finite freedom, adequate abundance, modest meaning, and limited happiness. Partial, finite, adequate, modest, limited— and yet worth working on, with, and for.

## Purity, and What the World Deserves

The not-simple "purity made simple" soap is one knot in a tapestry of products and ways of talking about the world. A hot-yoga studio franchise in my town, "Pure Yoga," enjoins people to become "pure yogis," offering a dizzying array of styles of yoga unmoored from any yoga tradition in particular;

the owners of the studios have also recently opened a vegan restaurant that serves killer gluten-free, vegan onion rings. Hot yoga, they say, "not only helps you to detox flushing toxins out of the skin through sweat, but heats up the muscles allowing you to approach the postures from a safe place" ("Discover Pure Yoga Ottawa" 2015). The shelves of ordinary food stores—let alone stores that self-identify as health-food stores—offer various products to detoxify our bodies. Cleanses, juice fasts, detox diets, ionic foot baths that draw poisons out through our feet, foot detox patches that you apply and that work overnight using herbs that activate "far infrared energy," bottles that offer pure spring water (with or without fluoride), and Himalayan pink salt-rock lamps—all offer ways to manage something, something experienced by consumers as a toxin that we can be free of. There is a clear and growing concern about material toxins accumulating in human bodies even as there is little clarity about what a toxin actually is, if ionic baths actually cleanse anything, or how we practically might personally manage the complex systems that affect the air we breathe, the water we drink, and the substances we touch.

Purity politics arise not only in our response to potential physical contamination; it is also an issue for our ethical and political situation in the world. How might our response to physical and political impurity be connected? Consider. Many of us are settlers living on unceded native land, stolen through genocidal colonial practices. We feed domestic animals more food than starving people lack, and spend money on the medical needs of pets while eating factory farmed meat and spraying our lawn with pesticides that produce cancer in domestic animals. We pay for cosmetic surgeries in a time when many people can't access basic health care. We recycle but take plane trips to Alaska. We worry about global warming and turn on the air-conditioning. We think slavery is wrong, but eat chocolate and fish produced in contexts that meet every definition of nonchattel slavery. We believe that people deserve good working conditions but buy clothing produced in sweatshops and maquiladoras because we couldn't afford equitably sourced clothing even if we could find it. We cannot look directly at the past because we cannot imagine what it would mean to live responsibly toward it. We yearn for different futures, but we can't imagine how to get there from here. We're hypocrites, maybe, but that derogation doesn't encompass the nature of the problem that complexity poses for us. The "we" in each of these cases shifts, and complicity carries differential weight with our social position—people benefiting from globalized inequality are for the most part the "we" in this paragraph. People are not equally responsible or capable, and are not equally called to respond. But however the bounds of the "we" are drawn, we are not, ever, pure. We're complicit, implicated, tied in to things we abjure. This is a kind of impurity implied in the sense of "compromised living" that involves making concessions.

In addition to making ethical compromises, we are also, as a recent self-help book about responding to toxins in our bodily environments puts it, "born pre-polluted" (Lourie and Smith 2013, 3). Our bodily boundaries are penetrated and traversed by viruses, chemicals, microbes. This way of being compromised names the sense in which we are liable to danger, vulnerable, potentially or actually damaged or sickened. Under contemporary regimes dictating individualist responses to pollution, we are made responsible for our own bodily impurity; we are called on to practice forms of defense against our own vulnerability. Charting the space between complicity and pollution, between righteousness and compromise, is difficult. If hypocrisy were the problem, really it wouldn't be much of a problem; at least on the surface, it is something we could give up. In contrast, being co-constituted with the world, ontologically inseparable, just seems to be our condition. And yet, contemporary imperatives to detox, to eat clean, to defend against pollution, or to avoid inflammation-causing foods imply the possibility that we could be pure in the relevant sense. I juggle a knee-jerk reaction to such personalized purity pursuits (individualizing, "not in my backyard"/NIMBY, capitalist, accepting of injustice in the distributions of harm) with the recognition that, indeed, there are substances in the world that none of us should, if we want to live, be coconstituted in relation to. Environmental racism is real, workers' bodies are wrongly incorporated as the detritus of capitalism, and militarism shapes the bodies and minds of everyone involved in war in the mold of trauma.

The "moves" involved in the not-simple "purity made simple" face wash, in NIMBY politics, in avoiding BPA, in eating organic (or vegan or paleo or sugar-free), or in doing monthly detoxifying "cleanses" may seem very different from each other. And they may seem very different in turn than other practices I explore in this book—practices of forgetting in relation to our implication in colonialism or the history of disease designation, for example. There are obvious real differences involved, but they are threaded together. Let's call the line that links them "purity politics," or "purism." What's needed, instead of a pretense to purity that is impossible in the actually existing world, is something else. We need to shape better practices of responsibility and memory for our placement in relation to the past, our implication in the present, and our potential creation of different futures.

I should say—since I try not to use the unsupported yet urgent imperatives so prevalent on the left ("we need," "we must"), instead shifting from categorical to hypothetical imperatives—*if* we want a world with less suffering and more flourishing, it would be useful to perceive complexity and complicity as the constitutive situation of our lives, rather than as things we should avoid. The action that comes out of the rather undefined idea of wanting a world with less suffering is, perhaps needless to say, a moving target, and one that raises more questions than it answers. Less suffering for whom? How is suffering measured? Who has the capacity to perceive entanglement, and who has the capacity to respond? To say that we live in compromised times is to say that although most people aim to *not* cause suffering, destruction, and death, simply by living, buying things, throwing things away, we implicate ourselves in terrible effects on ecosystems and beings both near and far away from us. We are inescapably entwined and entangled with others, even when we cannot track or directly perceive this entanglement. It is hard for us to examine our connection with *unbearable pasts* with which we might reckon better, our implication in *impossibly complex presents* through which we might craft different modes of response, and our aspirations for *different futures* toward which we might shape different worlds-yet-to-come.

In this book, I argue against purism not because I want a devastated world, the Mordor of industrial capitalism emerging as from a closely aligned alternate universe through our floating islands of plastic gradually breaking down into microbeads consumed by the scant marine life left alive after generations of overfishing, bottom scraping, and coral reef–killing ocean acidification; our human-caused, place-devastating elevated sea levels; our earth-shaking, water poisoning fracking; our toxic lakes made of the externalities of rare-earth mineral production for so-called advanced electronics; our soul-and-life destroying prisons; our oil spills; our children playing with bits of dirty bombs; our white phosphorus; our generations of trauma held in the body; our cancers; and I could go on. I argue against purism because it is one bad but common approach to devastation in all its forms. It is a common approach for anyone who attempts to meet and control a complex situation that is fundamentally outside our control. It is a bad approach because it shuts down precisely the field of possibility that might allow us to take better collective action against the destruction of the world in all its strange, delightful, impure frolic. Purism is a de-collectivizing, de-mobilizing, paradoxical politics of despair. This world deserves better.

## Living after Disturbance, Being Already Polluted

All of us on this earth are part of what Anna Tsing calls a *disturbance regime*—we're all living in *blasted landscapes* (Tsing 2014, 92). As she argues, referencing mushroom-growing in the shadow of the 2011 nuclear meltdown at Fukushima: "We need to be able to differentiate between forms of disturbance that are inimical to all life and those that offer multispecies opportunities. One place to start is by recognizing that not all human-shaped landscapes are as deadly as those spread by the Fukushima power plant. It is in the patchy difference that we can look for hope. Blasted landscapes are what we have, and we need to explore their life-promoting patches" (108).

Living in a disturbance regime means that we are all living after events that have changed, and frequently harmed, ecosystems and biospheres. Change is not the same thing as harm, and harm is not evenly distributed—famously, many forms of plant life only grow in the wake of forest fires, and the example Tsing engages is that matsutake mushrooms require disturbed forest to flourish—but mushrooms also happily take up radiation, and that is part of their response to the nuclear meltdown in Fukushima. They are signals for "exploring indeterminacy and the conditions of precarity, that is, life without the promise of stability" (Tsing 2015, 2). The question becomes, for Tsing and for me, how to delineate forms of disturbance in relation to what forms of life they sustain or proliferate. In the last section of this book, I offer normative guidance for life-promotion with the concept of flourishing—situated, historically placed, contingent. *How* we pursue flourishing, as I argue there, will always involve an in-process, syncretic, speculative fabulation, an improvisational engagement with emergence. The blasted landscapes of disturbance regimes are part of our everyday experience, and aiming for a more open field of the patchy differences where we might find hope is also going to have to be an everyday practice.

As I explore further in chapter 3, responses to herbicides and pesticides are very much like responses to radiation; though they are disparate discourses, they articulate a kind of purism. In these contexts the desire for purity is understandable and even politically activating. These examples show that being against purity does not mean being for pollution, and they illuminate key reasons we might sympathize with in the urge to find purity. The question is going to be *how* we conceive of and practice our relation to a world and a self suffused with otherness. Coconstitution with parts of the world we might want to protect ourselves from—parts of the world like radiation or herbicides or parabens—is difficult to disentangle conceptually or practically from coconstitution with the microbial others that populate our gut and allow us to digest food or the viral others whose descendants allow human placentas to function. We are in and of the world, contaminated and affected. As Eula Biss argues:

> If we do not yet know exactly what the presence of a vast range of chemicals in umbilical cord blood and breast milk might mean for the future of our children's health, we do at least know that we are no cleaner, even at birth, than our environment at large. We are all already polluted. We have more microorganisms in our guts than we have cells in our bodies—we are crawling with bacteria and we are full of chemicals. We are, in other words, continuous with everything here on earth. Including, and especially, each other. (Biss 2014, 75–76)

Being continuous with everything on earth is a starting point for critical inquiry, rather than an explanatory end. That we are coconstituted and thus polluted and impure hails us to make continually contingent and unsettled decisions about how to be in relation to the world, with no predetermined answer.

Biss's generative book *On Immunity: An Inoculation* is on one level about vaccination, starting from her thinking about vaccinating her own child, which always involves a decision about how to be in relation to the viral world and the other bodies who live here with us. On another level, it is a book about the impossibility of purity, and about how to reckon with realizing our entanglement and vulnerability in the world. Biss's book came out in a moment of increased attention to questions around vaccination and contagion in 2014 sparked by the rapid spread of Ebola and by a spike in measles cases that started with purposefully unvaccinated children at Disneyland. There is, as yet, no vaccine that protects against Ebola, and so responses to its resurgence centered not around who ought to be vaccinated but instead on the questions of whether (and how) to close borders to travelers who had been in infected areas (often framed simply as "Africa"), and what steps people could take to protect themselves individually against infection. Measles, by contrast, is an illness against which we have a standard and effective vaccine. Bundled with vaccines for mumps and rubella, it is one of the vaccines parents in North America first confront when they have young children. Biss begins by reflecting on her own process of deciding which vaccines to give her child, but she turns quickly toward a complex discussion of toxicity and purity.

It is easy to analyze vaccination discourse in relation to purity. Consider a report from CNN on a measles outbreak in Arizona, focusing on a pediatrician (Dr. Tim Sacks) who was appealing for people to vaccinate their children in part in consideration of his own child, ill with leukemia and thus with an immune system vulnerable to illnesses like measles and who could not be vaccinated. CNN focused on a doctor, Jack Wolfson, who argues against vaccination. In the interview, Wolfson affirms his commitment to not vaccinate his children, even if that refusal spreads diseases that make other children very, perhaps fatally, ill. He says: "I'm not going to sacrifice the well-being of my child. My child is pure. . . . It's an unfortunate thing that people die, but people die. And I'm not going to put my child at risk to save another child" (*CNN Report on Measles in Arizona* 2015). The belief that vaccinations introduce toxins that would make a child no longer pure is here closely allied with a species of defensive individualism, the sense in which the self is imagined as a fortress, separable from the world and requiring defense against the world.

Though she is not talking directly about this case, Biss articulates the two sides of thinking about impurity that Wolfson invokes here. She writes:

> Fear of contamination rests on the belief, widespread in our culture as in others, that something can impart its essence to us on contact. We are forever polluted, as we see it, by contact with a pollutant. And the pollutants we have come to fear most are the products of our own hands. Though toxicologists tend to disagree with this, many people regard natural chemicals as inherently less harmful than man-made chemicals. (Biss 2014, 39)

Toxicity is often framed as dose-dependent; the classic formulation is that the "dose makes the poison." In purity discourse, pollutants are rendered as a different kind of toxicity—mere contact makes the poison. As Biss notes, the conception of the violable but delimited individual body that undergirds this conception of a being who can be pure and protected from pollution is long-standing. She writes:

> Our contemporary belief that we inhabit only one body contained entirely within the boundaries of our skin emerged from Enlightenment thinking, which celebrated the individual in both mind and body. But what defined an individual remained somewhat elusive. By the end of the Age of Enlightenment, the body of a slave was allowed to represent only three-fifths of a person. Some people remained parts of a whole while others enjoyed the novel illusion of being whole unto themselves. (125)

As I'll explore below, in this way as in others, possessive individualism is densely racialized; the core idea that our selves are owned by us functions as a categorical move to lay out a map of who can own others.

I follow Biss in understanding the desire for purity as a wrong-headed response to the understanding that toxicity might just be our condition. This wrong-headedness is expressed in Wolfson's fiction that his child is pure, and his ready acceptance of the possibility that his faithfulness to that imagined purity might cause children to die. This move toward purity, as Biss frames it, appears in many other contexts:

> Purity, especially bodily purity, is the seemingly innocent concept behind a number of the most sinister social actions of the past century. A passion for bodily purity drove the eugenics movement that led to the sterilization of women who were blind, black, or poor. Concerns for bodily purity were behind miscegenation laws that persisted more than a century after the abolition of slavery, and behind sodomy laws that were only recently declared unconstitutional. Quite a bit of human solidarity has been sacrificed in pursuit of preserving some kind of imagined purity. (Biss 2014, 75–76)

I am concerned about the sacrifice of human solidarity in pursuit of purity, but I am concerned also with what we might think of as political solidarity with ecosystems, critters, bugs, microbes, atoms. Elsewhere I have forwarded a conception of aspirational solidarity—a "solidarity based on collective conceptions of worlds that do not yet exist"—as a norm that might guide action toward humans but also toward worlds in which all sorts of beings flourish (Shotwell 2013, 105). I explore this conception further in chapter 6.

## "We" Has Never Been Pure

Purity practices—in ideology, in theory, and in practice—work to delineate an inside and an outside; they are practices of defining a "we." Mary Douglas's 1966 book *Purity and Danger: An Analysis of Concepts of Pollution and Taboo* remains an important touchstone for thinking about purity. Fifty years on from its first publication, the book does throw up frictions for the anti-oppression critical theorist; Douglas refers consistently to "primitive cultures," by which she means mostly Indigenous non-Western cultures, and there are certain hiccups in her discussion of gender and sexuality. The book is usable in part because Douglas applies an ethnographic eye also to purity practices of the Christian Bible and critiques contemporary texts that attempt to use "primitive cultures to buttress psychological insights" (Douglas, 115). Douglas's investigation is at least in part structured around the idea that observing practices of purity can help us understand the symbolic work of social relations that stitch together society. She writes, "I believe that ideas about separating, purifying, demarcating and punishing transgressions have as their main function to impose system on an inherently untidy experience" (4). This imposition, in her analysis, is contingent and shifting—she does not think that cultural practices of purity indicate a timeless or iron-clad set of classifications. Rather, on her account, "rituals of purity and impurity create unity in experience. . . . By their means, symbolic patterns are worked out and publically displayed. Within these patterns, disparate elements are related and disparate experience is given meaning" (2–3). She frames managing "dirt" as a key move in creating these unities:

> As we know it, dirt is essentially disorder. There is no such thing as absolute dirt: it exists in the eye of the beholder. If we shun dirt, it is not because of craven fear, still less dread or holy terror. Nor do our ideas about disease account for the range of our behavior in cleaning or avoiding dirt. Dirt offends against order. Eliminating it is not a negative movement, but a positive effort to organize the environment. (2)

Concepts and practices of purity and impurity, in relation to dirt as well as other things understood as dirty, tell us something about how people understand the world they live in, and thus how they can imagine the world becoming. In other words, purity practices are also productive normative formulations—they make a claim that a certain way of being is aspired to, good, or to be pursued. Concepts matter for what we do and how we are in the world. As Donna Haraway puts it, "'Ideas' are themselves technologies for pursuing inquiries. It's not just that ideas are embedded in practices; they *are* technical practices of situated kinds" (Haraway 2008, 282). While current practices may well be connected to the forms of primarily religious purity practice Douglas discusses, in this book I am more concerned with the practices that characterize and structure key modes of life today. Both sorts of practices, though, deploy a particular idea-as-technology of parsing, cleansing, and delineating.

We can trace these practices back to a certain formulation of modernity, and from there to the practices of racialization that emerged with and in some ways coproduced the age of colonialism as in part a project of monitoring and managing the newly discovered realm of microbes and their effects. John Law, Geir Afdal, Kristin Asdal, Wen-yuan Lin, Ingunn Moser, and Vicky Singleton offer a productive manifesto for what they call "Modes of Syncretism," a way of being against purity (and, indeed, a way of being against the purity implied in being against purity!). They read Bruno Latour's claim that "we have never been modern" as in part a set of claims about the production of purity practices. They say: "[Latour's] argument is that modernity presents itself as gleaming, consistent and coherent; as something that is *pure*. Not fuzzy" (Law et al. 2014, 172). Law et al. argue that for Latour purity is a quintessentially "modern apparition"; the impossibility of purity is one reason that we have never been modern. So, "modernity presents itself as pure" even as *"it isn't pure at all"*—rather, *"modernity is a both-and"* (173). I follow one strand of the STS (Science and Technology Studies) genealogy which they characterize as cultivating "a *bias to impurity or fuzziness*; or if not a bias, then at least a *sensitivity* to that which doesn't cohere; and, as part of this, [STS] has a high degree of tolerance of mess" (175). Syncretism names a way to understand the way that different ways of being, traditions, priorities, and practices come to get on together—syncretisms are, for them, necessary to thinking about all practices in the real world, because practices always manage constitutive noncoherence—the fact that the world is made up of things that seem to hang together but that require work to hold in place. In chapter 5, I explore further implications of the normative conclusions they offer; for now, I affirm the possibility that attention to the various modes of syncretism by which noncoherence is lived "will be useful in a world in which it appears that the will to purity—and the conditions of possibility for purity—are in decline" (177). The stakes of purity discourses, and the theo-retical conviction that things are more coherent than they actually are, remain significant, even so.

It is commonplace now to understand the idea of natural purity as a racial-ized concept, particularly if we trace debates about the nature of human races back to questions that animated and justified the Atlantic slave trade—questions of monogenesis or polygenesis. These questions are of whether humans all descend from a single gene line (in which case some of us are less pure expressions of the line than others) or from many origins (in which case some of us may be made by nature for enslavement). As many philoso-phers have articulated, Kant's lectures on anthropology and race laid out one founding expression of racialization as centrally a project of purity, and to the extent that they forward a conception of pure reason as accessible only to the white race, they also delimit a racialized understanding of not only personhood but also rationality, descent, and the conditions for counting as human (Bernasconi 2000; Mills 1998; Eze 1997). But the formulation of racialization can be read, following Denise Ferreira Da Silva's generative work, in part through the tools (the "knowledge arsenal") used to measure the racial, which, as she writes, "institutes the global as an ontoepistemo-logical context—a productive and violent gesture necessary to sustain the post-Enlightenment version of the Subject as the sole determined thing" (Silva 2007, xiii). As Alexander Weheliye argues, in line with Da Silva's point, "There can be no absolute biological substance, because in the history of modernity this field always already appears in the form of racializing assem-blages" (Weheliye 2014, 65). Markers of racial purity are in turn entangled and coconstituted with biopolitical practices aiming to reduce or eliminate disability, poverty, and queerness at the population level.

To be against purity is, again, not to be for pollution, harm, sickness, or premature death. It is to be against the rhetorical or conceptual attempt to delineate and delimit the world into something separable, disentangled, and homogenous. With and following María Lugones, I am "firmly planted against the logic of boundedness." I follow her argument "for intercommu-nalism from the midst of impure subjects, negotiating life transgressing the categorical understandings of a logic of binaries that produces hard-edged, ossified, exclusive groups" (Lugones 2003, 35). Lugones critiques a meta-physics of purity, understood as separability, fragmentation, and standing outside culture and situatedness. The Man of purity, as a figure, "shuns impurity, ambiguity, multiplicity as they threaten his own fiction. The enormity of the threat keeps him from understanding it. So, the lover of purity remains ignorant of his own impurity, and thus the threat of all impurity remains significantly uncontaminated" (132). The metaphysics of purity is necessarily a fragile fiction, a conceit under constant but disavowed threat— to affirm a commitment to purity is in one move to glance at the entanglement and coconstitution, the impurity, of everything and to pretend that things are separate and unconnected. Kim Tallbear's important critique of the politics of DNA testing as a guarantor of Native American identity begins from the claim that "of course, mixing is predicated on the notion of purity. The historical constitution of continental spaces and concomitant grouping of humans into 'races' is the macro frame of reference for the human-genome-diversity researcher" (TallBear 2013, 5). Speaking of queer disability food politics but in a mode that we could take up more broadly, Kim Q. Hall argues instead for a "metaphysics of compost" since "there are no pure bodies, no bodies with impermeable borders. Because reality is not composed of fixed, mutually exclusive, or pure bodies, a metaphysics of compost is more conducive to food politics that remains accountable to real bodies and real foods/relationships" (Hall 2014, 179). As I'll argue in this book, a great deal of harm is done based on a metaphysics of purity; since it is false and because it is harmful, we do better to pursue metaphysics that do not aim to preserve fictions of integrity.

## The Plan of the Book

This book is organized around a predictable narrative line, tracing linear time—starting from the past, looking at the present, imagining the future. But time here is, as I hope to show, much less linear than this line seems to allow. The past involves the present and the future, the present entangles the past and outlines what is to come, bringing the future into the past, and the future rests on a situated past and can only "happen" in the present; tense intermingles. Part I, "Reckoning with a Fraught Past," focuses on disavowed or difficult histories. The central question I pose in this section is: What does it mean to think about those histories that are difficult to remember well— either because the present in some way requires erasing what happened in the past or because particular past events have become so taken-for-granted that it is hard to imagine that the world was once different, and how. This first part has two chapters. Because where we live and how we came to be where we are can be understood as a founding political narrative, the book begins with an inquiry into thinking about colonization and memory. I start with conceptions of critical memory practices as a way to think about how (primarily) white settlers can work with anticolonialism and decolonizing as praxis. The aspiration to this kind of practice has intimately to do with memory, and with the process of understanding the work of memory in two national contexts: Canada and the United States. I focus here on the practices of Indigenous sovereignty and critical whiteness as a challenge to forgetting. This chapter examines the memory of atrocities alongside state and nonstate responses to the past, asking how memory and forgetting are important to colonialism.

I then move to a chapter taking up more recent examples of relational remembering at the intersection of ordinary people's social movement activity with state classificatory work. I examine the official reclassification of AIDS by the U.S. Centers for Disease Control, a result of the activist work of a direct-action group, ACT UP. Thinking about activism and memory at this site shows us that it matters how we remember activism of the past in remembering in the present. It also points toward practices of responsibility that signal possible futures, futures in which activist work is remembered well. When classifications become commonsensical it can become difficult to recall that they were created and, sometimes, contested. Attending to contestation reminds us that what happened in the past was not inevitable. And since the past persists and consists in the present, no particular future is inevitable either.

It can be as difficult to understand and live with the complexity of our current world as it is to reckon with an unremembered past. Part II, "Living in an Interdependent Present," introduces the practical implications of theories of interdependence. Interdependence is, I argue, a useful way to think about current experiences of complicity and implication. I start with a case study of biological complexity and interdependence anchored in scientific and popular talk about frogs, toads, and what they tell us about pollution and toxicity. Amphibians are indicator species; they show the results of pollution early. I argue that they often stand in for and symbolize the threat of human gender and disability transformation as a result of industrial contamination. Asking what frogs and toads mean to us in thinking about pollution and toxicity, I examine the effects of this conflation of amphibians and humans, and what that conflation means for understanding the interpenetrations of toxicity.

The following chapter builds on the argument that interdependence is a key concept for thinking about compromise. I argue that being embodied places us in unresolvable relation to networks of other beings such that living our lives relies on the suffering and death of others. I investigate various ethical responses to this situation—veganism, conscious consumerism, environmentalism—concluding that a richer conception of interdependence allows us to rest better with constitutive impurity than ethical approaches aiming at individual purity. I formulate alternative conceptions of ethical and political responses to complexity. These chapters examine closely the distribution of toxicity and suffering, examining the ways in which people of color, people living in poverty, and Indigenous people are made to receive the externalities of capitalist production. The Fukushima nuclear disaster is one of my key examples here.

Part III, "Shaping Unforeseeable Futures," builds on Parts I and II. The point of reckoning with the social organization of forgetting—how and what gets remembered—and the differential distribution of present harm is, if it is anything, to craft a future different from the horrific past we have inherited and the resultant present we currently live. In this final section, I argue for aiming toward and creating future worlds radically divergent from this suffering-filled present. Under conditions of oppression and exploitation, how might we enact practices of freedom that can shape worlds we currently cannot imagine? I argue for what I call open normativities: collectively crafted ways of being that shape subjectivities oriented toward widespread future flourishing. I examine the critical disability performance troupe, Sins Invalid, and the legal support organization, The Sylvia Rivera Law Project, as examples of collectives currently shaping open normativities. The book concludes by elaborating the idea of "identifying into" queer disability politics. This is a model for taking current conditions seriously, acting toward and with them adequately, and through this praxis producing new social relations and material contexts. In the final chapter I take up an SF mode—speculative feminisms, science fictions, serious fabulations, to echo Donna Haraway—as experiments for an imaginative relation to worlds to come, which we can call into being in part through a playful and pleasurable imagining of what might be to come.

This is a theoretical book, a book focusing on theory in a number of registers. As such, it doesn't do much except say things. But it is "against purity" rather than for any of the many things that I am indeed for because precisely one of my imperatives is to be against without predicting all the things there are to be for. Being against in this way—having a "no"—involves also the Zapatismo invocation of the possibility of "many yesses." In this sense, I am allied with John Holloway's conception of "the scream." As he says, this is our starting point, this "rejection of a world that we feel to be wrong, negation of a world we feel to be negative" (Holloway 2010, 2). For Holloway, the scream "implies a tension between that which exists and that which might conceivably exist, between the indicative (that which is) and the subjunctive (that which might be). We live in an unjust society and we wish it were not so: the two parts of the sentence are inseparable and exist in constant tension with each other" (6–7). There is a forever unsettled collectivity involved in the scream (who is the "we"?) and an unpredicted outcome to wishing about the world that *it were not so*. To invoke the foundational "no" of being against purity means that when we talk about impurity, implication, and compromise we are also foregrounding the fact that we are not all equally implicated in and responsible for the reprehensible state of the world. But wherever we stand in relation to the world, we can scream "no!" and open the space for many yesses. And further, to say that we live in an unjust world is to hold a clear recognition that there are people who gain immense power and profit from this situation—and in real ways the people who benefit from the lie of purism are the ones who reiterate it.

# PART I

## Reckoning with a Fraught Past

# 1

# Remembering for the Future

## Reckoning with an Unjust Past

"Ask the colonial ghosts if they live in your bones," enjoins singer Rae Spoon. "Ask the colonial ghosts what they took." In places bearing the histories of imperialism and colonialism, these are good questions to ask. Whether and how ghosts live in our bones depends on our family histories; the colonial ghosts live in the bones of their descendants and inheritors, and not—or not in the same ways—in the bones of people indigenous to places. What the people of the past took, and from whom, is more stable. Any understanding of our place in the world rests on an understanding of the historical processes that have, in Antonio Gramsci's formulation, deposited in us "an infinity of traces, without leaving an inventory." And any reckoning with the past that we carry in our present involves crafting some way to inventory the ghosts in our bones, and some way to understand what colonialism took. In the Rae Spoon song, which is called "Come on Forest Fire, Burn the Disco Down," the colonial ghosts answer the question of what they took. They say, "you're dancing on it." In this chapter, I affirm that land and place—what we're dancing on—is the central thing colonialism attempts to take, while also affirming that land and place are relations more than they are locations.

The attempt to make a decolonizing inventory intimately entwines classification with memory. Here, I focus on the question of Indigenous sovereignty and the possibility of settler solidarity as a challenge to forgetting, following Roxanne Dunbar-Ortiz's formulation of the concept of "unforgetting." It is useful to connect the systematic erasure of memory to state classification practices. Classifying along various scales has been a central task of the colonizing state's work: it is in part through bureaucracy that colonialism takes form.[1] I start with an examination of the ways that categories of health, healing, and harm are used in managing histories and ongoing effects of Indian Residential Schools in Canada (or Indian Boarding Schools in the United States). These programs were explicitly attempts on the part of the state to, as the commissioner for Indian Affairs in Canada famously put it, "kill the Indian in the child." I argue for a connection between memory, classification, and racialization, grounding the analysis in current understandings of memory as relational and collective.

One way to understand a more usable mode of remembering the past that has harmed and benefited us, differentially, pervasively, is through a critique of the individualizing effects of what has been called "healthism." This names the idea that we are each responsible for maintaining our own individual well-being, even in contexts of collective harm, such as the current experience of colonial historical practices of removing children from their communities and families. I contrast such conceptions of health with an understanding of complex interdependence, which must involve a reckoning with our implication in unjust pasts. At issue in the process of reckoning with legacies of colonial harm is a struggle between incompatible classifications of health and personhood and incompatible understandings of responsible remembering. Understanding how to better practice memory and flourishing in the context of a decolonizing healing process points toward more adequate conceptions of health and flourishing in response to colonialism and its ongoing harms. I follow Sue Campbell in asking, "How can sharing the memory of harm and wrongdoing across pasts that are linked by (and in some sense) a common and toxic history aid reparative projects, and what form should this sharing take?" (Campbell 2014, 88).

The chapter has four parts. The first reviews connections between classification and racialization. The second examines individualizing effects of "healthism," contrasting such conceptions of health with an understanding of complex interdependence. In the third, I argue that a key issue in Canada's Truth and Reconciliation Commission process involves inadequate understandings of health, personhood, and colonization. Understanding how to better work with memory, including but beyond the context of the TRC process, points toward more adequate conceptions of health and flourishing in the wake of colonialism and its ongoing harms. I conclude with an argument for decolonizing memory practices as a key piece of resisting the harms of colonial practices that shape the conditions of our living and dying.

## Classification and Colonialism

Classification is, perhaps surprisingly, key to colonialism. While administrative practices can occlude the violence resulting from sorting people, getting them onto trains on time, and so on, and while bureaucratic violence may be difficult to perceive as violence, practices of classification have been coproduced with practices of colonialism. I am interested in subtler levels of classification than often arise in thinking about colonialism and classification—rather than looking at how whole societies are classified, this chapter looks at more fine-grained classificatory work, particularly around categories of health and harm. As a non-Indigenous, white, settler, immigrant citizen of the state of "Canada," currently living on unsurrendered Algonquin territory, I approach thinking about Aboriginal and Indigenous identity, health issues, and state policy from the desire for a decolonized future. I believe that in ways we cannot always predict, white settlers can play a role in transforming and challenging what are currently extremely oppressive social relations. One aspect of our role is actively participating in a politics of responsibility in our intellectual and social labor, actively challenging our own and others' ignorance and occluded thinking, and taking up practices of decolonization. I take inspiration here from Dale Turner's rendering of one account of the Two-Row Wampum in the Haudenosaunee/Iroquois Confederation: "The two participants in the relationship—Europeans and Iroquois—can share the same space and travel into the future, yet neither can steer the other's vessel. Because they share the same space, they are inextricably entwined in a relationship of interdependence—*but they remain distinct political entities*" (Turner 2006, 54). Attending to the specific histories buttressing the present context in which we live involves asking better questions about who the participants in the ongoing relationship of inheriting the legacies of colonialism are. In the case Turner mentions, they are specific Iroquois and specific Europeans who negotiated treaties, but there are many treaties (almost entirely disrespected), and also many relations not governed by treaty agreements. In resisting the classificatory work of past and ongoing colonialist practices, these relations could be a central concern.

Classification and its effects are intimately biopolitical, addressing how to sort people, group them, and how to manage what effect these activities have on population and time. As I'll discuss further in chapter 2, when classifications work well, they become infrastructure—they fade out, we cannot easily perceive them, and the social relations they shape become commonsensical. The movement of classificatory apparatuses into commonsensical background knowledge and practice is one of the main reasons we need a genealogical approach, with its attempt to bring to the level of critique things that normally go without saying, alongside a continued refusal to court finality and classificatory purity, or to lay questions to rest. White supremacist logics intensify the general operation of biopolitical power, requiring standards that can reliably create group differentiation and then group people into discrete and exclusive categories. The normalizing society generates disciplinary regimens to manage the inevitable supplements and excesses created by any classificatory work (McWhorter 2009, 51). The scientific project so central to sciences of the human—a project whereby one might determine definitively who was properly human, deserving of rights, who manifested as the surviving fittest at the peak of evolution's ladder—relied on the fiction of attaining classificatory adequacy. Creating, describing, and managing the abnormal and the aim toward classificatory purity thus entangle the social relations we call disability, racialization, and sexuality (along with all the excess that does not fit into these groupings).

Nodes of intensity such as racialization, sexuality and its relation to gendering, citizenship, or the production of disability are significant, in part, precisely because of the classificatory failures built in to their definition. Take "race," for example. As Ladelle McWhorter argues, accurate racial classification in eighteenth- and nineteenth-century science was both desired and despaired of, though in various ways. Delineating bright lines of difference between groups using traits such as "hair texture, eye shape, skull shape, facial angle, cranial capacity, brain anatomy . . . failed to yield hard lines of demarcation between groups of people various scientists thought really did constitute distinct races—meaning that there were no such empirically evident morphological lines of demarcation" (McWhorter 2009, 43). It is, as she shows, similarly vexed to demarcate racial grouping along any other of the available lines of explanation—geographical or ecological habitation (whereby place makes race), cultural grouping, lineage, and more.

Like most classificatory practices, the aim toward theoretical purity arose from particular practical imperatives (Who can one enslave? Who has political standing?) and was, or is, worked through on the ground. That working-through becomes, for us, infrastructure on which other things travel. Perhaps because race has been a problem in North America for a long time, it generates multiple commonsense understandings, which sometimes bump into and denaturalize one another. Unpacking the lines of descent that have shaped the social relations and material effects we call "race" gives "an awareness that things are as they are, not because God or Nature so decreed, but because of the balance of power at a given time, the pressures and strains of a historical moment. And one consequence of that awareness is the recognition that today's status quo was far from inevitable and need not persist into tomorrow" (McWhorter 2009, 295–96). Seeing that the world we treat as infrastructure is a product of history shows us that, as McWhorter argues, "we can unmake and remake what has been made" (328).

We can understand how disability, for example, is worked through—how it becomes what Foucault calls the "external frontier of the abnormal" (quoted in McWhorter 2009, 50)—by attending to the work of classification implicit in the purity discourses necessary to whiteness. The capacity to identify, treat, house, and manage the bodies and selves of people with disabilities was central to the work of "human development." And conceptions of human development were in turn important to colonization projects at various scales—determining scales of societal development in terms of more and less developed or degenerate races and then mapping individuals' development in turn. At the level of the individual, the nation, and the race, this productive work tied together salient categories of abnormality; classification and the conceit of classificatory purity are central to this process. Folk classifications interact with state and scientific classification. Racist systems that aim to produce "healthy babies" (code for "babies without disabilities") may seem just by accident to disadvantage people living in poverty, people living with disabilities, people of color. So, for example, we might understand the Children's Aid Society as an agency that in Canada continues to disproportionally take the children of Indigenous people from their families of origin. This process, even as it is less obviously motivated by genocidal desires than Indian Residential Schools, can be connected both to residential schooling and to the "Sixties Scoop" in Canada, during which an unusually high number of Native babies and children were taken from their families and put into foster care or adopted by, predominately, white people.

Classification shapes settler and Indigenous lives in the place we could call Canada, or Turtle Island (where the choice of term is itself an enactment of various forms of classification). In the Canadian context, the primary technology for this shaping over the last hundred years is the Indian Act. As Bonita Lawrence writes in her important study of the effects of classification on Native identity, the Indian Act is

> much more than a body of laws that for over a century has controlled every aspect of status Indian life. It provides a conceptual framework that has organized contemporary First Nations life in ways that have been almost entirely naturalized, and that governs ways of thinking about Native identity. To date few individuals appear to have recognized the depth of the problem that the Indian Act represents—its overarching nature as a discourse of classification and regulation, which has *produced* the subjects it purports to control, and which has therefore indelibly ordered how Native people think of things "Indian."
>
> To treat the Indian Act merely as a set of policies to be repealed, or even as a genocidal scheme that we can simply choose not to believe in, belies how a classificatory system produces a way of thinking—a grammar—which embeds itself in every attempt to change it. (Lawrence 2004, 26)

Regulation is, as Lawrence shows, productive. Former director of research of the recently defunded Aboriginal Healing Foundation, Chippewa scholar Gail Guthrie Valaskaks argues that "Indian membership policies are colonial codes that ricochet through time and space to cut across and construct Native identity and tribal affiliation. The codes that identify Indians in a matrix of blood or paternity circulate in conflicts over membership, in disagreements over who is an Indian, what signifies Indianness, and what being Indian means" (Valaskakis 2005, 212). As I'll argue below, if we understand classification itself as a central technology of colonialism, and colonialism as an ongoing process, we should worry about current strategies of reparation, response, and reconciliation that center classificatory work.

However, since classification has been a cross-continental racializing tool *and* since we rely on classificatory work in opposing oppression, we must reckon with it. This reckoning will involve understanding classification's differential effects. As J. Kēhaulani Kauanui has compellingly argued, U.S. government policy classifying Native Hawaiian peoples based on blood quantum deploys a logic in which whiteness functions as a process of "disappearance for Native people rather than signifying privilege" (Kauanui 2008, 10). Alexander Weheliye follows Kauanui in understanding the effects of racial sorting and articulates how such classificatory work shapes racialization. He argues that "the denial of personhood qua whiteness to African American subjects does not stand in opposition to the genocidal wages of whiteness bequeathed to indigenous subjects but rather represents different properties of the same racializing juridical assemblage that differentially produces both black and native subjects as aberrations from Man and thus not-quite-human" (Weheliye 2014, 79). In the final section of this chapter, I will examine the community-led database project, It Starts With Us, which represents a coalitional and generative reappropriation of classificatory practices. To get there, first let me lay out some key terrain in individualizing "moves" around health and healing and an account of the work of memory and forgetting in this context.

## "Healthism" and Responding to Residential Schools

"Healthism" names the tendency to think about individual health as a moral imperative—individuals are held responsible for their bodies, and obesity, diabetes, cancer, and other chronic conditions are rendered as moral failings. In this context, there has been a recent turn to think about "health" as a contested and troubled category, or at least a category that we ought not understand as automatically positive. As Jonathan Metzl and Anna Kirkland argue, "Even the most cursory examination of health in daily conversation, email solicitation, or media representation demonstrates how the term is used to make moral judgments, convey prejudice, sell products, or even exclude whole groups of persons from health care" (Metzl and Kirkland 2010, 2). The originator of the term "healthism" was Robert Crawford, in a 1980 article titled "Healthism and the Medicalization of Everyday Life." Crawford argued that "health" had simultaneously been individualized— made the property and responsibility of the individual and correspondingly moralized—such that we can be lauded or critiqued for "being healthy." For Crawford, without a political and collective conception of health, we fail to have an effective strategy for real health promotion. Notice again that a central aspect of health-as-healthism is its focus on the individual: even if we understand that many things that affect our health are beyond our individual control, we are held responsible for managing those collective situations individually (as I'll discuss in chapters 3 and 4, we can think here about pesticides in food, carcinogens in the air, our capacity to bus or bike instead of driving). Recent focus on a social determinants of health approach to understanding oppression has opened space for thinking about health as contingent, multivalent, and complexly intertwined with our social and material environments.

Assessing wrongs of the past with an eye toward how health is conceptualized shows that we might productively move even further into non-individualist accounts of the health of the individual. As James Daschuk has illustrated, the production of health or illness is a key piece of the history of colonization. Tracing disease vectors and avoidable starvation, he argues that "microbes cannot be separated from commerce; there is no way to envision the expansion of trade between the Old World and the New World without considering the impact of disease" (Daschuk 2013, 181). Considering this history, he says, calls on us to recognize that the "decline of First Nations health was the direct result of economic and cultural suppression. The effects of the state-sponsored attack on indigenous communities that began in the 1880s haunts us as a nation still" (186). In welcoming such a haunting, it is productive to examine the forced schooling of Indigenous children in terms of a conception of healthism; the "healing" people subjected to residential schooling are meant to experience is too often framed as an individual process. There are important links between the discourse of "healing" as it is deployed by the state to aim for closure on harms of the past as in fact a kind of healthism; a critique of healthism can be productively brought to bear as well on many discussions of healing, asking whether what is on offer opens space for collective responses to collective harm. We can perceive something useful about a colonialist purity politics operating through the intertwined practice of inadequate memory practices, classifications of health, and understandings of the political meanings of the past.

The history of forced residential or boarding schooling of Indigenous children has been a major focus of discourse around healing from the wrongs of colonialism in North America. In the current United States, the most active formation has been the National Native American Boarding School Healing Coalition, which has for many reasons not (or not yet) pursued individual legal cases as their main work. In the Canadian context, formal reparations for the legacy of forced schooling were pursued through a Truth and Reconciliation Commission (TRC) that was established as part of the settlement of a large class-action suit brought from people who experienced harms as a result of residential schooling. The Indian Residential School (IRS) system operated from the 1890s in Canada, with the last school closing in 1996. The residential school system was complex and has still-ramifying effects; here, I am going to focus on only one facet of the many things involved, asking how the pursuit for particular reparations has involved practices of memory and classification consistent with individualist healthism.

A key piece of thinking about classification in its enactment in the TRC is itself a limiting situation: the TRC's focus on an ostensibly time-delimited "sad chapter in our history," in the words of then Canadian Prime Minister Stephen Harper's 2008 formal apology, can be paired with Harper's 2009 statement that Canada has "no history of colonialism." Read together, it is coherent to understand the process of coming to "closure" through the TRC as itself a process of denying both the colonialism of the past and the ongoing colonizing practices of the present. Classification—both of the TRC as a process addressing residential schools rather than colonialism more broadly—is, here, a memory practice. The transition from apologizing for Indian Residential Schools to denying that Canada has any history of colonialism is also a purity practice—it is in part *through* framing residential schools as a sad chapter of our history that the prime minister can claim that Canada has no history of colonialism.

Among other things, classifications make people legible to/subjects of the state. In the case of the TRC process, dense classificatory frameworks were used as the basis for claims for recompense but also then as a means of state control of people who make claims. This is visible in the Common Experience Payment application process, and below I will examine some of the web of state classificatory work through which people were asked to articulate themselves as they make claims for redress. Speaking more broadly, though, we can say that one of the internal contradictions of the colonial space of residential schools involves a tension between individual and collective conceptions of selfhood. The work aimed to "kill the Indian in the child," in the now-infamous words of Duncan Campbell Scott, head of the Department of Indian Affairs (1913–32). Forcing Indigenous children into institutions—taking children away from their families, their language-communities, their home places—was a form of destructive violence, with the kinds of individual abuses and violences adding to the founding and systemic violence of colonialism. An attack on the conditions for interdependent self-formation of Indigenous children through disrupting their relations with family and place was, then, central. But that attack was made under the sign of a denial that selves are at root interdependent—the practice itself asserted a belief that people are independent, and, in the practice of enacting that assertion, profoundly harmed Indigenous practices of interdependence.

In the process of reckoning with one enactment of colonialism—residential schools—we see several current recapitulations of state practices of classification of the past. Consider three, figured through these questions: What is an Indian? What is covered under the recompense process? What kinds of harm and health can be conceived within it? On the first question (What is an Indian?), the language of classification itself matters. Taiaiake Alfred has discussed the production of the term "Aboriginal" as itself a classifying move situating peoples indigenous to places as irretrievably in the past, and thus needing to evolve in the context of the Canadian state. With Jeff Corntassel, Alfred critiques an embrace of "the Canadian government's label of 'aboriginal,' along with the concomitant and limited notion of postcolonial justice framed within the institutional construct of the state. In fact, this identity is purely a state construction that is instrumental to the state's attempt to gradually subsume Indigenous existences into its own constitutional system and body politic" (Alfred and Corntassel 2005, 598). Classifications of Aboriginal identity have since their inception had the overt aim or covert effect of classifying people *out* of the category now covered by the Indian Act. This process is most generally called "enfranchisement." This was first, under the (1857) Gradual Civilization Act, a supposedly voluntary process. Enfranchisement then became a kind of Orwellian "newspeak" term for the process of forcibly reclassifying people as not Indian when, variously, they left their reserve, took payment ("scrip") in place of treaty land, married white men, were deemed "half-blood," received university education, or a number of other conditions that morphed through various revisions. With the 1951 revision of the Indian Act, and its further revisions, the Canadian state removed some of the restrictions on traditional spirituality and movement, while simultaneously deepening its purview to determine who would have and maintain Indian status, and what material meaning that status would have. Since one material meaning of status is a claim—often via treaty rights—on the Canadian state by virtue of prior agreements, that state has an interest in limiting the rights claimed.

When Duncan Campbell Scott said that he aimed to kill the Indian in the child, then, he was (obviously) classifying "Indianness" as something different from the life of an individual—it would be possible to kill the Indian and keep the child, somehow. In residential schools, this death was too often literal—we will never know how many children died while forced to be in residence. Survivors suffered damage to language, access to culture, and, for many, a felt sense of resilience and dignity. The paradox here is that a people's existence as Anishnabeg, as Onkwehonwe, or as "the People" in any of the many languages naming this ontology, is not determined by the Canadian state. And yet that state's activities had and have an effect—through classification and its consequences—on the enactment of that identity. Indian Residential Schools were one site for attempted destruction—it was children classified as Indian who were taken to these schools, and it was these now-grown children who, when they were deemed eligible, might claim redress.

The second question important to the TRC asked: What is covered under the recompense process? Now, the TRC had an expansive mandate, which includes, as I quoted above, telling *the complete story* of the residential school experience. This telling continues, through making the stories of survivors available and through a new archive of the TRC process. However, legal redress currently takes the form of limited individual restitution, mobilizing different categories of harm and presupposing individualist understandings of health. Consider the Common Experience Payment, which was available (until September 2012) to anyone who could show that they had attended a residential school. The CEP was supposed to pay out $10,000 in recognition of the first year of residency and $3,000 for each year thereafter. A separate process, the Independent Assessment Process (IAP), was in place to assess survivors of physical or sexual abuse and to offer them some financial recompense.

These processes asked of the survivor: What kind of harm did you, personally, experience? How will you, individually, qualify for restitution? People who filled out the forms applying for the CEP or recompense under the IAP participated in multiple webs of classification. CEP applicants must "indicate which group you belonged to at residential school" (Status/Non-Status/Métis/Inuit[Nunavut or Quebec]/Inuvialuit/Non-Aboriginal). They were required to give proof of identity, and to identify the school they attended and the dates they were there. Schools not listed could be written in, and there has been substantial difficulty reported from survivors whose schools were not listed. As Michael Hankard has compellingly argued in his examination of access to Non-Insured Health Benefits for off-reserve applicants, the very fact of having to provide these kinds of self-classifications and the documents to support them entangles people in colonial categories and systems of validation (Hankard 2014). Filling out these documents also requires substantial material resources and administrative fortitude. The forms are not simple, and there are challenges identifying some schools, as well as further layers of classification around the questions of, for example, what forms of recompense day students ought to be able to access, and which schools are understood as having been residential schools for the purpose of the payment process.

The categories of formal redress center themselves on the individual—while also holding in view the fact that the harms experienced by individuals were harms to collective identities and worlds. There is a limited recognition of the fact that the kind of harms experienced by Indigenous people cannot be healed by giving individuals a small amount of money. Such understanding acknowledges that achieving a nonindividualist form of health would involve very complex and resource-heavy transformations. If we took seriously a notion of real interdependence of self with social world and ecologies, those worlds and those environments would need substantial redress. It is hard to conceive of what healing in this broader sense could be. The CEP and IAP can be read, in the place of more fundamental transformation of the world, as a form of healthism: the harms of residential schools come from the systemic violence of colonialism, but it is up to individuals to prove their effects and manage their response to these harms.

Taiaiake Alfred addresses the broader health situation in which all of this takes place. He writes:

> Onkwehonwe suffer health problems at rates exponentially higher than that of Settler populations; epidemic diseases, obesity/diabetes, HIV/AIDS, and the effects of Fetal Alcohol Spectrum Disorder are the primary concerns. . . . These social and health problems seem to be vexing to governments: large amounts of money have been allocated to implement government-run organizations and policies geared towards alleviating these problems in both the United

States and Canada, for example, but they have had only limited positive effect on the health status of our communities. But these problems are not really mysterious nor are they unsolvable. The social and health problems besetting Onkwehonwe are the logical result of a situation wherein people respond to or adapt to unresolved colonial injustices. People in indigenous communities develop complexes of behaviours and mental attitudes that reflect their colonial situation and out flow unhealthy and destructive behaviours. It is a very simple problem to understand when we consider the whole context of the situation and all of the factors involved. (Alfred 2000, 163–64)

The pursuit of healing in the wake of residential schools and their ongoing effects will require this sort of collective and decolonized approach to health. Many people are—and long have been—crafting these kinds of approaches within Indigenous communities.[2]

*Then*—in the nineteenth century, in the "Sixties Scoop" and in residential schools—the colonizing approach was to individualize, atomize, and decontextualize people, as a form of colonial violence. Given this, it is difficult to believe that the activities *now* (ostensibly to redress past wrongs), when they take the same form—a focus on delimited classification as a precondition for access to resources and a focus on the individual even in the context of collective harms—are not of a piece. The forms—the structures and technologies of sorting and managing identity—were developed in the work of colonization, and those are still the modes the state uses in its partial and incomplete attempts at righting those wrongs. Redressing the harms of colonization will require rearticulating our relationships with classification and its salient practices. A central problem remains how we understand the question of responsibility: What would responsibility for the future look like, as a collective practice of producing the conditions for flourishing (rather than the narrow conception of individual health)? What would it mean for the Canadian state to take responsibility and attempt to redress harm not merely for the wrongs of forced residential schooling, but for the histories and ongoing practices of colonization? What could it mean for resurgence from harm to arise without reference to the Canadian state? In other words, we ought to consider how might we pursue, in Alfred's words, a response to the *whole context of the situation and all of the factors involved* in order to resist, shift, and reconfigure the available classificatory frameworks toward true, complexly interdependent, flourishing.

## Unforgetting

To do this, we need to revisit how we remember and reckon with this past, opening different possibilities for the present and future. In the Canadian context, such reckoning perceives the continuity between then Prime Minister Harper's seemingly disjunctive statements: the apology and acknowledgment of Indian Residential Schools as a wrong, and the claim that Canada has no history of colonialism. Strangely, these statements—one that seems to acknowledge colonialism, the other that disavows it—are *both* forms of disavowing colonialism as a patterned and continuing network of social relations. Following Patrick Wolfe, we can understand this "move" as an attempt to frame colonialism as a fixed event; he argues that instead we should understand colonialism as "a structure rather than an event," existing as a complex social formation across time (Wolfe 2006, 390). Events happened in the past, and they are finished; remembering them is a form of closure, nostalgia, or recapitulation. Practices of colonialism are written into the infrastructure of the states founded through expropriation, and in this sense they ascend from the past as the infrastructure of the present. Patterns of social relations, as structure not event, then predict the practices of the future. Remembering how these patterns came to be is a practice of opening questions, defamiliarization, and (perhaps) refusal of the social relations that produced events of the past. As Glen Sean Coulthard argues:

> In settler-colonial contexts—where there is no period marking a clear or formal transition from an authoritarian past to a democratic present—state-sanctioned approaches to reconciliation must ideologically manufacture such a transition by allocating the abuses of settler colonization to the dustbins of history, and/or purposely disentangle processes of reconciliation from questions of settler-coloniality as such. . . . In such conditions, reconciliation takes on a temporal character as the individual and collective process of overcoming the subsequent *legacy* of past abuse, not the abusive colonial structure itself. (Coulthard 2014, 108–9)

How might we think and act in more adequate ways as we stand in relation to shared pasts and presents?

Historian of Indigenous struggles and revolutionary, Roxanne Dunbar-Ortiz formulates the beautiful concept of *unforgetting* as a part of resistance to colonialism. In this section, I dwell with conceptions of critical memory practices as a way to think about how white people can work with anticolonialism and decolonizing as praxis. For me, the aspiration to this kind of practice has intimately to do with memory and with the process of understanding the work of memory in colonial contexts. It is key to hold in mind that the stakes of memory and forgetting are not equal; while people, and white settlers in particular, benefit from forgetting the past that organizes the racist present, Indigenous people bear the weight of memory oppression. As Patricia Monture-Angus writes, drawing on Paula Allen Gunn's views on memory: "It must be remembered, especially by Aboriginal individuals, that the roots of our oppression lie in our collective loss of memory" (Monture-Angus 1995, 235). I'll focus here on the question of decolonization as a challenge to forgetting, which implies that this collective *loss* of memory could perhaps be understood as a theft of memory, a dispossession integral to the colonial process. Dunbar-Ortiz says:

> The definition of lying is what white South African anti-apartheid writer Andre Brink plays with in his book *An Act of Terror*. What's the opposite of truth? We think immediately "the lie." But in Greek, the opposite of truth is forgetting. This is a very subtle thing. What is the action you take to tell the truth? It is un-forgetting. That is really meaningful to me. It's not that the origin myth is a lie; it's the process of forgetting that's the real problem. . . . Alliances without un-forgetting at their core aren't going to go anywhere in the long run. So, it is a dilemma, but we have to find a way. (Dunbar-Ortiz 2008, 57)

Unforgetting, on this view, is an activity, just as forgetting is an activity. Political forgetting names an epistemology (a way of knowing) and an ontology (a way of being). Epistemically, forgetting is a core piece of colonial practice. Charles Mills and others call this an *epistemology of ignorance*: just as what we know arises from political situations and choices, what we do not know is actively shaped and carries politics (Mills 2007; Sullivan and Tuana 2007). Ignorance is not just an absence of knowledge; it is a way to (not) know things. In our being, ontologically, we become who we are in part through what we know and what we are made (or made able) to forget. Unforgetting, following Dunbar-Ortiz, can be an important part of resistance.

A central feature of white settler colonial subjectivity is forgetting; we live whiteness in part as active ignorance and forgetting. In situations where facts of the matter are routinely brought to our attention, forgetting must be an active and ongoing thing. In general, I believe that systemic oppression is, in fact, present enough in our world that the kinds of ignorance and lack of knowledge running alongside oppression deserve explanation. Consider that some people think that they "just don't see race," or that poverty doesn't exist in their community, or that Indigenous people aren't part of their national consciousness. One way to understand what is at play here is through imagining a kind of benign ignorance—people just haven't been taught the facts of the situation, and so they can't be held responsible for not under-standing how race, poverty, indigeneity, and more, are present in their lives. If this were the problem, just giving people more and better information would correct their knowledge problem. But we don't just have a knowledge problem—we have a habit-of-being problem; the problem of whiteness is a problem of what we expect, our ways of being, bodily-ness, and how we understand ourselves as "placed" in time. Whiteness is a problem of being shaped to think that other people are the problem. Another way to under-stand this dynamic is to realize the very complex entanglement of practices and habits of ignorance, repression, and active disavowal that constitute an active settler process of not telling, not seeing, and not understanding the truth of the matter, which is a truth of being shaped as the legacy of the harms of the past.

We unforget, actively and resistantly, because forgetting is shaped by forces bigger than ourselves. In their book about regulation of sexuality through state surveillance, Gary Kinsman and Patrizia Gentile say: "In part, capi-talism and oppression rule through what we call 'the social organization of forgetting,' which is based on the annihilation of our social and historical memories. . . . We have been forced to forget where we have come from; our histories have never been recorded and passed down; and we are denied the social and historical literacy that allows us to remember and relive our past, and, therefore, to grasp our present" (Kinsman and Gentile 2010, 21). We white people might, on some level, *like* living with annihilated social and historical memories—we might like to think that the present can be innocent of the past that produced it. We might like to think, though we're ashamed to admit it, that we don't need to tell or hear the painful stories of the actions that created the world we live in. That feeling, of wanting to be people un-moored from history, of endorsing the pretense that we have nothing to do with the past that constitutes our material conditions and our most intimate

subjectivities, is a feeling that defines us. The social organization of forgetting means that our actual histories are lost, and it means that we have a
feeling of acceptance and normalness about living with a lie instead of an
unforgetting.

How do we tell a resistant, anticolonial story without using colonial
frameworks? What would it mean to understand this history without foregrounding a conception of individualized and disconnected history that
may be completely unintelligible within Indigenous social and legal systems?
How can we tell histories of residential schools without replicating another
colonial trope, that of the innocent, pure, all-good natives corrupted by
colonial education? That is, how can we see the people forced to attend residential schools as victims of profound injustice, and also as people who
manifested profound resistance, then and now? How can we understand the
people who were forced to attend residential schools but who identify the
experience as a positive part of their pasts? In other words: How can we tell
the full complexity of this narrative in a way that foregrounds the needs and
interests of people most affected by vectors of oppression and vulnerability—
without reinscribing the very categories delimiting purity and impurity that
were deployed to organize this form of colonization, and without inscribing
an ontology of vulnerability as definitive of Indigenous being? What would
inhabiting the full complexity of that narrative do to settlers, white settles
in particular? When I, as a white settler woman living on stolen land, nar-
rate these questions or take up and amplify other people's engagement with
questions like these, can I simultaneously take responsibility for whiteness
and undo it?

These are not meant to be rhetorical questions, but they are difficult to
answer. They become even more difficult when the questions apply not just
to one school, or to one system of forced schooling, but to an entire area now
constituted as a country, Canada, and the entire network of relations thread-
ing through it. And it is this entire network and this complex and dense
history that the work of unforgetting would stand in relation to. Recall that
the TRC's mission statement states: "The Truth and Reconciliation Commission will reveal the complete story of Canada's residential school system,
and lead the way to respect through reconciliation . . . for the child taken,
for the parent left behind" (Truth and Reconciliation Commission 2012, 2).
Telling the complete story of Indian Residential Schools involves substantial struggle against a social organization of forgetting; in Canada, unlike in

places in transitional contexts such as South Africa in the wake of apartheid, there has not been widespread attention to the TRC process from white people and settlers generally. Also, and this is the key categorical point, the process itself has been delimited. It did not involve a reckoning with the entire history of colonialism and its violence—it addressed itself to the more historically and socially bounded wrong of residential schools. Residential schools have been a widespread colonial technology. In addition to Indian Residential Schools in the Canadian context, there were Indian Boarding Schools in the United States and the forced removal of Australian Aboriginal children, though they were held in more dispersed institutional housing and schooling situations.[3]

There is a way in which the TRC process contributes to a major struggle against the social organization of forgetting. Paulette Regan was research director with the Truth and Reconciliation Commission of Canada. In reflecting on the responsibilities settlers hold to undertake an engagement with this process, she quotes theorist Roger Simon. She says:

> Such an undertaking would enable us, as Simon states, not only to "correct memory" by "engag[ing] in an active re/membering of the actualities of the violence of past injustices" but also to "initiate remembrance of the discursive practices that underwrote the European domination, subjection, and exploitation of indigenous peoples." Engaging in these acts of "insurgent remembrance" makes visible to non-Indigenous people the colonial roots of historical patterns and structures that shape our contemporary thinking, attitudes, and actions towards Indigenous people: . . . my own act of insurgent remembering involves deconstructing the peacemaker myth, linking the discursive practices of nineteenth-century treaty making and Indian policy to a flawed contemporary discourse of reconciliation, and thus tracing the continuity of the violent structures and patterns of Indigenous-settler relations over time. (Regan 2010, 49–50)

Insurgent remembrance, unforgetting, reveals salient lines of history, dwelling with how the past shapes the present. For example, consider the presumption that the Canadian state keeps peace rather than practices violence, or that things were not already profoundly violent. This presumption is part of a dense process of forgetting. The Canadian military has been deployed relatively rarely on Canadian soil, but almost always against Indigenous peoples, and almost always in relation to land claims. From a different view, then, we can say that the military brings the violence, rather than quelling it. It would be a truer, less of a forgetting mode of thinking, to understand the historical context of the founding and grounding violence of the Canadian state—violences directed toward many immigrant and enslaved peoples, as well as toward Indigenous peoples.

Erasing the memory of past wrongs may be a key part of settler consciousness, even if disavowed. As Regan says, "[O]ur willingness to negotiate outstanding historical claims with Indigenous people is mediated by our willful ignorance and our selective denial of those aspects of our relationship that threaten our privilege and power—the colonial status quo" (Regan, 35). Unforgetting, in these terms, can be understood as requiring not only the acknowledgment (the coming into knowledge) of things that threaten the colonial status quo. Unforgetting, following Regan, will also require a willingness from those of us who partake in the legacy of colonialism and have the potential to affect what is remembered and why. This, again, involves a shift from *knowing about* particular things to *taking action* in particular ways informed by that understanding. This is because more is at stake than the truth; the colonial status quo involves vast apparatuses and histories that have a material effect of immiseration for many people and profit for few. As Donna Haraway argues, "Some differences are playful; some are poles of world historical systems of domination. 'Epistemology' is about knowing the difference" (Haraway 1991, 161). The point of reckoning with the social organization of forgetting is, if it is anything, to craft a future different from the horrific past we have collectively inherited and differentially live in the present. Such crafting would change the material conditions of our lives, though in ways that we cannot completely predict or determine. So this is an epistemic task, but it is also ontological, in that it aims to change the being of the social and political world. When I've taught university classes about Canadian colonial histories, my mostly white settler students worry that if we reckoned for real with the histories they're learning about, often for the first time in their lives, they and their families would be kicked out of Canada. They worry that Canada would cease to exist. Some of them know where their families came from, and many of them do not. But they consistently say, "Where would we go, and what country would take us in?" These responses are connected to the healthism narrative I outlined above; they assume that responsibility for harms of the past will (or should) be addressed through individual retribution.

The assumptions my students make in these worries tell me something about how they see themselves. My students assume that if Indigenous people were in charge of the geographical place now called Canada that they would expel and expunge all the white people and all the settlers of color. They assume that the social relations of oppression, violation, and dispossession would be merely reversed, and not transformed. They assume there is no way to reckon with the past that does not reiterate the founding violences that they have learned about for the first time. This tells us something useful about how people, even when they have not reflected on the problem very deeply, view whiteness and settler colonialism—these students see one part of the historical role of white people with accuracy, and it is a shameful role, one that terrifies them to imagine being reversed. Their response also re-deploys a classificatory rigidity, transposing the activities of settler colonialism into a settled identity that cannot be transformed but only rejected. I am profoundly sad about these conversations, and in this way working with well-intentioned mostly white settler young people has shown me something about my own experience of seeing whiteness as a problem. When we learn even small parts of the shared histories that constitute racialization, most of the time we encounter those histories as something above and outside us—as reified, settled, and unchangeable. This more often produces despair than actuates possibility. So we will need some way of working with what Sue Campbell calls the "present past," a concept that I will unpack shortly, understanding that mere reversal does not transform oppressive relations.

Unforgetting, then, if it can have the potential that Dunbar-Ortiz claims for it, to sustain alliances, has to be collective. And, as she notes, it cannot be elitist or only happening in academic or guilty liberal contexts. She argues that:

> It means organizing working-class whites. There's just no question about it. We've just got to do it. We've been trying to avoid it for so long. They're the carriers of the origin stories and the people who have the most invested in them, especially the descendants of the original settlers. But I think the commitment to getting history straight has to come first. If you're trying to change a society and you don't know its history, you will never get anywhere. (Dunbar-Ortiz, 58)

Kinsman and Gentile's reflections on the importance of resisting the social organization of forgetting are useful in thinking about how memory might be involved in this kind of organizing. They say: "Remembering and memory are produced socially and reflexively. The liberal individualist notion that memory is some sort of asocial and ahistorical essence is not consistent with how memory works as a social practice. Memory always has a social and a historical character. Our experiences are remembered through social language and through how we make sense of them to ourselves and others" (Kinsman and Gentile, 37). If memory is collective in these ways, it may be that unforgetting contributes to generating a will and an energy to act, and not simply an enhanced knowledge or understanding. The social and historical character of memory and remembering places our memory practices in political and social context, and opens the question of what the people implicated in a particular history can do in response to it. This is why thinking about history is useable in organizing.

If the will to take action is generated in collective contexts, if we can't self-generate it, it makes sense that my students feel frozen to the extent that they don't see what they might be able to do to *individually and personally* change the world. They can't be white, or settlers, all alone; our whiteness and settlerness only exist in the context of complex social relations. So unforgetting in relation to understanding and acting in response to the overwhelming complexity of everything, refusing the lie, only makes sense as a collective venture. Anything else is a kind of conceit.

## Decolonial Memory, Resurgence, and Taking Responsibility

I have been arguing so far that the Canadian state's practices in response to the history of colonization recapitulate two worrying moves: First, a classificatory practice that aims to delimit ongoing colonial relations, rendering them an event that happened in the past rather than an ongoing structure of violence. Second, there is an associated individualism regarding how healing ought to be approached, as something that could happen in a quasi-juridical space and with monetary compensation for a past wrong. If the "sad legacy" we have to confront is only residential schooling—though that itself is expansive and difficult to adequately address—we might imagine that the work of memory and restitution would end with the end of the TRC process. If we instead follow Leanne Simpson, Coulthard, Alfred, Daschuk, and others, in seeing the task of reckoning with the past as much less easy to delimit, we will need a richer understanding of colonialism and decolonizing practice. Along with this, we can ask some useful questions about the relationality of memory in the context of pervasive and harmful social relations.

As I'll discuss more in the next chapter, Sue Campbell's view of memory proves useful for thinking about the place of memory in understanding co-implication and relational self-formation. We—and perhaps specifically those of us who are settlers—can productively engage her thinking on memory in decolonizing work. Campbell argues that we should "regard remembering as itself a relational capacity interwoven with identity formation" (Campbell 2014, 91), giving an account of how such a relational conception of remembering helps us respond to the historical and present harms of colonialism. Campbell notes:

> Most non-Aboriginal Canadians have not participated in activities of sharing memory that would allow the memories of First Nation, Inuit, or Métis peoples to have any force in shaping the experience and significance of their pasts. Insofar as this is the case, many non-Aboriginal Canadians experience their own past from the colonialist perspective of their forebearers and communities—they have never engaged in the sharing of memory that could truly challenge this view of the past. (160)

And for this reason, we ought to think about better understandings of memory, which track the ongoing, "present past" quality that all memory has. As Campbell argues, "conceptualizing the possibilities of good relational memory is politically vital: relations of greater political equality require our capacity and willingness to re-experience the actions and events of our personal communal pasts, often conceiving their significance as quite different from what we do at present" (6). For people living on stolen land, in places where the treaties made in the past have not been respected, there is frequently a desire for a communal past not marked by genocide. This is one way to understand then Prime Minister Harper's claim that Canada has no history of colonialism, or my students' shock at discovering that history.

What happens if, instead of disavowing the history that has produced the situation we are in, settlers pursued a practice of memory grounded in a politics of impure responsibility? Asking this, I mean to disrupt two different purity moves, two different ways that people affirm a pursuit of purity. One is the simple lie Harper tells, but which perhaps many settlers in the

United States and Canada implicitly or explicitly believe: that we are not implicated in ongoing genocidal colonialist practices, either because there were never such practices or because they are a thing of the past. This move figures closure, sometimes through mourning, of sad past wrongs. It is easy to see this move both in the U.S. trope of Terra Nullius—the idea that Turtle Island was empty and unused before colonization, and that thus actually European colonialism was a good thing—and in the performance of mourning the disappearing Indian, apologizing for a "sad chapter" of history. Whether instantiated as official legal position or rhetorically deployed, the historical closure move frames "authentic" indigeneity as only ever a part of the past. And if authentic indigeneity is only in the past, so too are the wrongs of colonialism—land theft, primitive accumulation, and genocidal cultural practices are part of a "then" against which our "now" is separate and clean. Indeed, situating indigeneity as always of the past often grounds very real and present legal practices. In the Canadian context, proving claim to a particular historical treaty territory can require proving sole and continuous inhabitance and use of that place. This classification "defines out" many of the actual past Indigenous life-practices of sharing territory, moving from one place to another in seasonal ways, and other histories of movement, conflict, or mixing by adoption and cohabitation.

The second "move" appealing to a kind of harmful purity practice is a displacement of settler responsibility to take up decolonizing work. I have seen this most often in the desire of people who perceive the ongoing harms of colonialism to attempt to lay themselves down, symbolically, at the feet of an Indigenous Other—to repudiate their identity as settler colonizers through taking up Indigenous spiritual practices, discovering previously unknown Indian ancestry, or reifying a correct-line Indigenous politics. This approach matters much less than the first, since it has much less material and political effect than the legal or military enactment of the "sad past" closure narrative. Attempted settler self-displacement uneasily allies new-agey spiritual appropriation based on the belief that Indigenous peoples are closer to the earth, more real, or truly healing with a particular strand of self-righteous yet guilty leftism that loudly proclaims a rigorous anticolonial critique while failing to practice any politics in particular. These seem in content very different approaches to indigeneity. Their form, though, shares a crucial approach; in realizing their implication in the history of colonialism and formulating a critique of the lifeworlds available to them, settlers aim to repudiate that history through taking on Indigenous identity—spiritually, biologically, or politically. This is a problem because such an attempt to shed historic wrongs reenacts in form the attempted appropriation of culture, identity, and land that defines the colonial project in the United States and Canada (Andrea Smith 2005).

What other options might settlers pursue? And given the well-trodden critique of restrictively situating Indigenous identity in the past, how ought we think about memory as a politically usable resource for a practical and collective settler politic? I am aiming for a kind of settler politics of memory that does not try to stand outside the past in all its horror, that does not individualize the possible response to how we are implicated in that past, and that opens possibilities for collective action. I find one opening for such a politics in Campbell's notion of responsibility as an outcome of forward-looking memory.

Campbell argues that any useful understanding of memory as an ethical and political matter will resist essentializing, especially frozen-in-the-past, conceptions of Indigenous identity. She writes:

> Non-Indigenous Canadians can respect this non-essentializing imperative along with the very different and valuable models of sociable memory evident in Indigenous teachings. These teachings express and revitalize rich traditions of public remembering that assume remembering is most naturally an inter-active, collaborative, and profoundly ethical activity; that sharing the past is critical to the epistemic and ethical fidelity of memory; that memory plays a fundamental role in making and maintaining relations; and that it is an impor-tant way to renew and transform intergroup relations. (Campbell 2014, 111)

Settlers can take up sharing the past as an activity through what Camp-bell theorizes as "forward-looking responsibility." While she identifies this conception as arising out of an engagement with Claudia Card (1996), Iris Marion Young (2006), and others, I believe that the specific formulation is her own. Consider, she says, a very ordinary mess: someone has spilled some coffee. If I say that I will clean it up, she says, "I have made myself account-able for improving a situation that I did not cause, and for which I could not be held liable" (150). Forward-looking responsibility involves this practice of, repeatedly, making ourselves accountable.

Writing specifically about the Indian Residential School TRC, in a document commissioned by the councilors, Campbell writes:

> in the context of the IRS TRC, the forward-looking senses of responsibility are politically powerful because they give people a sense that there is action that can be taken for the future. To talk of taking responsibility can move non-Aboriginal people away from the sense that they are being blamed to think about what they can now do, and this language allows people to make themselves accountable where they would reject blame. Perhaps a blame/guilt dynamic is not a part of a person's cultural understanding of responsibility, perhaps she was born at a time when the Residential School system was being dismantled and angry at the suggestion of blame; perhaps she belongs to a group that has itself been the subject of political marginalization; or perhaps she is a new Canadian. Moreover, backward-looking responsibility may be appropriate for a situation that has a terminus—a harm that has been done and needs to be redressed. Forward-looking responsibility may be more appropriate to responding to ongoing structures of injustice that require reforming and dismantling. (151)

I agree with Campbell; often settlers very actively disavow responsibility for past actions to which we believe we are not connected. As an immigrant settler to the Canadian state, it has been useful to me to consider what obligations and responsibilities I inherit in light of standing in relation to this context—no matter how disavowed they are by the very state that bestows them on me. Some of these are codified in the form of wampum belts, verbal agreements, legal rulings, and treaties. Others arise in less codified relations of care for land that I am a guest on, friendships, or action in political solidarity.

Telling an unforgetting narrative and resisting the social organization of forgetting is useful to projects attempting to reckon with the colonial situation we are in; memory is important, and in contexts organized by a socially sanctioned forgetting all of us will have to acquire memories of events and relations that we did not ourselves experience. Those of us working to hold histories of the attempted genocide of Indigenous people in our consciousness might encounter a habituated difficulty: a key colonial trope situates Indigenous people as always in the past, already lost in the mists of time, civilizationally underdeveloped, or incapable of existing in the "modern world." Resisting these tropes is important, and Campbell's notion of "remembering for the future," taking forward-looking form of responsibility, productively reconfigures how memory can be understood. We should think of memory as a relational and situated process through which we collectively determine the significance of the past for the present as a form of forward-looking responsibility. And coming to collectively determine what should be remembered for the future, and who can hold memory, is itself a dilemma. This dilemma involves classificatory delineation of who is inside community and who is outside, who has standing to determine what should be remembered and what should not be remembered, or what action memory can cue. Memory is about the past, but it triangulates with dilemmas of the present and unfixed futures to come.

In order to approach memory responsibly, then, it is important to also hold in mind the fact that people do not engage shared histories on the same footing. As Campbell points out, non-Indigenous people have the power to refuse to share memory in the relevant sense because we benefit from ongoing histories of colonial theft, murder, and betrayal. In this sense, if settlers want to take responsibility for the past that has shaped the conditions of our lives, we will have to start from an understanding that we are implicated in a past we abjure. We are, in the terms I offer in this book, never pure, never innocent. Any capacity we have to resist colonial oppression is in part based on benefiting from colonial oppression—the differential access to health, cultural situatedness, family continuity, and more. Any practice of relational, forward-looking responsibility may involve some form of purification (in the sense of attempting to redress ongoing wrongs), but it will not be pure. As Claudine Rankine puts it, in her lyric engagement with U.S. American racism: "The world is wrong. You can't put the past behind you. It's buried in you; it's turned your flesh into its own cupboard. Not everything remembered is useful but it all comes from the world to be stored in you" (Rankine 2014, 63). While Rankine is here referencing Black U.S. American subjectification, I take her sense that the wrongness of the world incorporates us, differentially, in classificatory practices of sorting, boxing, cupboarding.

When the *world is wrong*, and our *flesh is its cupboard*, it might be difficult to conceive of where a forward-looking responsibility can be grounded. The most compelling conceptions of such practices of responsibility have been and are being formulated in Indigenous practices of decolonization. One strand of these practices brings forward an analysis of dispossession as a fundamental operating feature of colonialism. Resistance to dispossession, on this analysis, centrally involves practices of responsibility. As Kanien'kehá:ka scholar Patricia Monture-Angus compellingly argued at many points in her writing, practices of responsibility are central to decolonizing work. She writes:

> We have to learn how to live our rights because that is our responsibility. . . .
> Do you know what kind of rights you have? Elders taught me that I have only
> one. Do you know what that one right is? It is the right to live as a Mohawk
> woman because that is the way Creator made me. That is the only right I have.
> After that I have a series of responsibilities, as a Mohawk woman, because that
> is how I was made. (Monture-Angus 1995, 87)

Moving away from the framework of rights granted by the state based on citizenship, Monture-Angus formulates an account of responsibility as a practice of relationality that constitutes sovereignty. She defines sovereignty as a right to be responsible, which

> requires a relationship with territory (and not a relationship based on control
> of that territory). . . . What must be understood then is that Aboriginal request
> to have our sovereignty respected is really a request to be responsible. I do not
> know of anywhere else in history where a group of people have had to fight so
> hard just to be responsible. (Monture-Angus 1999, 36)

Here, "responsibility" articulates beautifully the sense in which being responsive to the whole situation we find ourselves in, to reprise Alfred's words, is simultaneously far beyond and counter to the classifying and delimiting terms offered in state practices around land and people. It is also specific to context—our responsibilities will shift depending on how we are placed in the web of relations that constitute who we are.

Coulthard has offered an intervention further exploring the importance of taking responsibility as a decolonizing practice. He conceives of colonialism as centrally involving dispossession of territory and disruption of the relations of place that come along with being grounded in a situated history. And he argues that "in the Canadian context, colonial relations of power are no longer reproduced primarily through overtly coercive means, but rather through the asymmetrical exchange of mediated forms of state recognition and accommodation" (Coulthard 2014, 15). As I outline above, these forms of recognition closely articulate with classificatory apparatuses that by design disenfranchise Indigenous people in relation to the state, whether under the Indian Act or through land claims processes that attempt to shift collectively held places into property simple (property owned by individuals). Dispossession can be understood both in the most obvious cases relating directly to land and also in situations that affect the relationships that constitute place and identity. So, when the Canadian state violates treaties or agreements about land usage, when it restricts people into "reserves" or requires them to live a certain distance from cities, it is fairly clear that a form of colonial dispossession is happening—colonies require the appropriation of physical territory. This process is historical and it is ongoing; the Canadian state's two primary forms of engagement with Indigenous claims (legal challenge and land claims) both aim to extinguish future title and claim.

However, we can also understand the sense of dispossession that I see Coulthard and others invoking in broader terms, which could track the theft of Indigenous relationships to place and people. In these terms, from the earliest iterations of the Indian Act to very contemporary revisions, the aim of "classifying out" Indian identity is a kind of dispossession. Similarly, we ought to understand residential schooling, which aimed to cut children out of their language communities and away from the places they would otherwise have come to know as an everyday part of their relations as a form of colonial dispossession. We can see the "Sixties Scoop," in which children were "adopted out" of their communities and moved to places far away as a form of colonial dispossession. We should see current practices of clear-cutting, strip-mining, and using traditional hunting and fishing territories as dump sites for mining waste as a form of colonial dispossession. We can understand current practices of imprisoning large numbers of Indigenous people, frequently moving them far away from their home communities, as a form of colonial dispossession. For example, when people from the north are arrested and their sentence is longer than two years, the state mandates that they be imprisoned in a federal institution. But the only federal institutions are in the south of the country, which means that it is prohibitive to the point of impossibility for their family to visit, and on release in general people do not have resources to make their way home. We should also understand conceptions (or legal definitions) of indigeneity as only "real" outside cities, in reserves, as a form of colonial dispossession.

Notice that all of these forms of dispossession only exist within the frame of the Canadian state. They begin from legal fictions that have material effects. Ontologically, though, I follow many Indigenous thinkers in understanding that the Canadian state's classificatory attempts, its work toward dispossession, does not have standing in determining who is Indigenous, who has what sort of relation to place, and what constitutes community and right relation. However, to reprise the paradox of this situation, colonial powers have effects on Indigenous peoples through regimes of recognition and force. Resisting the effects of these attempts at dispossession is generative. As Coulthard writes, speaking of Sioux theologian and writer Vine Deloria, it is important to

> explicate the position that land occupies as an ontological framework for understanding *relationships*. Seen in this light, it is a profound misunderstanding to think of land or place as simply some material object of profound importance to Indigenous cultures (although it is this too); instead, it ought to be understood as a field of "relationships of things to each other." Place is a way of knowing, of experiencing and relating to the world and with others; and sometimes these relational practices and forms of knowledge guide forms of resistance against other rationalizations of the world that threaten to erase or destroy our senses of place. (Coulthard 2014, 61)

Understanding place as a relationship opens terrain for the decolonizing practice that Coulthard calls "grounded normativity," by which he means "the modalities of Indigenous land-connected practices and longstanding experiential knowledge that inform and structure our ethical engagements with the world and our relationships with human and nonhuman others over time" (13). Recall Monture-Angus's conception of ethical engagement as a relational practice of responsibility. She writes: "Sovereignty, when defined as my right to be responsible, is really a question of identity (both individual and collective) more than it is a question of an individualized property right. Identity, as I have come to understand it, requires a relationship with territory (and not a relationship based on control of that territory)" (Monture-Angus 1999, 36). The relationships to place that constitute identity on Monture-Angus's view are fundamentally different from relations of ownership.

How, though, might non-Indigenous settlers take responsibility for *the whole situation* we are in? Our practices of responsibility do not arise from the web of relationships with people and place that Monture-Angus draws on when she inhabits being Kanien'kehá:ka. And there is, almost by definition, no practice of responsibility that respects and lives alongside Indigenous sovereignty in the relevant sense. Indeed, the Canadian state's practices of engaging with Indigenous practices of responsibility aim in quite thorough ways to destroy the grounds of those practices. Practices that recall responsibility and a relation to place will, it seems, be important forms of decolonization. How, then, ought settlers stand in relations of forward-looking responsibility without attempting to stand in the place of Indigenous people? How, if we don't attempt to walk the same path, recognizing that impulse at itself a colonizing one, can we share responsibility for the situation we have the bulk of responsibility for creating and benefiting from? Beginning to answer these questions opens a space for a renewed relation to memory and a renewed practice of forward-looking responsibility.

As Andrea Smith says in her article "Soul Wound: The Legacy of Native American Schools," reckoning with the past will likely not involve a wholesale rejection of classification and institutionalized memory practices altogether. She notes, "Although there is disagreement in Native communities about how to approach the past, most agree that the first step is documentation." Through beginning to call the state that mandated boarding schools and the churches that ran them to accountability, the National Native American Boarding School Healing Coalition projects founders hope that "Native communities . . . will begin to view the abuse as the consequence of human rights violations perpetrated by church and state rather than as an issue of community dysfunction and individual failings" (Smith 2007). I close this chapter with one example of documentation that insists on classification as a part of decolonizing work—community databases of Missing and Murdered Indigenous Women in the Canadian context.

There is more to say about #MMIW, as it has come to be shorthanded, than I can discuss here, including important questions about how and whether people call for justice from the state that has brutalized them. This issue arises in thinking about missing and murdered Indigenous women (as a phenomena, rather than a hashtag) because often the experience of families of women who have disappeared or who have been killed involves dismissive or disrespectful treatment from the police who might otherwise be expected to investigate crimes like murder. Proving that women who are missing haven't voluntarily left their home and family, or that if they did leave voluntarily their disappearance still deserves investigation, or that their murders were not invited, has involved setting up mechanisms to track who is gone and what happened to whom. It has involved multiple classificatory schemas normally applied as part of state-mediated relations: who "counts" as Indigenous, what is a crime, and who is responsible for tracking widespread harms to Indigenous women.

The organizations No More Silence (NMS), Families of Sisters in Spirit (FSIS), and the Native Youth Sexual Health Network have launched a community-led tracking database of missing and murdered Indigenous women under the name "It Starts With Us" (online at http://www.itstarts withus-mmiw.com/). This work carries on aspects of a database and story-gathering initiative that had been held by the Native Women's Association of Canada called "Sisters in Spirit" documenting details of the disappearance and deaths of Indigenous women in the Canadian context. This initiative ended when the federal government defunded SIS, redirecting the money that had been allocated to them to the Department of Justice and the Ministry of Public Safety (Sterritt 2010). In 2011, Families of Sisters in Spirit was formed to continue some of work SIS had begun. It is thus possible to see continuities between these databases, as well as with the daily work out of which the databases arise—the work of remembering people who have been lost and working to make sure that others are not lost. As the website of It Starts With Us says:

> We acknowledge the women, families and communities who have been doing this organizing themselves for decades, especially when police and governments have failed to acknowledge, listen or act despite Indigenous women, Two Spirit and Trans people that have continued to disappear or be murdered. Generations of work have brought us to where we are and continue to teach us how we must work forward in achieving justice together. (2015a)

They thus place the work of memory in a long historical context of colonialism and its effects. At the same time, they argue for an infrastructure of resistant remembering that cannot be cut by the government that perpetrated genocidal colonialism in the past and that continues practices of land and cultural dispossession in the present. They say:

> It's time for community to build our own structures independent of govern-ment and institutional funding. The purpose of this database is to honour our women and provide family members with a way to document their loved ones passing while asserting community control of our own record-keeping. ("Why a Community-Led Database?" 2015)

Alongside documentary and memory practices tracing the myriad stories that manifest the social relation that is colonialism, It Starts With Us thus uses key classificatory practices as a form of remembering for justice. This work also suggests that for memory to be politically transformational it may be necessary to have certain institutional forms that resist institutionalized forgetting.[4]

Remembering for justice is, I think, a practice of resisting dispossession. Holding the memory of people who have gone missing or been murdered is a practice of refusing to accede to the idea that Indigenous women have already disappeared. It can take the form of the kind of grounded normativity that Coulthard discusses. Resisting dispossession from our position as settler colonizers who want to repudiate these relations, as the inheritors of pro-found ongoing wrongs, will not take the form of grounded normativity in the sense that Coulthard outlines. We do not have those specific relation-ships. Still, taking up an unforgetting approach, revisiting the question of what and how we remember, we can understand ourselves as relationally con-stituting power-saturated relationships of differential but forward-looking responsibility. I believe that such responsibility will start with a commitment and practice that asks: How does this potential action resist or reinforce colonial dispossession in any of the relevant senses? How does any proposed action resist healthism and hold in mind a collective web of relationality? Answering these kinds of questions will involve a lot of listening and a kind of productive uncertainty. We cannot predict, as we shift toward such a memory practice, how these kinds of relations of responsibility will unfurl, or if they will end.

## 2

# "Women Don't Get AIDS, They Just Die From It"

## Memory, Classification, and the Campaign to Change the Definition of AIDS

Ordinarily, we may not think about the processes by which diseases are defined. Perhaps we also don't often see disease classification as political. And yet, the process of ordering the complexity of bodily experiences of vibrancy or sickness into categories of health or disease imbricates social, political, and practical questions in an assemblage that comes to appear as a neutral expression of what's really happening in the natural world. There are real things happening in a real world, but how we sort, name, and manage those happenings cocreates the ontologies that we then render as natural.[1] Medical classifications are also keys to memory, offering themselves as a technology for managing what in the past presented itself as a confusion instead as a diagnosis. It is difficult to perceive the messy histories behind established disease categories at the point at which they are no longer emergent or in categorical crisis, but it is sometimes worth our attention to ask how they came to be what they are.

In this chapter, I examine a specific activist campaign to change the U.S. Centers for Disease Control surveillance case definition of HIV and AIDS, which will help us think concretely about the politics of medical classification.[2] This campaign's effects included a profound shift in how AIDS is understood, and thus in some real way in what it is. One strand of my argument here is that classification should be understood as a political formation with material effects. I ground this part of the argument in the words of activists, most of them women, who contested the way AIDS was defined in a moment when no one else thought the definition needed to be changed. A second strand of the chapter examines the question of what it means to remember the history of currently stable classifications that were once very different. I argue that Sue Campbell's work on the importance of understanding memory and feeling as relational helps understand the histories of death and loss, resistance and fierce joy, crystallized in activist responses to HIV and AIDS. I begin by arguing that Campbell's accounts of feeling and memory are compatible and connected. Then I connect Campbell's conception of "remembering for the future" to the specific project of resistant remembering as a kind of activist project. Finally, I will examine the interaction of memory with the politics of classification in this specific case study, followed by the idea that how we remember the past matters for our capacities to do justice to the present and future. Impure politics require memory projects like this, which can recognize that the present was not inevitable, and that the future we are now shaping can likewise be different than the present.

My central archive in this project comes from the ACT UP Oral History Project (AUOHP). This project has so far collected more than a hundred interviews with people involved with the New York branch of the activist group ACT UP (the AIDS Coalition to Unleash Power). ACT UP still exists in many cities, though in different forms than its early days; it was and is a direct-action activist group agitating to transform the lives of people living with HIV and AIDS through researching and spreading information about drug treatments, acting to set up now commonly held practices such as needle exchanges, helping people have access to treatment, confronting the stigma attached to AIDS, and much more. One of the core activists who worked with ACT UP NYC reflects on it: "The beauty of ACT UP was that it was about the fact that medicine is political" (Wolfe, 97).

Remembering the nomenclature of the disease we now call HIV/AIDS is political as well. Such memory tracks salient social histories, and attending to how people conceived of the virus in the days before it had a standard epidemiological story is an interesting project in itself (Treichler 1999). It's hard now to hold in mind—hard to remember—what it was like to live in a time before AIDS, where "AIDS" signals here both certain medical ontologies (what the disease is) and social practices (what it means). This moment comes after a reasonably widespread understanding of what HIV was and how it was transmitted, at least in communities most heavily affected, but before mainstream audiences necessarily understood what was involved.

President Ronald Reagan only publically spoke the word "AIDS" in 1987. By the late 1980s, there was an established set of criteria by which HIV and AIDS were defined. In January 1993, that definition changed in significant ways.

Here is the official Centers for Disease Control explanation of the change: "To be consistent with standards of medical care for HIV-infected persons and to more accurately reflect the number of persons with severe HIV-related immunosuppression who are at highest risk for HIV-related morbidity and most in need of close medical follow-up, the surveillance definition was expanded on January 1, 1993" (CDC). The expanded definition included CD4/T-cell counts, pulmonary tuberculosis, recurrent pneumonia, and invasive cervical cancer in people living with HIV. Crucially occluded in the official account is *how and why*, exactly, this definition changed. As written, it looks like the CDC changed its definition as part of a routine process of making sure that designations kept pace with science, instead of as a response to mass protests, a substantial legal suit, media attention, a letter-writing campaign, and more. The definitional shift in fact came out of work by ACT UP activists, and it had profound effects, which continue today. Activists's commitments to respect the people affected by HIV/AIDS made the CDC change its definition, and this change shifted far more than a definition.

Following Cathy Cohen's important work on racial formation and AIDS, I see the Centers for Disease Control as a dominant and life-shaping institution in the United States and beyond, particularly in the early days of AIDS. This is in part because the CDC's surveillance definitions serve as lynchpin concepts with cascading social effects. As Cohen writes, the CDC functioned, particularly in the "early years of this epidemic, as the most important informant on the progression of AIDS. The epidemiological work of CDC staff members constructed the 'facts' of this disease. The CDC helped to define who was at risk, as well as the appropriate paths of research, reporting, and response that others would follow" (Cohen 1999, 121). As Cohen emphasizes, it's worthwhile to attend to these effects *not* because of the "personal intentions of researchers and staff members at the CDC." Rather, it was the "structures and procedures of the CDC which served to bias the system, making some groups invisible to this institution" (131). The ACT UP campaign to change the CDC's AIDS surveillance definition can be understood as an important historical example of engaging with effects of systemic injustice.

Many readers will have heard of this campaign without knowing it. Steven Epstein's science studies book, *Impure Science*, discusses it, as does Ann

Cvetkovich's *An Archive of Feeling.* The redefinition campaign is narratively central as well to the popular 2012 documentary, *How to Survive a Plague.* But for the most part the campaign is rendered in terms of its import to the history of the internal dynamics of ACT UP, rather than as a significant moment in other, bigger contexts. Details about what the campaign was and why it mattered are obscured. So, for example, Cvetkovich devotes a central chapter to discussing the context and fallout of a key moment in the surveillance classification work, during which internal struggles produced a substantial institutional split within ACT UP. She frames this moment this way, noting that it highlighted "already existing tensions within ACT UP between working on the inside and working on the outside, between negotiating with government officials and engaging in direct action. . . . One of the critical moments in ACT UP's history occurred when the CDC Working Group proposed a moratorium on all negotiations with government officials for six months until the definition was changed" (Cvetkovich 2003, 198). Cvetkovich—and I believe she is representative of a broader tendency in how this moment is rendered and remembered—focuses on the effects on ACT UP of this proposal for a moratorium. These effects were significant, and they are well worth studying. The responses of ACT UP people involved both with working directly with the scientists and government officials around HIV and AIDS and those working on what was framed as the social, direct-action "side" of things reveal a lot about an important moment in movement history.

But Cvetkovich does not discuss the campaign itself, or its effects outside of ACT UP—and she devotes more attention to the campaign itself than most.[3] There are thus important things that remain persistently untold and unremembered about this moment, even in central texts discussing this time. One of the problems with the standard narrative about this campaign, as it's rendered, is a curious allegiance to a particular kind of narrative, which I read as a purity move—the assumption that it's possible to cleanly separate out the politics informing working on the science or the activism "sides" of AIDS. Another problem is simply that telling the histories of this campaign through looking at only the effects of the call for a moratorium, without attending to the specifics of what was being fought for, loses a key piece of the history of AIDS activism. It might seem, to readers of these texts, that it has always been the case that AIDS was defined as (among other things) having a particular T-cell count, or more broadly, having or not having the opportunistic infections that now classify the disease. But the formation of

AIDS as it is now lived was in fact a product of very particular struggles to shift both the social imaginary of AIDS and how "having AIDS" is experienced. In telling a different version of this history, I am interested in what an allegiance to the impurity and complexity of social movement work can help us understand about the past.

## Memory, Affect, and Relational Personhood

In order to access some of what is important about the campaign, I begin with Sue Campbell's early work on feeling and expression. Campbell argues for the importance of what she calls "free-style" or unsanctioned feeling—modes of feeling that do not fall neatly into the boxes offered by classic emotions, such as anger, love, jealousy, and so on. In conversation with theorists of emotion who attend to "outlaw" emotions (Jaggar 1992; Spelman 1989), Campbell argues that expressive possibilities are important to affective experience. She also disrupts the supposed transparency of even "classic" feelings, showing how they too are collectively shaped and stabilized. But she is most interested—and I follow her here—in the feelings that are not given social sanction and the coproduction of free-style selves and feelings. Such feelings are especially interesting to me in thinking about heterodox activist activity, which may amplify or create such feelings.

Feeling and expressive uptake require one another, which is to say that we require certain kinds of worlds in order to have certain kinds of feelings. "To understand affect," Campbell argues, "is centrally to understand both the activity of expression and the risks of expressive failure" (Campbell 1997, 6). We "form our feelings through acts of expression, and, in doing so, attempt to make clear to others, or even just to ourselves, the personal significance of some occasion or set of occasions in our lives" (131). Campbell's understanding of affect is inherently public—our capacities for feeling rely on others. This means, among much else, that oppression disproportionally affects feelers and knowers who are not accorded dignity in their expressive potential. Our affective lives can be the site of oppression. This is, in Campbell's words, "especially the case when people cannot secure adequate uptake or do not have the power to determine how the occasions of their lives are viewed" (180). One piece of oppression, then, is the constraint and torquing it wreaks on affective and expressive possibility.

Campbell's later work on memory, discussed in chapter 1, may seem to be simply a different area than the work on expression and feelings. And yet if we follow her thinking about expressive uptake and the capacity to form feeling subjectivities, we see that her understanding of memory is profoundly connected to her account of the political dimensions of affective expression and the ways that affect is always relational (and therefore always also political). The relational and political dimensions of affect are fruitfully understood in terms of relational conceptions of selfhood. Consonant with relational accounts of self-formation, Campbell emphasizes the social or relational nature of personhood: we cannot understand persons, she thinks, as atomized and isolated individuals. Campbell argues: "We develop and live our lives as persons within complex networks of institutional, personal, professional, interpersonal, and political relationships—both chosen and unchosen. We are shaped in and through our interactions with others in ways that are ongoing" (Campbell 2003, 155–56). The work of memory is part of the network of interaction that shapes us as persons. Memory is held not only, or perhaps even not primarily, in our skull. Rather, it might be best understood as "held" within precisely the complex network of relationships that shapes affect and personhood. In thinking about Campbell's claim that we need a relational view of memory, recall her argument that having a discursive community can help us express free-style feelings and that expression is in key ways involved in having feelings that do not fit into preset, well-established emotions. Campbell frames memory as collaborative, too.

Campbell discusses a shift in understandings of memory from a storehouse or archival view to a dynamic or relational view. Conventional Western accounts hold that memory is a mechanism for recording information, keeping it in inert form, and offering it back to rememberers essentially unchanged. On such views, the "goodness" of memory lies in its stability, its purity, its resistance to change over time, its individuated character. Memories that change in conversation with others, that shift meaning with time or perspective, or rely on collective construction for their existence are suspect, contaminated, corrupted, impure. Campbell argues, in contrast, for a relational account, stressing the "dynamic, embodied, reconstructive, and social nature of human recollection" (Campbell 2014, 73). She highlights modes of remembering that see memory as situated in the invested and particular present, as changeable, as collectively shaped and (sometimes) collectively held. This conception of memory, which she also sometimes calls "reconstructive," is not necessarily new—it also expresses certain Indigenous modes of honoring the past in the context of the present. Understanding memory as relational involves, in part, valuing the work others can do to help us articulate and understand our past. It involves thinking of memory as inherently impure in relevant ways, and holding that impurity up as generative and, actually, good.

Campbell's work on memory took two tracks. Her book *Relational Remembering: Rethinking the Memory Wars* made substantial interventions in debates about "false memory" syndrome, responding particularly to the ways that understanding memory as dynamic and relational has been critiqued by "false memory" skeptics. Campbell observed that women who recovered memories of past abuse were often discredited by people—often in courts of law—who claimed that their memory was unsound because they had fashioned their memories in conversations with therapists. In these cases, women are rendered unreliable or sullied rememberers through, among other things, storehouse, individuated conceptions of memory. Campbell's claim here is that memory is not a storehouse, nor individual. So it is not a failure of memory that we need others to articulate and understand our past experiences; others are necessary to our memory. In her later work, Campbell began significant thinking about the usefulness of social conceptions of memory in Canada's Truth and Reconciliation Commission inquiry into the history of residential schools. Here, Campbell offered nuanced reflections on the politics of memory, forwarding the idea of "remembering for the future" and discussing the question of how memory is used in crafting livable futures in the context of systemic and ongoing oppression.

In her work on the TRC, Campbell extends her analysis of the social and political nature of memory into a powerful set of reflections on state and collective memory practices. She argues that "the reconstructive view of memory does not suggest that we can undo or remake facts about the past, or will away the damage of the past by thinking about it differently. It rather stresses that how we remember can change the significance of the past for the future" (Campbell 2014, 148). If we understand memory as situated in the present, as at least partially collective in nature, as reflecting present interests and needs, and as offering multiple ways "in" to respecting the past, we might begin to do justice to that past in all its relationally constituted richness. In this kind of memory project, accuracy is determined by fidelity to the past as it is collectively understood, and with an attention to the political salience of what and who is remembered. It also matters who does the remembering. In this case, the people who lived can remember, and this matters because as with any health catastrophe, living and dying is partially torqued by social relations—how much support do people have, how much money, what kind of access to information about their illness. As I discuss below, forms of relational and collective memory can be more accurate to this complexity than dominant accounts. Here as in chapter 1, thinking about the past is important to the account of being against purity for two reasons: First, recognizing the contingency and malleability of what happened in the past reminds us that the world we experience now is a product of complex social relations, which continue to have ramifying effects in the present. Second, attending to how we remember the past calls on us to consider how and why we remember, and to recognize that these practices are situated and invested rather than natural and inevitable.

## Memory as Forward-Looking

Campbell's theory of memory can be usefully put into conversation with contemporary oral history work. As I write, I am working on just such a project, the AIDS Activist History project, alongside queer sociologist and historian Gary Kinsman; the interviews we have done so far and the archival documents we have collected doubtless inform my reading of the CDC reclassification. In this chapter, I turn to the oral history project that inspired our work, New York ACT UP Oral History project. Run and curated by writer Sarah Schulman and filmmaker Jim Hubbard, this project shows us an enactment of complex memory about densely interwoven scientific and social pasts. Schulman narrates its origins:

> I accidentally tuned in to NPR's commemoration of the 20th anniversary of AIDS.
> "At first America had trouble with People With AIDS," the announcer said. "But they then came around." I had long been disheartened by the false AIDS stories told in the few mainstream representations of the crisis. Gay people are alone—hurting each other and causing our own oppression—until benevolent straight people bravely overcome their prejudices to help us.
> Bravo!
> But now, that lie was being extended beyond the arts to actual history. We were being told that AIDS Activism never existed. Instead, the dominant culture simply "came around."
> That is not what happened. I know, I was there. (Schulman 2003)

Schulman articulates the dangers of allowing knowledge of what ACT UP was, and what a broader coalition of AIDS activists did, to be erased from history and to fade from public knowledge. Using Campbell's analysis, we might understand this commitment as recognizing that one site of oppression is the closure of the space for affect and memory. History matters, and when the history involves resistance to systemic harm, it matters to defend our current capacities to remember that history. A recent book on the memory-effects of the AIDS crisis captures this harm through an analysis of "de-generational unremembering," the cutting off of continuities between our present and a complex past (Castiglia and Reed 2011, 9). Schulman says that she wanted to keep the knowledge of what ACT UP achieved in "public memory." Thus, she and Hubbard began collecting and archiving interviews.

It may seem that such archiving bolsters the storehouse view of memory that Campbell critiques—creating a blank and settled repository that can then be accessed by future researchers. This would be an incorrect reading of the intention and effects of the project, I think. The salient capacity to generate the archive, and to help others remember, relies on the relations generated though personal involvement and political work. Those connections are necessary to the memory. In many of the interviews, the people Schulman speaks with talk about knowing her in the past, the work that she did, the people she knew. A web of relationships allows memory to function in the present, and that in turn allows researchers who were not involved in the work of ACT UP NY to read and interact with the interviews. The repository is mediated, situated, invested, just as the work it documents was and is. It is explicitly set up to allow researchers and activists from diverse positions and with varied interests "in" to the project, aiming to create multiple sites for remembering for the future.

Activists' reflections on their work in those early years of understanding and shaping the ontology of AIDS underline why it matters to remember this time. Shifting the knowledge practices of AIDS, scientific knowledge production, bodily memory, what disease does to our bodies, getting drugs into bodies, knowing what wasn't known, caring for one another, and more emerged from and simultaneously crafted complex ways of living and re-membering. When interviewees talk about memory, though, they tend to bemoan how little they remember and render themselves as bad rememberers. To take just a few examples: Robert Vazquez-Pacheco says, "That's what we were doing—I'm sorry, I can't even remember my own history, let alone anything else (Vazquez-Pacheco interview, 10); Greg Bordowitz says, "I'm really embarrassed to admit I don't remember what the issue was" (Bordowitz, 11), and "I'm embarrassed to say that I remember faces, but I don't really remember names. It's terrible" (45). Heidi Dorow says, "These interviews make me nervous primarily for one reason: my memory, I don't always think is accurate, and it's also, it's not only colored with time, but then also my opinion. But I'll just say what I remember" (Dorow, 46). Every one of the interviews I've read has a number of instances in which interviewees bemoan their inability to remember the things they're trying to talk about.

In fact, they remember a huge amount, and in remarkable detail. Often protestations of being unable to remember cascade into dense, richly detailed, compelling accounts of ACT UP's work in New York. In part, the reclamation of history signaled by the ACT UP oral history project, and indeed other projects that focus on social movements as historians and theorists of their own activities, is illuminated by Campbell's account of memory as a relationally interpreted and shaped situation. Campbell sees memory as being about the past, but as also, at least potentially, as a way of being orientated toward the future. She argues that "one of the most specific and important ways in which memory is forward-looking is that capacities to take responsibility for the present and future require our ability to re-remember and re-feel our past" (Campbell 2014, 148). It is, then, salient to attend to who creates and narrates occasions, just as it is generative to consider what forms of responsibility forward-looking memory might generate. In the case of ACT UP, the occasions were and are complex, bridging communities of affect, with labs, with day jobs, with political actions, and with time in jail. How we tell and understand that history matters to meaning. And meaning matters, in turn, to the material conditions and affective experience of our lives, particularly for subjects erased and disempowered by overlapping and coconstituting social relations of oppression.

I think that the number of interviewees who protest their faulty memory indicates in part an implicit self-classification as in some way not "good rememberers." Of course, many of us simply have difficulty remembering things when we have not thought about them for some time. This prosaic fact is surely part of the picture involved in interviewing people about activist work they did many years earlier. Also, it may be that interviewees' protestations about not having good memories connect to conceptions of queers as those people who don't need to remember because they have no future

(Edelman). Or, more practically, in a time when the activist work animating people's lives was in full swing, so many people were dying that many activists had a hard time imagining that they themselves would live. The memories the people who lived on are asked to unfurl may be, then, experienced as a past from the point of view of an unexpected future. Their cocreation of remembering happens within a perhaps unimagined future anterior from the point of view of an actual future that they created through activist work in the past. In thinking about the memory status of interviewees, three points are important:

First, memory is about knowledge and a particular conviction about one's own capacity to know. Campbell's discussion of the troubling ways people are "sorted" into reliable and unreliable rememberers and the corollary effects of (de)valuation of memory practices help us think about the epistemic competency assumed and to a degree created via the coproduction of the oral history interview itself. Being interviewed calls on the rememberers to be, to become, the kinds of subjects who remember. Alongside the repeated assertions that the interviewees are incapable of memory comes the manifest presence of memory. Being asked these questions places ACT UP people in relation to a history they shaped through activism and are shaping through memory work; the act of interviewing enacts, then, a relational formation of them as feelers and rememberers.

Second, interventions in memory are political: they reclassify what happened in the past and what's happening in the present. In relation to ACT UP, Campbell's understanding of the politics of affect and memory helps us understand how vital it is to tune in to idiosyncratic memories and feelings—and, perhaps especially, the kinds of tangle of both that we experience in trying to remember the early days of AIDS while holding in view its continuing presence. Such a tuning-in contests the kind of memory involved in the NPR story—that the straight world spontaneously came around to caring about queers and our deaths. It may be possible, too, to understand the kinds of activist work involved in ACT UP itself as about memory: Who counted as "having" AIDS? What should the disease be called, and what effects would those names and classifications have? How could those people not yet dying do justice to the lives and deaths of those without access to treatment? I discuss this in detail below.

Third, these interviews affirm connections among feeling and memory. The suffusiveness of feeling that animated the work ACT UP did, in New

York and elsewhere, is palpable in the interviews—in how people talk and what they say. The intensity of the work was political and it was affective, and at the same time was inchoate and dynamic (Gould). The feeling of doing activist work in that context was entangled with relationships with other people, through whom the cadence of memory took its beat. People and how interviewees felt about them shaped the work, and the feeling of that work shapes memory about this history.

## Remembering Changing the CDC Definition

Remembering for the future is a politically charged act. And, like anything political, it is impure—it has a stake in something, an urgency, a desire directed toward some other future or against some current present. In turn, the question of memory is intimately involved with classification and its effects—how to sort people, group them, and what effect these activities have on population and time. Geoffrey Bowker and Susan Leigh Star define classification as: "*a spatial, temporal, or spatio-temporal segmentation of the world.* A classification is a set of boxes (metaphorical or literal) into which things can be put to then do some kind of work—bureaucratic or knowledge production" (Bowker and Star 1999, 10). The abstract or ideal classificatory system uses unique classificatory principles, deploys mutually exclusive categories, and completely describes all areas it treats. Of course, no classification system ever meets all (or, probably, any, completely) of these criteria. The work of standardization aims to manage the inevitable failure of classificatory systems to do their work. When classifications work well, they become infrastructure. They fade out, we cannot easily perceive them, and the social relations they shape become commonsensical. The work of classification has been central to understanding HIV and AIDS. Folk classifications interact with state and scientific classification, as in the case of the CDC definition, always in terms shot through with conceptions of deviants/deviance, probable dangers, and the difficulty of tracking a condition whose etiology shifted from identity markers, to tracking behaviors, to viral load. At the base of ACT UP struggles around classification was the outraged, clear knowledge that classificatory practices in research, political priority-setting, and hospital care-giving were killing people—even if it seemed that they were simply being allowed to die earlier than they otherwise might. Classification schemes, as Bowker and Star note, "have the central task of providing access to the past" (255). In providing this access, classification practices also organize selective forgetting. Some forms of forgetting are instrumentally useful, others are actually beneficial in their capacity to unsettle "reification or projection" (257)—but classification in general is entangled with the politics of memory.

I turn now to examine the memory practice involved in tracking and tracing one site of this cultural and scientific transformation: the 1993 CDC reclassification of HIV/AIDS. Just as there is no permanent and solid medical classification of AIDS, there is no solid and permanent social classification of the sexual and gender identity of who might care about or struggle around AIDS. Reflecting on the campaign to change the CDC surveillance definition reveals both the subtlety and complication of identity categories *and* the complexity of medical classifications. Although I focus here on the work ACT UP did to change medical classification, note that while this work was happening, activists also engaged with one another in a multilayered struggle within the organization. Although they accomplished brilliant things, AIDS activists were not saints or paragons, and I would not want to give the impression that I think of them as queer minor deities. The social history of movements is more interesting than hagiography.

I aim here to understand ACT UP activists as rememberers in ways that show the complexity of affect mobilized in the activism of the past, remembering in the present, and the opening to a practice of responsibility that signals possible futures, futures in which AIDS activists' work is remembered well. Among other things, attending to their struggles to change the surveillance definition of AIDS pulls into view the work that has become now part of our unmarked classificatory habits of thinking about AIDS. When classifications become commonsensical, it can become difficult to recall that they were created and, sometimes, contested. Attending to contestation reminds us that what happened in the past was not inevitable.[4] And since the past persists and consists in the present, no particular future is inevitable either. But perhaps futurity requires an attention to the past as a mode of figuring the future, which I discuss further in chapter 6. Such an attention to the past as a way of crafting more livable futures requires a particular mode of attention to the present—one that can somehow stay with sadness and live with complex and impure classification. In telling AIDS history, oral history projects such as the AUOHP contribute, in imperfect and permanently partial ways, to such a crafting.

The CDC definition campaign brought together ACT UP activists, doctors, lawyers, and people trying to access disability benefits working to expand the definition on the books. An important piece was lawyer Terry McGovern, who brought a class-action suit against the Social Security Administration for wrongfully denying disability benefits to HIV positive women who, in many cases, were sick and dying of AIDS without ever being diagnosed as having developed full-blown AIDS. The campaign slogan was "Women Don't Get Aids, They Just Die From It." As one activist reflects:

> The definition had been arbitrarily developed through an observational, sort of systematized collection of diseases that were being seen in gay men alone. And meanwhile, people involved with drug users and women were seeing all these other diseases. And if you got an AIDS case definition, you were entitled to benefits, Social Security Disability benefits. And without that AIDS case definition, you didn't have that. And it could literally mean the difference between life and death, and between not having any income, and having a little bit of your disability payments, which you had paid into. (Banzhaf, 74–75)

Because the Social Security Administration was using the CDC's definition of AIDS, people needed to meet that definition to get benefits. But because the definition was skewed toward a gay male model, specific groups would never meet the definition. McGovern, a poverty lawyer in New York, encountered a number of clients who had problems as a result of this situation and, in working with ACT UP, formulated a legal strategy to address the definition via the Social Security Administration. McGovern says she ended up "surveying all the poverty law offices and gathering a big group of plaintiffs who had been denied Social Security disability" benefits and then filing the suit on their behalf (McGovern, 19).

This legal strategy was connected with direct-action protest actions, including a large initial demonstration at the Health and Human Services building in Washington, D.C., Jean Carlomusto, a videographer with DIVA TV (Damned Interfering Video Activists) and ACT UP, says about that action:

> I remember that was one of the times that I remember just crying and doing camera work. Because at one point during the action in front of HHS, whenever a woman was going to speak about her case we sounded these horns and everybody sat down and shut up. And it was really notable, because before that we were all chanting, we were marching and chanting. "How many more have

to die before you say they qualify," was one of the chants I remember. But when that horn went off, everybody shut up. And I remember specifically when Iris De La Cruz took the megaphone and spoke about not being able to get health care. She said her physician didn't take food stamps. (Carlomusto 29–30)

The push to change the CDC definition came significantly from the Women's Caucus in ACT UP, and one way the campaign was framed highlighted the fact that women as a group were excluded from the definition. As Karen Ramspacher remembers, HIV positive women were getting diseases that in women should be signaling increased immunodeficiency, or the development of full-blown AIDS: "They're opportunistic infections. They were dealing with thrush on an ongoing basis, vaginal thrush, and they were dealing with pelvic inflammatory disease, and that was actually turning out to be quite dangerous. They were spiking a fever. It was a bacterial infection. It was incredibly difficult to fight and some were dying from it, and they weren't getting any services. They just had HIV. So it was like, oh, man, we've got to change this" (Ramspacher, 43–44). These were gender-specific manifestations of AIDS, which were difficult to see and name *as* AIDS because the classificatory habit tracing and defining the disease was rooted in a historical focus on gay men.

In the end, the only gender-specific criteria to make it into the changed definition was cervical cancer. But the struggle to change the definition was significant in terms of its effect on multiple constituents. In the United States, funding to cover AIDS-related medical needs for underinsured people affected by AIDS falls under the Ryan White Comprehensive AIDS Resources Emergency (CARE) Act. So local health departments had an interest in expanding the definition. As activist Marion Banzhaf says, "Health departments were recognizing these other diseases, too, and they wanted access to the more money that they would have if they had more people with AIDS identified in their own states. Then they could get more funding streams, right? Because the allocation of the Ryan White money was based on people with AIDS, not people with HIV. And so they had an interest in changing the case definition" (Banzhaf, 75–76). Since the CDC definition was a gateway criteria, meeting it affected one's access to ADAP (AIDS Drug Assistance Program), housing subsidies, Medicaid, and more. So although the campaign focused on shifting the paradigm definition from what many people frame as a "gay male model" to include women, in key ways the shift in orientation tracked social relations other than gender. The focus on gender was in part a political decision—perhaps focusing on people living in poverty or just out of prison would not have had the same effect.[5] As Terry McGovern says, "I mean, the thing is, everybody always focuses on women because that was very obvious. But the original AIDS definition was not looking at the concept of converging epidemics. So tuberculosis wasn't in it; bacterial pneumonia wasn't in it. So it wasn't just women; it was lots and lots of poor people, if you had to pick a denominator" (McGovern, 24–25). The legal push to change the definition thus intersected with funding interests at local scales. Classification has, in these cases, direct material consequences for who counts as having AIDS. And changing the classification ramifies the effects of a broader definition beyond the bounds of the original gender-based analysis of the campaign.

Of course, the reason activists started the three-year campaign to change the CDC definition was precisely because even when people weren't classified as having AIDS, they were dying from it. Their experience of sickness motivated the legal redefinition work, and that move in turn relied on medical evidence for conditions that were not yet medically recognized as evidence. This meant that the activist work could not be only legal or involving direct actions and phone zaps. As McGovern remembers: "It was like, it was crazy—taking on the government on this thing. So we had to do a lot of work. We had to get doctors to publish what they had seen in their clinics so there was evidence. It was a lot of things. There was the ACT UP piece, but there was also the creating-the-medical-evidence piece. There was a lot to be done in that moment" (McGovern, 31). Maxine Wolfe, one of the key people in the CDC campaign, expands on the further research implications of these classifications:

> And one of the issues that we always had, even within the group that was doing that was that terror was very focused on the disability benefits, but there were other outcomes of this, that were just not about disability, which is that, if you don't define a kind of infection that's associated, you don't do research. You don't do research, you don't get any treatment. So, it's not just that you don't get disability benefits, because who wants to get disability benefits and die. It's that you want to make sure that if people are doing research or developing treatments, they're also developing treatments for the things that you get and not just what somebody else gets, and that they're not giving you drugs that haven't

been tested on you that can cause cancer of the cervix, when that's something that you're going to get. (Wolfe, 84–85)

In the case of changing the definition, several activists remember that anecdotally Pelvic Inflammatory Disease seemed to be more prevalent than cervical cancer in HIV positive women dying of opportunistic infections. Wolfe's point is illustrated here: because there was no data from the scientific community on PIDs and HIV at that point, but there was some data about cervical cancer, cervical cancer ended up being the sex-specific criteria in the redefinition. Research, treatment, classification, and lived effects intertwine and mutually—but with unequal standing—condition one another.[6]

## Doing Justice to the Past and Remembering for the Future

Recall Campbell's argument that "memory is about the significance of the past for the future" and that it changes in relation to our current and future needs (Campbell 2014, 139). In the case of women who were dying without an AIDS diagnosis, we can see how a commitment to knowing what was happening to them takes the form of a commitment to remembering significant pasts. But in what way is this remembering for the future? Why does it matter that we remember that ACT UP, with others, forced the change of this definition? There are two ways to answer these questions: First, we can take an almost emic approach, which is to understand how the CDC reclassification operated as a struggle with the present in the context of the three-year campaign to change the definition. Second, we can consider how the reclassificatory work of the past created conditions for different futures, which we, who live in the future created by their struggle, should recognize and honor as a way to better understand our own histories and craft potential futures.

In its own time, the multifaceted campaign to change the CDC definition of AIDS was, obviously, a struggle over classification. Like any classificatory struggle that matters, it arose because there were material effects of the classification: people were suffering more and dying earlier under the pre-1993 system. That fact connected complexly to research priorities and folk classification about who was expected to develop AIDS, a web of classification that mutually picked out gay men as the expected AIDS subject. The tendency to "pick out" gay men, and implicitly white gay men, as the "normal" person with AIDS also reveals a complex classificatory struggle within the social worlds in which the CDC campaign took place. In a moment before "queer" was an accepted identity category, "gay" and "lesbian" markers carried classificatory politics that were themselves the site of struggle, perhaps particularly within ACT UP. And these struggles in turn connect to further sites of negotiation and conflict in the realm of medical categorization of sexuality, sex, and gender. Categorization is never only oppressive, whether it concerns disease or gender—sometimes we categorize and recategorize in liberatory ways. It is important to the narrative I tell here that the struggles over the CDC definition did not simply pit a unified, homogenous, angelic activist group against a powerful and heartless government agency. Rather, attending to the CDC campaign shows something about complex challenges to the community of people fighting AIDS, including their own self-understanding.

The campaign to change the definition can be seen also as a struggle over memory. Since HIV positive women were not counted as having AIDS, when they died they were not remembered as having died of AIDS. Interviewees in the AUOHP note that there was a feeling that the epidemic was being systematically undercounted (though equally there was significant contestation within ACT UP about the question of testing and counting HIV positive people). So there was an issue about classification as about remembering in the near term why people were dying, and holding as a political insight that it was not only gay men dying of AIDS. Attempting to remember these moments calls us to consider the complexity of medical classification, identity categorization, and multiple forms of resistance and hope.

The in-the-moment reclassificatory imperative was also a question of changing the treatment options available to people living with HIV or developing AIDS. If, as Maxine Wolfe argued, you want to not simply get your disability benefits and then die but rather have expanded treatment options so that you might not die yet, the set of opportunistic diseases and infections you experienced themselves needed solid treatment research. Reclassifying what was happening to people was thus about much more than recording more accurately death statistics—it was instead trying to produce the medical and social conditions under which people as rememberers might live into their own future. One of the losses frequently marked in oral history projects collecting the stories of AIDS activism is the perspectives and memories of people who died before treatment options opened that would have kept them alive.

Consider Katrina Haslip, for example, who was one of the key organizers of the AIDS redefinition campaign, and had worked on it both inside and outside of prison. She died December 2, 1992—days before the CDC announced that it would change the definition. Because she had been centrally involved, Haslip was one of the people invited to make a statement about the redefinition. Terry McGovern recounted that Haslip wrote a statement, which another HIV positive woman read at the press conference announcing the change, "basically saying, I'm not going to smile. This is only happening because of us, and you let us die." McGovern says about Haslip's words: "It's a very moving statement" (McGovern, 40). She continues:

> Katrina . . . didn't qualify. She didn't have AIDS, even though she was dying. She had bacterial pneumonia. And she had no T-cells, but the definition hadn't been changed. So bacterial pneumonia wasn't there. So she actually didn't qualify for Division of AIDS Services, and therefore couldn't get a home attendant. And she kept falling in her house. And I kept sending positive women who were volunteers with HIV Law Project to pick her up and take her to the hospital.
>
> So she was a victim of the AIDS definition, actually. She really didn't get the care that she needed. She had to fight every step of the way to get anything. And it was incredibly tragic, actually. (41)

Haslip is one example of many: a woman who directly supported and educated other people living with HIV, supporting them in prison and in their transition outside, who led the campaign to change the definition, and who suffered and died in the way she did because of the pre-1993 classifications and their effects. Counting her in the moment could have changed many things, and failing to remember her and people like her mattered.

How can we change the significance of this past for our present and future? I have argued that the reclassificatory work of the past created the present we now live and thus conditioned possibilities for futures we might craft. In this present, the memory of the CDC redefinition as a multifaceted struggle is occluded, erased: it is not remembered. This is visible in the official timelines, the CDC's own description of what happened, and popular media representations of the history of HIV and AIDS. As McGovern says, reflecting on the discourse she encounters in her work on AIDS with the Ford Foundation: "I'm at presentations all the time. I see AIDS timelines. And it's never there. My first day here, there was a big fat timeline, you know:

Rock Hudson. No mention of it. And even more amazing is, I sit through these conversations about the epidemiological history in the U.S., and amazingly, in 1993, there's this huge rise in the number of cases. And it just happened organically. Isn't that so interesting?" (McGovern, 41–42).

If we fail to remember more than the official story—if we accede to the account where *the dominant culture simply "came around,"* in Schulman's words—we lose more than historical accuracy. We lose the understanding that our own reality is the product of passionate struggle. We fail to honor the people who loved the possibilities of changed futures enough to work toward them even while they were themselves dying. We repudiate the interdependence and coconstitution required for memory projects that can do justice to the past we have inherited. We lose sight of how we might, in our own present, take queer responsibility for shaping different presents and more livable futures. And, perhaps centrally for this discussion, we let slip that insight that medicine, like memory, is political and never pure—and thus is something for which we can collectively take responsibility. The queer work of remembering for the future centers the possibility of remembering this kind of reclassificatory work as a promise for worlds to come.

# PART II

# Living in an
# Interdependent Present

# 3

## Shimmering Presences
### Frog, Toad, and Toxic Interdependencies

Attending to the present moment implies, necessarily, understanding that the present we move through—a perpetually shifting bubble-node that we cannot fully grasp but that simultaneously is the only thing we can experience—is a reliquary of the past, holding traces of everything that has happened and everything that has been erased. The present is also necessarily a continually receding seed for the future. Whatever happens *now* shapes the conditions for what can happen in any given *then*. This quality of the current moment is beautifully if terrifyingly manifest when we think about toxins, pollutants, and, as I explore in chapter 4, nuclear by-products with half-lives that stretch beyond our capacity to understand their scope. The things we experience now as toxic dangers are often the remnants of past innovation— the DDT that cleared mosquitoes later producing cancers and fragile eggshells, bedbug resurgence, and so on. We are now producing and consuming things that later will, if history is any guide, sicken and kill us and others. If we live that long.

In this chapter, I think of the present situation as *interdependent*, manifesting a kind of toxic connectedness. I forecast here a network of understandings of interdependence that I will unpack further in chapter 6, where I argue for disability interdependencies as a key for crafting different futures. There, I draw on certain Indigenous, Buddhist, and disability-theory conceptions of interdependence. For the purposes of this chapter, I am relying on a smaller-scale notion of interdependence. Here I understand this concept to mean that feature of our organic life such that we are physically constituted through the stuff of the world. We are coconstituted and in that sense interdependent, made up of the materials around us. Such literal interdependence is perceptible in thinking about the ways that substances we call toxins cross barriers, shaping current bodies and predicting future embodiments when they affect reproductive possibilities. In this chapter, I take an approach to the toxic present grounded in conceptions of queer relationality. As Samuel Delany and José Esteban Muñoz have helped me understand, queer practices of relationality are also practices of temporality—being in the present with a relation to the past and future offset from the normalizing progression of both subject formation and the accumulation of capital as an always-increasing progress narrative. Mel Chen, another keystone for this chapter, frames queer and racial temporalities as "a kind of shimmering presence. They are less easily bound to capital or to any other regimented time; or perhaps we could say that the time of capital is also no longer in the form it might once have been" (Chen, 219). In this chapter, I work with the shimmering presence of the present with an eye toward the possibility of different futures—a notion I discuss more in Part III of this book. The title of this chapter also intends to invoke a culturally specific memory of the Frog and Toad children's books—cross-species friends, probably queer, with very different characters, anthropomorphized through their suit-wearing, cookie-eating, kite-flying behavior. For me, reading Frog & Toad stories as a kid predicted my assumption that anurans—frogs and toads—are interesting and friendly.

Now an adult, I doubt that anurans are friendly (or unfriendly)—they aren't, I think, registering on affective scales I can understand, though we can be in relation to one another, with attention. But the stories we tell about them continue to be interesting. I will attend both to the tropes of gender-bending or disabled amphibians and to their actual bodies and lives. I will argue for a queer disability attention to the toxic present as a kind of responsibility. Anurans have, over the last ten years, been frequently held up as warning signs for biological dangers inherent in many of our practices around food, climate, and mining. Industrial production, of corn or petroleum or most anything else, has significant effects on the world around it. As I'll explore below, one of the main ways people argue that these effects are too harmful to justify current production practices evokes gender and disability danger; humans, the warning goes, will be born disabled, queer, or genderqueer if we continue using or producing certain substances. And the way we know this, the narrative continues, is that frogs and toads are being born with bodily anomalies including ambiguous genitalia, changed voiceboxes, extra limbs, and more. My agenda here is not to argue that we should not be worried about toxins and their effects—worry and anticapitalist action are both, I believe, at least justified and perhaps necessary. Rather, I argue that we ought to cultivate practices of responsibility for the toxic present we are implicated in creating that do not rely on antidisability or trans-hating tropes and that simultaneously do not attend to anurans merely as indicator species. Further, practices of perceiving interdependence may nourish an ethical relation to complex ecologies in which we are implicated and through which we are formed.

The chapter begins with a description of the context in which I started thinking about anurans—a small mining city—as a way to ground my discussion of the more general issues involved in this area. After that, I give a reading of Mel Chen's understanding of toxicity, attending to their account of the queer relationality we might find in toxic interdependence. I then examine two sites: first, a controversy around the herbicide Atrazine, exposed as a danger by biologist Tyrone Hayes, and second, practitioners of what Anna Tsing has called "arts of noticing on a damaged planet"—civilian/amateur naturalists who attend to their local environments and who model ways of being connected to anurans and our mutual ecologies. To conclude the chapter, my guide is poet and field naturalist Jim Maughn, an old friend who has taught me a lot about what it means to notice the world as a practice of responsibility.

## Toxic Contexts

For five years, I lived in Sudbury, Ontario, Atikameksheng Anishnawbek land. Classified for purposes of auto- and industry-emissions standards and urban-rural hierarchies as "The North," Sudbury is both far and not far away from big cities. A five-hour drive up a two-lane highway from Toronto, Sudbury feels further. You see the smokestack of the main mine's smelter while you're still miles away, driving into town. Sudbury is very close to all of us, though: home to the second-largest nickel-mining operation in the world, odds are that at least some of the metal in my computer, your phone or stainless-steel sink, the wiring in the walls, is Sudbury nickel alloy.

Smelting is toxic, any way you do it, and because Sudbury is among the longest-running mines in the world, the land, water, and air there bear the traces of more than a hundred years of industrial offcasts. This is true for any mining town, but it is more layered there simply because of time; most mines tap out after thirty or forty years. In Sudbury, we tested the ground before planting anything in it that we might eat, before letting babies play in the dirt. The water in the lake in the middle of town, the primary sources of drinking water for the humans of Sudbury, takes in runoff from a parking lot on its edge made of slag fill—mining detritus gradually leaching copper, nickel, arsenic, lead, manganese, and other metals into the lake's ecosystem. People there generally avoid eating bottom feeders, as they bioaccumulate parts of the slag runoff. Acid rain, that relic of the 1980s, was "discovered" in Sudbury. Creeks, lakes, and watersheds bear the imprint of still-significant acidification, and acid-water environments alongside potentially toxic trace metals shape the situation for all the inhabitants of the area. Rocks that were pink and sandy-white before industrialization, shot through with quartz, now are charcoal-black, and animals and fish carry biologically (temporarily) secured deposits of various elements. Blueberries, which happen to like more acidic soil, grow in profusion in northern Ontario. Parts of the ground are crusted with a kind of black bubbling coat, and what vegetation grows in those parts is sparse, perhaps a response to the products of smelting carried in the air and water, perhaps a legacy of widespread clear-cutting during the period when the area was a major source of lumber. I lived in the part of town where everyone knew "the air was bad"—more often downwind from many of the mines, even with the "superstack" that diverts more of the by-products of smelting higher into the atmosphere than the old, shorter stack used to. I went running on trails through land owned by the mining company, passing through alternating patches of verdant life and gray ground in which little grew. My chemical reactions and nickel allergies amplified in that place—I was very sick often, kind of sick a lot, tired almost always. This is one way that interdependence manifests: the places and ways we live show up in our bodies as sickness and health.

Sudbury also bears the marks of struggle, and one of the wonderful things about living there was the experience of seeing how people who care about the world they're in can shape it against the imperatives of capitalist depredation. A periodic queer women's party was called "Super Stacked," the flyers modeling a hot, curvy woman alongside the phallic main smelting stack, its plume of smoke—which in real life is visible at a great distance from town—drifting off. Workers' struggles, smuggling air-testing kits into the mines in their lunchboxes and taking action based on the data they gathered, provided key footholds in early workplace safety legislation (Steedman, Suschnigg, and

Buse 1995). Thirty years ago, the landscape in Sudbury was denu
tion hardly grew, a response to what one report calls a "multip
environment. An often-told story says that the people preparing for the first
Moon landing walked first in Sudbury, to get a visceral experience of what
walking in a place without living things felt like. Now there are trees and
bushes, and when you go out walking you can see the effects of years of people
scattering alkalinizing lime powder with their hands. The lakes aren't dead
anymore; the air is breathable though sometimes sulphurous. These changes
are traces of activism and sometimes of social movements—those miners
carrying air-quality-assessment test kits secretly underground, working-
class people who wanted to be able to hang laundry outside without it getting coated with black sticky something, other, often immigrant, ordinary
people taking political action about lakes that had lost all their fish, liberal
environmentalists with good intentions, scientists in the very early days of
understanding the effects of industrial off-products, and others. People are
justified in lifting up and honoring the work that every clear-ish stream and
every green tree manifests. Another way of understanding interdependence.

Perhaps especially since leaving I have begun to think through some of
my experiences of being constituted in and with the material situation of
Sudbury as a kind of interdependence. Five years living there shaped my
consciousness, perhaps permanently, of being a product of what Anna Tsing
calls "contaminated diversity" (Tsing 2015, 33). As she argues, "Everyone carries a history of contamination; purity is not an option" (27). I follow Tsing
in understanding contaminated diversity to require us to attend to stories
that are not easy tools for knowing the world. As a relational condition, contaminated diversity might unsettle us; Tsing argues that it is "complicated,
often ugly, and humbling." She continues:

> Contaminated diversity implicates survivors in histories of greed, violence,
> and environmental destruction. The tangled landscapes grown up from cor-
> porate logging reminds us of the irreplaceable graceful giants that came before.
> The survivors of war remind us of the bodies they climbed over—or shot—to
> get to us. We don't know whether to love or hate these survivors. Simple moral
> judgments don't come to hand. (ibid.)

We all participate in situations and worlds unavailable for simple moral
judgment; attending to stories about the effects of substances, lively though

inert substances, that change bodies and ecosystems but are useful or needed, opens one way to form more adequate ethical judgments.

The multiple lively substances that shape the conditions for existence in Sudbury are, in aggregate, almost certainly more harmful than not. There are, people told me, cancers that show up in the lab and in Sudbury—I carry the effects of those years in my body, maybe to come to fruition later. Such effects matter, and having better ways to think of that mattering is important. Now that I live in a very "clean" city, I think such thinking is perhaps especially important for those of us who can live further away from the depredations of capitalist production, those of us who might imagine that there is a raw substance existing before or beneath its incorporation into systems of exchange. Once living in a place where the effects of mining and clear-cutting are present and obviously involved in people's lives has shifted my experience of *not* directly experiencing the production of products I still buy and use. Being against purity, as I think about the effects of mining and clear-cutting in Sudbury, involves recognizing that even if we live in a city where the air does not make us sick, we are still implicated in the air, land, and water of contaminated places.

As I discussed in chapter 1, colonialism is centrally a practice of dispossession and displacement—land is expropriated and pollution is distributed. "Clean" cities achieve their status in large part through downloading the effluents and excreta they require into other places and other bodies. This is global: Sudbury, for example, "cleaned up" its air through building the main stack higher alongside adding more "scrubbers" to filter the smoke produced in smelting. Pushing the stack higher sent the off-gasses further into the atmosphere, leaving the area near the stack (the city itself) cleaner at the cost of sending the unwanted substances on to other places. And scrubbers that capture some of those substances on their way out of the stack also must go someplace—the substances exist, whether they're in a part of the atmosphere higher up than we breathe or captured in a filter, and so it's just a question of *where* they exist. Purity in this context is a fiction, and one tracking a decision about how to store and host pollution, and who will bear the effects of that decision. Coconstitution poses a perpetual problem, a struggle: if we want things made, in this example, out of metal, how will we determine the distribution of harm involved in its production? In an impure world, interdependence will always mark a site for struggle.

## Toxic Presents

Let me turn to frogs and toads as a node for unpacking the idea of inter-dependence as a site of struggle, starting again with Sudbury. There is a long and fairly big creek there: Junction Creek. Appropriately though unimagina-tively named, Junction Creek connects many smaller towns that were forci-bly amalgamated during state austerity measures in the 1990s that aimed to reduce government spending and that now make up the city. There is a small civilian activism committee that has taken stewardship of the creek, with activities including creek cleanups, fish releases, and lobbying for watershed-related policy changes at city council. They are not a particularly radical group, nor queer, and they don't have a sharp analysis of interlocking oppres-sions. They have a project called "FrogFind," which, as they say, "encourages local Citizens to take an interest in the amphibian life present throughout Greater Sudbury." Their aim is to protect "frogs and toads" (anurans), but interestingly—in a way that may seem at first pass very simple—the activity we could take up if we lived there and took an interest would be learning the calls of frogs and toads, and reporting their prevalence based on these calls. I will return to this kind of project in the section below on naturalism.

On one hand, the FrogFind project simply (and obviously) uses frogs and toads as indicator species. They are understood as beings immersed in water, therefore in chemical soups, membranous, obviously (and, the implication is, more than we are) experiencing what Nancy Tuana calls "viscous poros-ity" (Tuana 2008). Amphibians are framed explicitly as useful for telling us something about situations we cannot see or understand, if we can access that telling through a dispersed network of dog walkers, smokers out for a quick one, and joggers willing to pause and take off their headphones who later input data into an online survey. Amphibians' function here as an indi-cator species is not only human-centric (and putting them in an instrumen-tal relation); it to a certain extent ignores that they are their own beings with their own worlds, differentially taking in the toxic load we create and dis-tribute. And yet because of the differential distribution of chemical harm, surely also we who cause that harm ought to track it. Further, the people who take up this work take it up as a noninstrumental kind of joyful atten-tion to the world they are in—a mode of attention that manifests also when people are not formally involved in FrogFind, but just spending time near water—fishing, walking, sitting on the deck. This is an extremely specific and local example, and honestly in the context of how deeply messed up the land and water of Sudbury are, it feels very minor. But read in a bigger context, the situation in Sudbury and the attempt to access and understand it through amphibians and their voices is part of an interesting shift in understanding our connection with the impure, toxic world.

As Mel Chen has compellingly argued, toxicity offers a usable case study of a mode of being in which it is not possible to stably distinguish between the experiencing subject and some imagined ontologically separate "other" that affects the subject. As Chen points out, "There seems to be a basic semantic schema for toxicity: in this schema, two bodies are proximate; the first body, living or abstract, is under threat by the second; the second has the effect of poisoning, and altering, the first, causing a degree of damage, disability, or even death" (Chen 2012, 191). This is intuitively compelling as a schema, constellating as it does a conception of bounded individuality requiring defense from outside pollutants and purification of the toxins already taken on. The model of separable bodies—one affected, one affecting—is insufficient for understanding the kinds of coconstitution Chen has in mind. Instead, we might engage "toxicity as a *condition*, one that is too complex to imagine as a property of one or another individual or group or something that could itself be so easily bounded. . . . How can we think more broadly about synthesis and symbiosis, including toxic vapors, interspersals, intrinsic mixings, and alterations, favoring inter-absorption over corporeal exceptionalism?" (197). Animacy theory, as Chen unfurls it, allows repeated iterations of this move from delimited-though-affecting-and-affected bodies to an understanding of multiple, mutually shaping complex conditions. Both the material and social ontologies we engage are marked by constitutive interpenetration.

Eula Biss connects the wish to dissociate ourselves from that which we call toxic to an earlier attention to regimes of defense against filth. She writes:

> Where the word *filth* once suggested, with its moralist air, the evils of the flesh, the word *toxic* now condemns the chemical evils of our industrial world. This is not to say that concerns over environmental pollution are not justified—like filth theory, toxicity theory is anchored in legitimate dangers—but that the way we think about toxicity bears some resemblance to the way we once thought about filth. Both theories allow their subscribers to maintain a sense of control over their own health by pursuing personal purity. For the filth theorist, this

meant a retreat into the home, where heavy curtains and shutters might seal
out the smell of the poor and their problems. Our version of this shuttering
now is achieved through the purchase of purified water, air purifiers, and food
produced with the promise of purity. (Biss 2014, 75–76)

I agree with Biss and Chen that the discourse of toxicity attempts to secure
a rhetorical space for individual purity that would allow us to imagine that
we can succeed in not being altered and shaped by the world. The practices
that come out of this—in the overdeveloped world including all the filtra-
tion money can buy—replicate the redistribution of externalities away from
some bodies and toward others. Rich people have an easier time enacting
the kind of redistribution or avoidance of poison in their bodies than poor
people. But, as Chen and Biss help us understand, these practices are tem-
porary and illusory; we cannot in the end be separate from the world that
constitutes us. Corporeal exceptionalism cannot be sustained because inter-
absorption is the way things actually are.

Where do we find normative guidance for orienting ourselves toward
meeting the future organisms we are becoming in coconstitution with complex ecological situations that range from pH-altering elements in the rain
to the slag heaps of nickel mines to endocrine-disrupting compounds in our
waterways?[1] What approaches might we take that do not revert to antidisability or human-centric political orientations? Whatever answer we give,
it cannot rest with some wholesale approval of pollution, contamination,
or toxicity. Whatever answer we give, it has to reckon with the differential
distribution of harm. Whatever answer we give, it should not treat frogs and
toads as mere indicators, or as mattering only because of human concerns.
Chen's conception of toxicity helps me think about this problem. I agree that
we can

in a sense, claim toxicity as already "here," already a truth of nearly every body,
and also as a biopolitically interested distribution (the deferral of toxic work
to deprivileged or already "toxic subjects"). Such a distribution, in its failure
to effectively segregate, leaks outside of its bounds to "return," and it might
allow a queer theoretical move that readily embraces, rather than refuses in ad-
vance, heretofore unknown reflexes of raciality, gender, sexuality, (dis)ability.
In assuming both individual and collective vulnerability, it suggests an ulterior
ethical stance. (Chen, 218)

The *ulterior* here signals forms of knowing and being not articulate but often obvious; weighty and dense node points that shape and inform the space around them. Understanding vulnerability as not something we must (or can) defend against, but instead as a constitutive fact of our lives, a world-shaping mattering, offers us something. Chen argues that "thinking and feeling with toxicity invites us to revise, once again, the sociality that queer theory has in many ways made possible. As a relational notion, toxicity speaks productively to queer-utopian imagining and helps us revisit the question of how and where subject-object dispositions should be attributed to the relational queer figure" (207). Central to formulating an ulterior ethical stance, a subject-object variable orientation, we might adopt queer practices of relationality. Such practices turn aside from narratives organized around an expected line of descent, denaturalizing "fitness" and modeling something more interesting about what it might be to survive and thrive in disrupted landscapes. As I'll articulate below, such practices might learn much from forms of loving attention to our proximal ecosystems and coinhabitants.

## Atrazine, Hayes, and the Gender and Sexuality of Toxic Effects

Eva Hayward's work informs how I think about one particular use that frogs have come to be put to in expressing one kind of response to complex and toxic coconstitution. Such responses are perceptible, for example, in media representations of biologist Tyrone Hayes's work on the sex, reproductive, and voice-box changes in frogs exposed to the herbicide atrazine, which I discuss in this section. The fear evoked in these articles is primarily directed toward frogs as a different kind of indicator—a cohabitant of toxic worlds who might show us what sex and gender dangers we're courting through our chemical habits. In a short editorial about sex-changing frogs and fish, Hayward writes: "Is there a way to re-evaluate ecological resilience—such as the sex-changing response—and meet the future organisms that we are becoming? . . . We are all in chimeric borderlands where new forms of life are emerging" (Hayward 2014). With Malin Ah-King, Hayward has articulated an approach to "toxic sex," understanding "sex as an ongoing process influenced by endocrine disruptive chemicals, describing our shared vulnerability to one another; our bodies are open to the planet." This dynamic and emergent conception of sex conceives of bodily response and "ecological resilience that reframes the toxicity without reasserting a politics of purity" (Ah-King and Hayward 2014, 2). Ah-King and Hayward compellingly argue that we ought to understand "endocrine disruption as an unavoidable co-presence in the liveliness of organisms. . . . Neither utopic nor dystopic, toxic sex opens the realization that bodies are lively and rejoinders to environments and changing ecosystems, even when those same engines of changes provide exposure to carcinogens, neurotoxins, asthmagens and mutagens" (8–9). In this section, I connect this kind of approach to thinking about endocrine-disruptive compounds (EDCs) to the story I've been telling above, about Sudbury and its frogs.

A central claim in assessing the effects of toxins focuses on the harms of environmental racism, of the disproportionate distribution of pollution and carcinogens in racialized communities, is that their kids are born with disabilities and that adults are made disabled. This worry resonates with and is frequently supplanted with a complex queer-phobic worry that EDCs, especially herbicides, are making us, or imagined future children, queer or trans, or, depending on the document, influencing sex development so that there is a disproportionate number of females (of whatever species) born. A surprisingly hard-hitting investigative article into industrial pollutants and their effects appeared in the magazine *Men's Health*. The article's lead offers a warning: "On an Indian reserve in Canada, girls rule the day-care centers, the playgrounds, the sports teams. The reason: For the past 15 years, fewer and fewer boys are being born. It may be the leading edge of a chemically induced crisis that could make men an endangered species" (Peterson 2009). Low male birth rates, in this article and in others, are the flashpoint and a key indicator of danger—but also mentioned are "deformed rabbits and weasels scuttling through their woods" and air that the article's writer can hardly breathe as she enters Aamjiwnaang. There are many reasons to write an investigative article about industrial pollution in this area, also called Sarnia—it is commonly identified as a "cancer valley," for the carcinogens that leave the array of plants in the area. It is a case study for environmental racism, and for the specific genocide by industrial fiat that distributes poison in the water and foodways of Indigenous peoples on Turtle Island (Murphy 2013). And so it is notable that the hook for this piece, what the writer returns to over and over again, is not death, or pain, but rather a maldistribution of sex selection proportional to the norm.

Giovanna Di Chiro has compellingly argued that the focus of environmental activism against toxins recapitulates a limited conception of what will count as "normal." She argues that the dominant anti-toxics discourse deployed in mainstream environmental-ism adopts the potent rhetoric that toxic chemical pollution is responsible for the undermining of perversion of the "natural": natural biologies/ecologies, natural bodies, natural reproductive processes. This contemporary environ-mental anxiety appeals to cultural fears of exposure to chemical and endocrine-disrupting toxins as troubling and destabilizing the normal/natural gendered body of humans and other animal species, leading to what some have called the "chemical castration" or the "feminization of nature." (Di Chiro 2010, 201)

Drawing on Eli Clare's generative theorization of the interconnections among a class analysis, environmental activism, disability justice, and queer gender and sexual flourishing, Di Chiro notes that if you "scratch a liberal environ-mentalist and you might find polluted politics enforcing 'eco(hetero)norma-tivity' lurking underneath; disability becomes an environmental problem and lgbtq people become disabled—the unintended consequences of a con-taminated and impure environment, unjustly impaired by chemical trespass" (202). I agree with Di Chiro that the focus on supposedly inappropriate sex formation seriously occludes possibilities for appropriate response to envi-ronmental harms arising from the chemical context we inhabit. Like her, I turn to a consideration of a key chemical, and scientist, in this story.

Consider, then, the talk around atrazine. Atrazine is an herbicide, one of hundreds of kinds of chemicals currently in use in industrial food farming to tilt the scales toward the kinds of plants humans want to grow and eat and away from the plants classified as weeds or unusable. As Sandra Steingraber outlines in her account of the environmental conditions of cancers, atrazine (as a triazine herbicide) intervenes in a particular chain reaction of photo-synthesis in non-grass-species plants. It is usable in industrial food produc-tion in part because species like corn, widely consumed by humans and the animals we feed to later eat, are less susceptible to its effects than other plants we call weeds. Atrazine, like other herbicides, is toxic because it is dispersed and taken up in water. Steingraber says,

> Applied directly to the soil, atrazine is absorbed by the roots of plants and trans-ported to the leaves. It poisons from within. Atrazine is thus water soluble. And because of its solubility, it tends to migrate to many other places. . . . Atrazine-sprayed fields are leaky fields. And atrazine's capacity to inhibit photosynthesis does not stop once it leaves the farm. It has demonstrated a remarkable capacity

to poison plankton, algae, aquatic plants, and other chloroplast-bearing organisms that form the basis of the whole freshwater food chain. . . . Once it enters the water cycle, atrazine becomes a component of precipitation, so that raindrops themselves are now laced with a chemical that possesses the wily ability to blow up chloroplasts. (Steingraber, 157)

Much of this is true of other herbicides, and the fact of solubility and wide dispersion of chemicals is true also of many pesticides. For example, think of the widely used pesticide permethrin, which has been around since 1979 and is now infused in much sport and outdoor clothing as well as military uniforms. These clothes usually carry a warning label to not allow contact between the clothing article and any water systems because of the chemical's toxicity to marine invertebrates, bees, and amphibians (and, when wet, felines)—but they never explain how wearers of the clothing are supposed to launder it without sending permethrin out into the water system. Atrazine, however, has become a more well-known flashpoint than its siblings largely because of the efforts of scientist Tyrone Hayes.

Hayes is a biologist whose work focuses on how steroid hormones may effect the development of frogs and toads; he has become well known as a result of a more than fifteen-year-long dispute with the agricultural chemical firm Syngenta about the question of whether atrazine (one of its products) creates environmental conditions that affect frogs' reproductive capacities. Hayes argues that his research shows that atrazine affects the voice box of male frogs, leading them to have difficulty signaling their availability for mating, but more directly that atrazine affects their gonadal development. As Hayes writes on his website: "My laboratory showed that the herbicide atrazine (the number one selling product for Syngenta) is a potent endocrine disruptor that chemically castrates and feminizes exposed male amphibians at low ecologically relevant concentrations" (Hayes, n.d.). Syngenta argues that there is not sufficiently rigorous scientific evidence for these claims, and the company has spent years attempting to discredit Hayes's work (*Democracy Now!* 2014; Aviv 2014). There is a lot to say about the conflict between Syngenta and Hayes that I will not address here, including a complex story about the ways that racialization, science research culture, and graduate student funding structures have shaped the narrative. As a Black man at an elite but public university who speaks about the conditions in which primarily people of color are exposed to herbicides, Hayes is complexly positioned in relation to these things. He has performed and emailed explicitly rap-influenced and confrontational communiqués to Syngenta employees that have been responded to in quite racist ways. Here, I focus on the substance and rhetoric of the claim that Hayes is making: that these chemicals cause feminization in frogs, and that they may have the same effects on humans.

Consider the language in an interview with the news program *Democracy Now!* Amy Goodman, the program's host, asks: "And, Professor Hayes, talk about exactly what you found. What were the abnormalities you found in frogs, the gender-bending nature of this drug atrazine?" Hayes answers:

> Well, initially, we found that the larynx, or the voice box, in exposed males didn't grow properly. And this was an indication that the male hormone testosterone was not being produced at appropriate levels. And eventually we found that not only were these males demasculinized, or chemically castrated, but they also were starting to develop ovaries or starting to develop eggs. And eventually we discovered that these males didn't breed properly, that some of the males actually completely turned into females. So we had genetic males that were laying eggs and reproducing as females. And now we're starting to show that some of these males actually show, I guess what we'd call homosexual behavior. They actually prefer to mate with other males. (*Democracy Now!* 2014)

The set of assumptions at work here about what threat we face are not spelled out, but they come up over and over. They rest on the idea that there is an uncontaminated, pure, natural state that is being affected by artificial chemicals. On this account, we see the effects in the harms manifesting in frogs: first, feminization, and then, homosexual behavior. As one 2011 public radio program puts it in an introduction to the situation, "Scientists are continuing to sound the alarm about some common chemicals, including the herbicide atrazine, and link them to changes in reproductive health and development. Endocrine disrupting toxic chemicals have been found to feminize male frogs and cause homosexual behavior. Ashley Ahearn reports on how these substances may be affecting human development and behavior" (*Living on Earth* 2014). I am tempted to quote the entire transcript of these episodes of *Living on Earth* and *Democracy Now!* because they so richly illustrate a very troubling approach to depicting the relations among frogs and humans, gender and disability—but let me just pick out a few key points.

Consider Goodman's framing of atrazine as a "gender-bending" chemical. Now, Hayes's research is on frogs. Frogs may have social relations that we understand as gendered, but certainly those relations aren't the same as human gender enactment. As Bailey Kier notes (speaking of fish in the Potomac River): "'Transgender fish' are transgender only because we signify them as such culturally, and this signification disrupts clear distinctions and an imagined knowledge progression of the categories of sex, gender, and sexuality" (Kier 2010, 304). Sexuality, and homo sex, certainly has various things to do with gender (in humans)—but if the finding is that frogs are feminized, and "completely turned into females," it is not clear how or why we should understand the sex they're having with male frogs as homosexual. And while we may all, frogs and humans alike, experience these chemicals and respond to them in predictable ways, the meaning of that response may well be different depending on whether we exist in frogly or humanly ways.

The "Living on Earth" segment extends some of the worrying tendencies of the DN! dialogue with a discussion of not only the supposed gender and sexual effects of atrazine but also the threat of disability. The host again introduces this shift, beginning with a comment from Hayes:

> HAYES: People go, well, it's frogs. I go, yeah but look, the estrogen that works in this frog is exactly, chemically exactly, the same as the estrogen that regulates female reproduction. Exactly the same testosterone that's in these frogs regulating their larynx or their voice box or their breeding glands or their sperm count is exactly the same hormone in rats and in us.
>
> AHEARN: So, what about us? Could endocrine disruptors be having feminizing effects in humans? No one knows for sure, but some believe that rising rates of one birth defect could be an indicator. (*Living on Earth*)

The program goes on to interview a pediatric surgeon who performs surgeries on children diagnosed with hypospadias, in which the urethral opening on the penis emerges along the shaft of the penis as well as, and sometimes instead of, emerging at the tip. Hypospadias is one of the most frequently performed operations to change or—in most surgeons' terms—"correct" where the urethra emerges in any given penis. Intersex activists have identified hypospadias as one of a number of often-unnecessary surgeries performed on babies and children. For most people the condition is not harmful at all, carrying the "threat" simply of needing to sit down on a toilet rather than standing to urinate, or needing to clean the penis along its shaft perhaps more carefully than in nonhypospadias bodies. This threat is, of course, a gender problem manifesting in the practices of bathrooms, where what it means to be a man can come down to standing at a urinal rather than sitting on a toilet. For most people, the physical condition of hypospadias is, then, not a threat at all; hypospadias is a threat only because of the social conditions that monitor and punish people's use of bathrooms. So it is notable that the radio program moves from framing the dangers of atrazine to frogs around sexual and sex dysfunction to hypostatizing, or rendering as the material and direct cause of, danger to proper penis formation. Here, again, note that the dangers held up, the reasons we are hailed to worry about atrazine, are that the supposedly deviant sexual formation and expression effects on frogs—sex switching or change to homosexual behavior in particular—might also affect humans.

Allow me to restate that Hayes—and indeed anyone who takes up his work on frogs and the effects of atrazine on their lives—is *not* a malicious person villainously deploying ableist, sexist, and queer-hating tropes to simultaneously drum up fear of trans people, disabled people, queers, and all the impurity we signal. Rather, there are two things that I believe structure this pattern in thinking about the harms of impurity: first, as I mentioned above, research funding structures have shifted, particularly in the United States, toward a particular metric of relevance that—unless research has military potential—to some extent relies on showing that the "ordinary public" cares about the issue the scientist examines. Since culture is so deeply imbued with oppression, and since people are remarkably prone to believing evidence that confirms their already-existing beliefs, it makes sense that research confirming views that are antitrans, ableist, homo-hating and so on would have popular uptake. At the same time, researchers of all sorts are able to direct their attention toward fundable areas, in a process that Jeff Schmidt identifies as cultivating "assignable curiosity" (Schmidt 2001). Schmidt compellingly examines the process through which professionalization shapes the lives and interests of people who go through graduate school and, perhaps especially in the case of research scientists, through postdoctoral programs. A piece of this, he argues, is the coproduction of "fundable" areas and scientists' interests. When companies or government agencies make their technical needs known, Schmidt finds that "scientists, through a process of self-adjustment, get interested in the appropriate topics" (57–58). This is not conspiracy theory, but reflection on the implications of attaching research priorities to fundability. Also perhaps involved in this particular example is what Julie Guthman identifies as "problem closure," or "'coproduction'—a situation in which the investigation of a phenomenon uses tools or techniques that already presume much about the nature of the phenomenon, which then brings it into sharper existence" (Guthman 2011, 34).[2] As an endocrinologist and someone focusing on the hormone function in metamorphosis, Hayes was predisposed to notice hormonal shifts as they affect gonadal development in part through the directions of his curiosities and in part through the apparatus he has assembled through which to examine (and thus assemble) the world (Barad 2007). Consider the findings of scientist Rick Relyea, who has studied the effects of the herbicide Roundup on frogs. Relyea investigated the effects of Roundup on morphological shifts in tadpole developments in response to indicators that predators are present in their environment. Roundup (or perhaps the surfactant in it that breaches the cell wall of plants) seemed to cause tadpoles to develop larger tails, something they also do in the presence of dragonflies and newts (some of their predators) (Relyea 2012). Relyea and his team frame this in terms of "morphological changes" and "trait changes"—terms that could also be used, with different effects, to talk about the changes frogs and toads take up in response to atrazine. That is, a key difference between Relyea and Hayes, aside from the fact that Hayes has gotten much more airtime in popular and academic writing, is that Relyea's research and findings focus on a different set of questions—morphology and function rather than hormone-intensive sex transformations—and thus his findings are structured by a less overdetermined set of political descriptors.

If we want to have more adequate understandings of the world, we need ways to talk about why atrazine and other chemicals used in industrial food production might be bad for us and the world that do not rely on the assumption that sexual bodily transformations, nonstraight sexuality, and disability are wrongs that must be avoided. The subtext of this discourse is that feminization or queerness are harms to be avoided and reasons to pursue noncontaminated waters and bodies. The logic here is that straight and non-disabled body formation—heterosexual practice and a hypostatized cis/gender-conforming body that lines up with current classifications of who is disabled—are the norm from which any form of difference deviates. If we want to pursue less-toxic interdependent worlds while simultaneously thinking that sex-changing bodies, queer behavior, and disability are great, we need to have better ways to understand harm. Atrazine might still be very bad, a chemical in relation to which we want to avoid being coproduced. But the reasons for avoiding it or other body- and ecology-shaping chemicals cannot be read directly off of the fact of certain bodily transformations. Assessments that do the job better will rest on an embrace of the fact of interdependence rather than an attempt to avoid it. But within accounts based on an account of interdependence, we still need clear ways to understand and resist harm.

One way to think about harm is in terms of Ruth Wilson Gilmore's definition of racism as the differential distribution of group vulnerability to premature death (Gilmore, 28). This approach works well in thinking about who bears the effects of chemicals like atrazine and permethrin, as well as more conventional pollutants—the beings who absorb these things often being far away from those who make decisions to use them. In the groups made vulnerable to premature death, I would include the bees and the anurans along with the humans who are often migrant workers or communities of color downwind from industrial processing plants in the form of fields or factories. I follow Guthman in this, using her conceptualization of the body as a "spatial fix" of capitalism. Expanding on David Harvey's account of how capitalism addresses crises of overaccumulation through geographical expansion—moving the problems and externalities of production somewhere else—Guthman argues that in the current context, along with the soils, seas, and air, bodies (both human and animal) are absorbing much of capitalism's excess. . . . In effect, individual bodies are absorbing the so-called *externalities* of production processes, so that food companies most definitely do not have to pay the full cost of doing business. And then bodies became a site for commodifiable cures to the conditions and illnesses created through these foods and exposures." She argues that "the body is wrapped up in the material processes of capitalism quite apart from the 'decisions' that human subjects make around production and reproduction. Rather, bodies as material entities are literally absorbing conditions and externalities of production and consumption" (Guthman, 182). Following Gilmore, we can understand that using the body as a spatial fix of capitalism unevenly distributes impurity, tending both practically and metaphorically to pollute supposedly already impure bodies. Racialized and Indigenous people bear the harms of being simultaneously a spatial fix for toxicity—living in polluted sites, breathing that air, drinking that water—and a metaphoric reservoir for pollutants.

Guthman's focus is on the problems with what I discussed in chapter 1 as "healthism"—the belief that individually we ought to manage our health to minimize or mitigate the effects of being immersed in the toxic soup that constitutes our everyday world. The idea that we can (or should) eat organic food, drink alkalinizing water from personal water filters, or take up other practices meant to manage the effects of exposure to pesticides and herbicides is a version of an individualizing purity politics. Such an approach perpetuates the difficulty of perceiving how bodies are embedded in and fixes of the flows of capitalist production—in the cases I discuss in this chapter, the industrial production of food with all its side effects for anurans and for us. Healthism as a possible practice is heavily racialized; people who live at the site of multiple vectors of vulnerability have less possibility for individually managing their health to resist the structural context that produces premature group-differentiated death. We should, then, understand calls for personal responsibility for health as racist as well as classist, and deeply imbricated with the purity logics that delineate whiteness as a social location. Responses to the distribution of harm not based on healthism—particularly healthism in the form of naturalizing and transposing understandings of sex, sexuality, and disability in an attempt to mobilize action about herbicides and pesticides—may be more effective.

Sandra Steingraber's complex book, *Living Downstream*, which I discussed above, details a lot of what I am identifying as impurity, which is one way to think about coconstitution. Consider again Nancy Tuana's formulation of the production of "viscous porosity," a way of talking about what she calls *emergent interplay* (Tuana 2008, 189). Writing about what happened during and after Hurricane Katrina's effects on the Louisiana coastline and on New Orleans, Tuana examines the interaction between social relations, the levees, the sea, and more, on down to our cells. She frames the material interplay among these sites as a dance of interacting agency:

> The dance of agency between human and nonhuman agents also happens at a more intimate level. The boundaries between our flesh and the flesh of the world we are of and in is porous. While that porosity is what allows us to flourish—as we breathe in the oxygen we need to survive and metabolize the nutrients out of which our flesh emerges—this porosity often does not discriminate against that which can kill us. We cannot survive without water and food, but their viscous porosity often binds itself to strange and toxic bedfellows. (198)

Tuana details the many ways we can perceive the toxic, polluted space that became particularly palpable in the friction of the storm—the superfund sites that may or may not have been breached, but also the long-lax regulations governing industrial pollution in what is known as Louisiana's "cancer alley."

Considering industrial offcasts (easily understood as pollutants) and substances like atrazine (a chemical framed as useful, harmless, and only in some contexts legible as harmful), we might find that they are more easily analytically than practically separable. As Tuana puts it, "There is a viscous porosity of flesh—my flesh and the flesh of the world. This porosity is a hinge through which we are of and in the world. I refer to it as viscous, for there are membranes that effect the interactions. These membranes of various types—skin and flesh, prejudgments and symbolic imaginaries, habits and embodiments" (199–200). Because of the ways materials in the world are taken into our body, the fact that there is always only a complex system that we name collectively "a human" becomes a little more obviously coconstituted.[3]

Unfortunately, this coconstitution becomes obvious because of effects that we don't want—estrogen-responsive cancers, insulin resistance, and other effects. If we care about shifting some of those effects, *or* if we worry about framing nonstraight sex, gender, and sexuality as threats, we ought to attend more to harms that don't happen to reinforce already entrenched social stigmas. Hayes's work on hormone-intensive transformations, sex-selective response, and atrazine tells us a lot, perhaps much of it beyond the presentation of his work in the popular media. And Syngenta's extraordinary efforts to discredit, defund, and defame Hayes could be a study in the forms of capitalist evil that distribute death to the many in the interests of profit for the very few. Even as I love the stand that Hayes has taken on atrazine, and stand with him against Syngenta, I would love more to see reasons for this stand that don't recapitulate old narratives that, as Di Chiro frames it, "appeal to pre-existing cultural norms of gender balance, normal sexual reproduction, and the balance of nature. The deployment of the anti-normal or anti-natural in anti-toxic discourse is questionable political-ecological strategy and can work to reinforce the dominant social and economic order (the forces actually behind environmental destruction and toxic contamination of all our bodies and environments) by naturalizing the multiple injustices that shore it up" (Di Chiro 2010, 224). Next, I offer some paths toward more adequate responses to the human consequences of hormone-effecting additives through attending differently to nonhumans.

## To the Frogs Themselves

In this chapter I have been raising concerns about the gender and sexuality tropes deployed to raise human alarm about the effects of products such as atrazine. Since scolding people for using oppressive examples rarely works to shift either examples or practices, I will focus on alternative approaches to the problem of toxicity in our shared ecologies. I argue that holding an ethical regard for anurans for themselves holds out promise for the rest of us. My touchstone here returns us to the Sudbury FrogFinder practice I discussed above: civilian naturalist practices of attention as a form of ethical response.

Jim Maughn took me on many walks and hikes when I lived in northern California, always showing me parts of the world around me that I was not capable of perceiving without his guidance. He is involved in one of the thousands of groups of people, more and less organized, on this continent who systematically observe their local ecosystems. Sometimes these groups are informal (hunters, farmers, gardeners); more often they are explicitly organized as civilian naturalists—observers of and carers for their proximal ecology. Jim is part of a formal project tracking the presence of designated endangered species in areas developers have applied to alter, work that involves counting members of those species. In order to count members of a species, you have to recognize them, and in order to recognize them Jim has developed a kind of attunement to the world that Tsing calls an *art of noticing* (Tsing 2015). I regard this kind of attunement as a rich resource for countering the dangers I have identified above: using frogs and toads as merely indicator species for potential human dangers and falling into harmful tropes around sexuality, sex, gender, and disability.

In a conversation with Jim, we talked about his love of amphibians, and how that love manifests in practices of noticing. He said:

> I think that's kind of what all of my interest in learning things and learning the names of things and stuff like that is really, just about *seeing things differently* and they're somehow—learning what the Latin name for a particular thing is—sort of makes you see it differently. And, it, it stands out from the landscape in a particular way. I think because you start to notice the uniqueness of the creature, the uniqueness of the species . . . and so, the world comes into a sharper focus.

I read this kind of attention as a form of placing oneself in a community of other people who have cared enough to know about species and to recognize individual members of species. Caring and noticing are also ways of placing oneself in community with the objects of care. Taking the time to get to know something about the frog, the bird, the flower is for Jim a matter of seeing the uniqueness of things, which allows perception of the thing as it is to emerge. Think here of the FrogFinder project, which is a method of training people to learn to be attentive to their environment in a way they weren't before— you go on the website and you listen to the calls, and then you can partici- pate in the study. There are large networks of these kinds of naturalists, attending to everything from sea turtles to sea birds to amphibians, all shap- ing their arts of noticing and their self-formation in relation to the specific organisms and ecologies within which the cared-for species can be found.[4]

There is a possible narrative here in which practices of noticing and nam- ing are simply parts of Man's God-given right to name the beasts of the field and the fowls of the air (Genesis 2:20), exercising dominion over the natural world—the ultimate in holding the rational, classifying, mode as mastery and use. Against this picture, I want us to understand this form of attune- ment, even as it uses practices of classification and naming—Latin names, common names—as a practice, perhaps paradoxically, of resisting human exceptionalism while at the same time thinking that humans have responsi- bilities. As Kier argues: "The point in interrogating these classificatory infra- structures, in order to de-centre the human, is not to put animals or other things on a pedestal or to include them, but to begin to map our interde- pendencies in larger systems of relational re/production. To simply include or valorize non-humans would deny the obligations humans bear as com- plexly thinking animals capable of solving some of the major social and eco- logical problems we've created" (Kier 2010, 306). What is it to care *humanly* without thinking that humans are the most important thing in the picture? If we want to do both, we need to have some way of caring about atrazine's effects on humans while also caring about its effects on frogs. So, to take an indicator species model is to care instrumentally—we think about the frogs because of what they might tell us about what could happen to humans. As Jane Bennett argues, "to acknowledge nonhuman materialities as partici- pants in a political ecology is not to claim that everything is always a par- ticipant, or that all participants are alike. Persons, worms, leaves, bacteria, metals, and hurricanes have different types and degrees of power, just as dif- ferent persons have different types and degrees of power, different worms have different types and degrees of power, and so on, depending on the time, place, composition, and density of the formation" (Bennett 2010, 108). Naming and noticing might be a way to care humanly, but not instrumentally, to recognize and value the fact that the frogs and the toads and the lizards have their own life that we are just tuning into. This is why I'm interested in projects of ordinary people (which doesn't mean that people can't have training in ecology and still be ordinary people). They, we, you, are using ways of noticing and technologies of noticing, like naming, that don't fundamentally have an allegiance to apparatuses of thinking shaped as a practice of dominion over the natural or social world.

In practice, I have observed that naturalists like Jim, even when they're just going for a walk, go for walks that help them to see the world differently. And when I've been out walking with them, I have, in turn, a different walk. Jim's capacities to attend to things sharpen and deepen and heighten my capacities to attend to things, on the level of actually being able to perceive previously imperceptible critters and flora. Sometimes these skills include walking in particular ways, knowing how to pick up a lizard to see the color of its belly, and more. I am identifying this as naturalism, which I think can be complementary and perhaps even necessary to the kind of biology Hayes and other laboratory scientists practice. This is not because I hate science, or think that it is cold, soulless, useless, or the usual other critiques. On the contrary: scientists and their work offer some of the most important sites for ethical attunement to the world. However, because of the ways funding structures, citation practices, and lab practices manifest now, it is not, I hope, rude to claim that practicing scientists might need help in critically examining the narratives that structure their exploration of the world and their exposition to nonscientists of why what they find matters. In a funding situation where scientists have to justify the importance of their work, it is no surprise that prurient or predictable narratives structure the presentation of their findings.

It is also no surprise that the narratives that seem to be available to show that a particular situation is worthy of attention fall in line with normalized forms of gender and sexuality. Jennifer Terry productively examines what she calls the "scientific fascination with queer animals," arguing that we humans "look to the sexual behavior of animals to give meaning to human social relations, and by doing so, we engage in imaginative acts that frequently underscore culturally dominant ideas about gender and sexuality" (Terry 2000, 152). The stories we tell to make sense of the world shape what sense we make. As Donna Haraway has argued, in many ways, "*Both* the scientist and the organism are actors in a story-telling practice" (Haraway 1989, 5). The stories scientist and nonscientist observers use to understand the world have an effect on what kind of work and noticing they do. As Martha McCaughey puts it, "Scientific storytelling is a consequential political practice" (McCaughey 1996, 263). Reflecting on heterosexist narratives about evolution, she continues: "Evolutionary theories, as scientific stories of the biological origin of species, harness an imaginary past and in so doing specify "natural" aspects of contemporary human sexuality—"perversions" of which can be theorized, condemned, or mocked by those who consider themselves properly and primarily heterosexual" (261). But since scientific stories are "inescapably value-laden, making values more invisible only enables irresponsible storytelling" (281). I am interested in what it means to take seriously the impossibility of telling value-neutral stories about the world, scientific stories or otherwise, holding in mind the ethical necessity for response that I believe attends human complicity in the damage done to the critters and biota with whom we share damaged ecosystems.

As Jake Metcalf argues, "Stories serve important epistemological and political functions by making the world intelligible. In order to adequately interrogate our ethical practices, we humans must interrogate our stories for which worlds they make possible" (Metcalf 2008, 100). Metcalf very usefully thinks through the stories about bears, considering especially what it means to hold an ethical relation with companion species that are neither innocent nor guilty, but that are enmeshed in human lives. Rather than attempting a return to a mythical past in which humans and bears did not coexist, Metcalf calls for an analysis that would "lead to a recognition of our obligation in the present for mutual flourishing, an obligation whose contours arise out of our entanglements, not despite them" (117). I find a model for such obligation in the caring practices of a kind of naturalism. Recognizing that this is a fraught term, I think of this as a naturalism without nature. This will need to be a naturalism based not on a separation and custodianship between humans and Nature, or the idea that the best form of care for the world is killing off the humans (an old Santa Cruz bumper sticker summed this up: "Save the planet! Kill yourself!"). It will need to be a form of practice arising from a thick conception of entanglement and coproduction, practiced as an obligation toward mutual flourishing.

We can draw on a naturalist's attention to the world around us if we want to have access to narratives that do not replicate and reinforce the way suffering is currently distributed in the world. The narrative we use to explain the world structures what we do in it. So we can ask, what happens if we use *this* narrative to make *these* changes in the world? If we say: atrazine is bad because gender and sex switching is bad, same-sex sex is bad, bodily changes we call disability are bad, and especially sex selection that results in fewer boy babies is bad, what happens? If the badness that we're pointing to happens to line up perfectly with the way *we tend to organize power in human life* already, then two things seem to be a problem. One is that this narrative reinforces the way we currently organize power in human life. The other is that if there aren't reasons to do things *for the love of the frogs*, we reinforce the ways humans organize power in the world altogether, which is currently ruining our shared world.

Consider the bullfrog, another example from Jim. Bullfrogs are not native to California, but they are everywhere. Jim noted:

> Primarily, they are spreading because it's the frog that people tend to like to dissect in high school biology classes. And there's always people who feel bad about dissecting them, or they raise them from tadpoles and then rather than killing them they'll take them out to the local stream and let them go. Well, and the problem with that is that the bullfrog devours all the native frogs. It will just decimate the native frogs—the West Coast has lost almost all the native frogs, the populations are all either threatened or endangered, and one of the main reasons is bullfrog predation and also that the bullfrog passes along a fungal disease that the bullfrog is actually unaffected by but that can [harm other frogs].

This example of the bullfrog is helpful for thinking about how we might take responsibility for pushing a system out of livability without resorting to sexist, heterosexist, trans-hating, and ableist narratives. It is not that there is anything wrong with bullfrogs themselves—as Jim says:

> Here's the thing: I like bullfrogs as much as I like California red-legged frogs. Bullfrogs are really neat. They're huge, and that's kind of neat, too. The problem is that there shouldn't be bullfrogs in California because the fact that we've released bullfrogs in California means that the ecology has changed in such a way that we are either going to be okay with the extinction of all the other frogs, or we're not.

Probably many people who release bullfrogs in California also would value the lives of California red-legged frogs, and might make different decisions about releasing them if they understood the effect they have. High school teachers might stop raising bullfrogs from tadpoles, using them in dissection, and so on. Again, thinking with Jim:

> I can appreciate a bullfrog for what it is, but it's concerning to me that there are bullfrogs in the environment *here*, because although I don't think of the environment as a static thing, I do think that there is something tragic about the fact that we're losing these other frog species because people can't tell the difference between a bullfrog and a red-legged frog. They are distinct organisms.

Not having good understanding of what a bullfrog is and how it might effect the world means that people think they're being nice when they spare the bullfrog and release it. If the limit on our ability to perceive the world, or the scope of our narrative, is "frog"—rather than "bullfrog," "red-legged frog," or other more nuanced stories, we will fail to have the kind of attention that can even begin to take action adequate to the world we're in. Toxicity is not only about invisible chemicals that cause transformations in the breeding capacity of frogs—it is also about bullfrogs eating tree frogs, or transmitting fungal infections to them. How can we attend to those conditions for the living and dying of amphibious friends?

Consider another example of attention, which I encountered through Hugh Raffles's book *Insectopedia*.[5] Cornelia Hesse-Honegger is an observer of the world, an artist who illustrates the damages experienced by insects who live near nuclear reactors. This is a different case than the kinds of toxicity narrated or experienced in exposure to herbicides and pesticides, but it tells us something about arts of noticing as a productive supplement and spur for scientific attention. Hesse-Honegger started her work as a scientific illustrator, a practitioner of a craft that some might have imagined would be replaced by photography. Scientific illustration is a form of nonphotographic realism, deriving its accuracy from the fact that it selectively renders aspects of the physical world, showing different parts of them to be salient depending on the theoretical question at issue. It is thus a form of epistemically interesting scientific practice, though often understood as not "Science" properly construed.

Raffles writes about Hesse-Honegger: "I don't want to tell a hero story. But let me tell you what she did" (Raffles 2011, 27). In its simplest form, what she did was draw leaf bugs, also called true bugs, living near nuclear reactors. Her close attention to their morphologies showed the bodily difference manifesting in them. Believing that these bodily differences are a result of the bugs' exposure to low-level radiation, Hesse-Honegger has been campaigning for scientific attention to what is happening in these places. Thinking more closely, or complexly, about what she did—the reason Raffles is tempted to tell a hero story—Hesse-Honegger initiated a very interesting and profound shift in understanding the effects of nuclear radiation. One piece of this is changing how we understand what's at stake in living in disturbed landscapes, to echo Anna Tsing's reflections on the landscape disturbance necessary for wild matsutake mushrooms to flourish (Tsing 2014). This shift starts with a mode of attention that displaces or defers habits of thinking. Raffles quotes Hesse-Honegger: "I realized that I had to free myself from all my prior assumptions and be completely open to what was in front of me, even at the risk of being considered mad" (Raffles 2011, 21). A key prior assumption concerns "dose dependency," a commonplace way to measure harm.

Dose-dependency is a core premise in conventional conceptions of toxicity. As the saying goes, the dose makes the poison—a little of something can be harmless, easily processed by our bodies, or even medicinal. I believe that conceptions of dose-dependency serve as foundational assumptions in much of our thinking about toxicity—hinge propositions, on which whole arguments, practices, and ways of understanding the world turn. In practices around radiation, dose-dependency theory establishes a fixed threshold beyond which it is dangerous to accumulate radioactive exposure. These practices rely on measuring and tracking the effects of the atomic bombs exploded at Hiroshima and Nagasaki—high-level, short-term nuclear exposures. Taking this event as the benchmark/reference point traces a linear exposure curve. As Raffles says:

> The resulting curve emphasizes the effects of exposure to artificial radioactivity at high values. Low-level radiation, such as that emitted over long time periods by normally operating nuclear power plants, appears relatively, if not entirely, insignificant, its effects falling within the range of the "natural" background radiation emitted from elements present in the earth's crust. The assumption is that large doses produce large effects; small doses, small effects. (23)

But this assumption seems to be quite incorrect. Instead, it seems that cells respond to radiation differentially depending on their stage of quiescence, growth, or repair; if cells experience radiation in a period of replication, they will respond. Raffles takes an analogy from Hesse-Honegger: if bullets are fired, "it doesn't matter how many are fired, whom they're fired by, or even when and where they're fired; you need only be hit by one at the wrong time and in the wrong place to suffer its effects" (25). If high-level, short-term radiation is like standing in a thick hail of bullets (some of which are bound to hit you), long-term, low-level radiation is like being shot at by perhaps more bullets—even though they are more widely distributed, if you're in their way you'll be hit.

So, effects from radioactive exposure are emergent, context-dependent, and not understandable using our most widespread, conceptual apparatus. This means that if we want to understand and act with more adequate resources, we need a different approach. Methodologically, I draw inspiration from Hesse-Honegger's artistic practice: resolutely attending to the shapes of the bugs as they appear, refusing to paint what she (or we) might expect. Critics of the kinds of theories of the effects of low-level radiation have argued that a problem with the approaches taken so far is that it lacks scientific rigor. In particular, making claims about the effects of something on something else (say, the effects of low-level radiation on leaf bugs) usually requires a reference population that can be demonstrated to not be affected by the agent in question—a pure, unaltered baseline from which we can track difference (leaf bugs that experience no radiation would be a reference population). But if the work that Hesse-Honegger is doing is right, we must follow her in arguing that "there can be no reference habitat on a planet thoroughly polluted by fallout from aboveground testing and emissions from nuclear power plants" (35). Astrid Schrader has articulated the kind of attention following from the form of attention, which I have followed Tsing in thinking of as an "art of noticing on a damaged planet" as a practice of nonteleological care. Such care "articulates a relation to the other and a mode of attention" (Schrader n.d., 5). In a piece reflecting on teaching the Chernobyl entry in Raffles's book, Schrader persuasively argues that Hesse-Honegger is able to perceive and think about a biological situation unthinkable by conventional scientists—she is able to "perceive the unexpected"—as "part of her technology of care, a particular mode of attention. In systematically complementing precision with randomness, Hesse-Honegger's self-withdrawal is no longer opposable to judgments about the exposure of deformities, but becomes its condition of possibility, such that the insect may contribute to its visible renderings" (26). But it is only an opening to a condition of possibility. The vital insight here is that merely noticing is not the same as acting on the basis of that observation.

I take great hope in reflecting on the people who are practicing arts of noticing in a damaged world, who manifest the kind of complex care and responsibility we need now. I believe they are legion, stretching from people living, fishing, and hunting in the far north who attend to how the biosphere is changing with global warming to the people who care for the frogs in Sudbury's damaged landscapes to the civilian naturalists who attend to the sea turtles on the South Carolina coast. I echo Ah-King and Hayward's artic-ulation of their motivations for giving an account of sex as already shaped by toxicity:

> It is not that we are promoting pollution, but rather, offering ways of coming to terms with the real conditions of everyday life. Rather than reinvesting in purity politics—the hope of some environmental movements—we wonder how resilience and healing can occur in the context of transnational capitalism and its monstrously under-regulated dumping and pumping of various by-products into air, water, and earth. As opposed to simply positioning oneself as an ideologue—the world is doomed unless we clean it all up—we offer a more pragmatic, if you will, and practical theorization for understanding the organisms we are becoming and the changing nature of the ecosystems to which we belong. (Ah-King and Hayward 2014, 6)

Consider, in closing, the etymology of the terms "pesticide" and "herbicide"—the suffix that marks these as deadly is from the Latin *cida*—slayer, killer, cutter. These substances cut, and at the same time they introduce something. Perhaps we can understand them to manifest an agential cut, in Karen Barad's sense, that process through which an apparatus that materially reconfigures the world delineates what is acted upon and what acts—boundary making and breaking agents. In toxic mattering, the compounds that we use to dis-rupt photosynthesis in undesired plants then disrupt the formation of human bodies: they are classic boundary objects. As Barad frames them, "Appara-tuses are specific material reconfigurings of the world that do not merely emerge in time but iteratively reconfigure spacetimematter as part of the ongoing dynamism of becoming" (Barad 2007, 142). Endocrine-disrupting compounds are apparatuses in this sense. In order to engage their effects without obscuring the decisions about what will count as a salient harm, worth attending to, we need to make different agential cuts that allow us to generate different narratives and different nodes of attention. Again: I highlight here the naturalist's art of attention not because scientists don't have rich and complex modes of attention. Rather, we might do better science—attend better—if we have better narratives, grounded in arts of noticing that open to and allow for noticing in contexts that are already disturbed, already impure.

# 4

## Consuming Suffering

### Eating, Energy, and Embodied Ethics

This chapter investigates the claim that embodiment produces ethical implication. What is the experience of recognizing ourselves as impossibly situated in interdependent relationships of suffering? I argue that to be embodied is to be placed, sustained, affected by the world, and in turn to affect the world. I fill out the ethical demands embodiment implies, focusing on the ethical entanglement of one's body with suffering bodies that at first pass seem to be quite far away. That is to say, intimate others may show up intuitively as touching and touched by our bodies and thus as ethically demanding. But we are also ethically entangled with more distant others. To say we are entangled is to say we have responsibilities by virtue of our relationships with near and distant others. Although these responsibilities arise from our particular and situated context—our individual lives—they are not resolvable individually. An ethical approach aiming for personal purity is inadequate in the face of the complex and entangled situation in which we in fact live. Individualism, in the context of relations perceptible through considering embodiment, is an ethical problem because it constitutes ethical success as personal purity. A central argument of this book is, of course, that personal purity is simultaneously inadequate, impossible, *and* politically dangerous for shared projects of living on earth. While personal purity may be a winnable aim in some ethical situations, it is impossible in situations such as energy use, climate change, and eating. We do better to aim for different sorts of ethical practice more consonant with the entangled and complex situations we meet.

One way to think about the ethical implication of embodiment is thus: that we have bodies means that we must sustain them—we must eat, and we

107

must maintain a physical situation that allows us to stay alive (we must use energy). Embodiment as a form of implication means that to live, we rely on others intimately—we use them, and our actions shape the conditions for their lives and deaths. Here, "use" often means "kill." Our eating bodies have permeable boundaries and unstable, dynamic relations with taking in nourishment and expelling waste. Ethical decisions about being an eating body often focus on vegetarianism. In this chapter I affirm an ethical orientation to and regard for the effects of our eating, but reject the idea that any particular eating practice will solve the conundrum eating evokes. Our bodies also rely on a relatively narrow range of temperature and environment, and to hold that range many of us heat or cool our houses, grow food in greenhouses, and otherwise render ourselves extravagant endpoints in a process of energy transfer. In order to explore this aspect of our consuming bodies, I will focus here on the nuclear production of energy, looking in particular at what the 2011 Fukushima meltdown can tell us about our bodily entanglement with other beings and ecosystems. I argue that in the case of energy usage, in ways similar to the use of others in eating, embodiment produces an unsolvable but urgent relation in which we consume suffering. To address the relations necessitated by our embodiment, we must reach toward a nonindividualized ethical practice that can address the problem of unresolvable ethical entanglement.

Framing ethical entanglement as a problematic implies that there are ways to think about ethics that do *not* involve entanglement or implication. I will argue that, indeed, our canonical theories revolve around a moral agent who is not ontologically relationally implicated with others. Instead, moral actors are commonly understood to act as *individual* knowers, willers, and actors. I will also explore the cases of the Fukushima nuclear catastrophe and eating as examples of nonindividualized ethical situations. Then I will discuss the question of whether embodiment can ever be understood as an individual problem and will offer theoretical resources for thinking about the work of encountering suffering and responding in some adequate way. Finally, I suggest two models that, extended, help us think about how we might orient ourselves toward responding well to near-infinite complexity and the near-inevitability of failure: distributed cognition and existentialist ethics of uncertain freedom.

## Ethics and the Individual

No ethical system, even one expounding ethical egoism, holds that individuals do not exist in the context of social relations. It is near-axiomatic that the reason we must think about ethics at all is the problem of other people, however people are defined. Every major ethical system assesses individual moral formation and activity in the context of certain collective considerations. And yet each predominant system takes as its unit of analysis the thinking, willing, and acting individual person. Ethics, as it has historically developed, aims to help individuals in their personal ethical decision-making, and we continue to assess moral rights and wrongs at the scale of the individual human. Take some canonical figures in ethics as representative examples:

Aristotle's articulation of how to live well begins from the measure of human excellence and the question of what our lives aim toward. He writes that "a human being's function we posit as being a kind of life, and this life as being activity of soul and actions accompanied by reason, and it belongs to a good man to perform these well and finely, and each thing is completed well when it possesses its proper excellence: if all this is so, the human good turns out to be an activity of soul in accordance with excellence" (Aristotle 2002, 1098a15). For us to craft our lives such that we develop the habit of responding to complex ethical situations in the right way, to the right degree, at the right time (and so on), requires a social context in which we develop our virtues. Aristotle marks the significance of sociality in his attention to everything from close friendship and family bonds to the most impersonal strictures of justice and political structure. While there is much in his account that might help us think about how moral capacity is shaped by social and collective context, the salient locus of moral excellence remains the individual. Individual people aim for the mean, and it is as a singular person that someone possesses excellence.

Immanuel Kant's work centers the moral agent for very different reasons. If the central question in ethical decision-making asks *What ought I do?* Kant answers via our capacity to reason, and thus to freely and autonomously choose in accord with the moral law. That reason is collectively shared by and definitive of everyone we can understand as human, and that rationality commands a regard for others means—on my reading—that this sort of autonomy is not individualist. Both in terms of the imperative to consider the universalizability of our actions and the clear sense that rational deliberation involves affected others, there is a sense in which Kant's work commands a certain sort of collectivity. Still, the capacity to act in accord with reason depends on the capacity to reason, and reason is explicitly understood as held by agents. ("Only a rational being has the capacity to *act in accordance with the representation* of laws, that is, in accordance with principles, or has a *will*" [Kant 1993, 4:412]). Even when we will in accordance with reason and test that accord by standards of universalizability, the locus of reason and morality remains an individual who thinks, wills, or acts.

Consider finally John Stuart Mill's utilitarianism—perhaps the ethical theory most clearly associated with collectivity. The idea that actions are "right in proportion as they tend to promote happiness; wrong as they tend to produce the reverse of happiness" for the greatest number explicitly holds that we ought to consider the well-being of others in our moral decision-making. Still, as Mill writes, the "greatest majority of good actions are intended not for the benefit of the world, but for that of individuals, of which the good of the world is made up; and the thoughts of the most virtuous man need not on these occasions travel beyond the particular persons concerned, except so far as is necessary to assure himself that in benefiting them he is not violating the rights, that is the legitimate and authorized expectations, of anyone else" (Mill 2001, 97). The individual is the locus of ethical analysis, and the conglomeration of individuals does not produce a collective standard of good different in kind from what produces happiness for the individual.

There are other ways to parse the guiding conceptions of the locus of moral agency—evolutionary accounts that see our moral actions arising from the need for individuals to get on together for the survival of the species, religious accounts that locate the origin of ethical behavior in our accord with one form or another of divine law, and so on. However we trace the lines of descent that produce this formation, though, the site for moral activity remains the individual. When we look to assess ethical decisions or actions, when we attempt to hold someone responsible, when we recommend action, we look to individuals. Even on an expressive-collaborative model like Margaret Urban Walker's, the locus of responsibility and agency is held, to a significant degree, by the person making a relevant decision—though, as Walker recommends, that decision may be made more effectively in consultation with a collectivity. There is a sense in which this concern with individual agency is interestingly not in play when we aim to hold entities like corporations responsible, or call for them to take ethical action. Whether under the frame of corporate social responsibility or the attempt to bring companies to court on criminal charges, in these cases I believe we treat incorporated bodies as conglomerates in ways that might be ethically interesting. Ladelle McWhorter's recent work on the disjunction between rhetorics of liberal individualism and the practice of protecting conglomerate corporations is instructive here (McWhorter 2013).

Reasoning about moral matters at the scale of the individual is entirely appropriate in many, many situations. Much of the ethical terrain considered in ethics and bioethics does indeed come down to the question of how a person ought to act in the face of morally difficult (or simple!) circumstances. The sorts of circumstances I have in mind include those in which my own ethical orientation toward the world is at issue, in which my decision-making relates primarily or only to my own life and the people near me, or in which there is an identifiable agent responsible for the action in question. When I decide whether it is acceptable to steal something, lie, kill someone, assist someone in suicide, and so on, in many circumstances it will be meaningful for an individual agent to make those decisions and take action appropriately.

There are, though, circumstances in which we need far more than an ethics at the scale of the individual; in this sense, the individual as the unit of analysis for ethics is not a "scalable" unit. Anna Tsing defines scalability as "the ability of a project to change scales smoothly without any change in project frames" (Tsing 2015, 38). She argues that organizing time and space in relation to scalability has shaped capitalist modernization, as things become "exchangeable at market value" (40), effacing their specificities and delimiting the scope of questions we might ask about social relations of exchange. Ethical approaches that hold a putatively separable individual as their core unit of analysis similarly take it that individual ethical purity will be scalable, producing societal harmony. This is not the case.

Rather, the terms of ethical thinking must change in relation to the scale of the ethical problem. As Susan Sherwin argues in her call for bioethics to address the worldwide global catastrophes facing us, ethics and bioethics "have been developed to deal with questions concerning the moral responsibilities of individuals and questions of the form, 'what should an agent do in circumstances of the sort x?'" (Sherwin 2009, 15). Sherwin's nonexhaustive list of the kinds of circumstances that cannot be addressed by attending to the moral responsibilities of individuals includes: "climate change; air and water pollution; rapid disappearance of growing numbers of species, including many that are crucial to human food supplies; a desperate shortage of (clean) water for many people; enormous disparities between the rich and the poor, both nationally and internationally" (8). To address these and other "big" problems, Sherwin persuasively argues that we need to formulate and practice a public, collective ethics. The density and complexity of the threats currently facing humanity and our biosphere means we must examine the values we use to make our collectively experienced ethical decisions. The complexity of global dangers we collectively face "requires us to have ethical tools that enable us to critically explore the multiple levels of moral responsibility with respect to complex human practices" (17). The kinds of dangers Sherwin identifies cannot be addressed only by changes in individual, personal behavior. And while it might be possible to aim for personal ethical purity at the scale of the individual, when we understand our relation to the broader contexts of our embodiment, it's clear that purity is an incoherent and impossible aim.

## Illustrative Cases—Energy and Eating

Take the example of the Fukushima nuclear disaster in the wake of Japan's 2011 earthquake and tsunami. A debate has arisen in many contexts about who bears responsibility for the harms still unfolding from this disaster: the CEO of the company, TEPCO, who perhaps could have done various things differently? The government policies that shifted energy production toward a 30 percent reliance on nuclear energy? The regulatory body that did not require pre-1975 cores to be shifted over to a gravity-fed water-circulation system that would come into play in the case of a long-term power-down? Or the Japanese citizens who use the energy produced through fission reactions? If we think that consumers bear some culpability for using energy— and this is a core question—how ought we evaluate that responsibility? In the 1970s, when there were widespread protests against nuclear energy usage, there were not equally widespread discussions about the effects of using coal to produce energy. Today we have good data that coal—which in Canada comprises 20 percent and in the United States takes up more than 50 percent of energy consumption—produces particulates like sulfur dioxide and nitrogen oxides, as well as significant greenhouse gas emissions implicated in global warming. Additionally, coal mining carries well-known health risks to miners such as pneumoconiosis, or coal-miner's lung, along with grosser health risks such as mine collapse or flooding (Jennifer Duggan 2013). There are significant environmental effects of open-pit mining to local communities. When some of the environmental regulations on burning dirty coal to make electricity came into effect, places like Nova Scotia started buying cleaner-burning coal from, for example, Colombia. The trade-off is that the environmental devastation and worker exploitation in Colombia is sufficiently extreme that many call coal mined there "blood coal." Whether through the creation of open pits for mining where very little can live, or flooding to create hydroelectric dams, or in the wake of nuclear disasters, creating energy to heat and light our homes creates what in the context of a nuclear disaster are called "exclusion zones." At the end of this chapter, I will discuss the example of two farmers who remained behind in the Fukushima exclusion zone to care for cattle formerly destined to be food.

Before turning to the complex enfolding of issues of radiation and eating those cows figure for us, consider eating ordinarily conceived. Eating situates us in relation to a social world, such as when eating or refraining from one thing or another is undertaken in order to place oneself in religious tradition or to retain certain cultural food practices. People also frame themselves based on their eating practices (as when they say "I'm a locavore, a vegan, a freegan, an ova-lacto vegetarian, a pescatarian, an omnivore, a carnivore, a raw foodist, a breathetarian"). Or on what they do or do not eat: this is not to be eaten (meat, fish, dairy, grain, soy, food from more than 100 miles away, cooked food, carbs, fats, bad fats); this is to be eaten (organic food, vegetables, meat, fish, dairy, grain, soy, food from less than 100 miles away, carbs, cooked food, good fats). These are ways of classifying the eaten world and ourselves in it, and they fail in the ways that most classificatory schemes do— they cannot describe the world completely, there will always be things beyond the schema, there are non-unique identifying criteria. Or, rather, they fail at such systems not out of the general principles in the way most classification does, but because of challenges at the heart of eating. Kim Q. Hall characterizes the attempt to manage the ills of the world through changes in personal eating behavior as it manifests in the "mainstreamed alternative food movement" as "a neoliberal hygienic eating project fixated on the achievement of virtue, health, and good citizenship through appropriate consumer choices at the table and in the (farmer's) marketplace" (Hall 2014, 183). If we orient toward eating as though we can personally exempt ourselves from ethical or physical ill-effects, we're engaging in a perpetually failing purity project.

In addition to the kinds of classifications individual eaters make about themselves and their food (and the ways those classificatory decisions co-produce each of these terms), there are many, many classificatory systems invisibly in place around our most unconsidered eating practices. Many of these take the form of state practices and policies, while some involve the accretions and effects of habits. Others have to do with side-products of capitalism, such as considerations about how long food can be in a shipping container, or whether it is a food fetish object. But all ways that we orient ourselves in relation to eating are also ways to place ourselves in material and immaterial systems that on some level we understand to be in play. The tomato we eat was a seed, then a sprout. It was planted by someone, and it relied on either a complex living web of microbes, insects, clay, humus, sunlight, water, or perhaps a complex web of petroleum derivatives, presterilized fields, seeds with fish DNA spliced in, sunlight, and water. Someone picked it, someone packed it, someone drove it around, someone placed a sticker on it, someone weighed it and told us how much it would cost to buy. When we bite into the tomato, we bite all of that and more (Harvey, Quilley, and Beynon 2003).

Similarly to the considerations involved in energy use—which, to be comprehensive, ought to include thinking about the waste products generated alongside heat, light, or electricity—eating implies waste. If petroleum-based fertilizers were used on that tomato, and they probably were, generating those products produced by-products. As what we eat moves through our body, it produces some ephemeral things—the energy to move our body, a tomato-eating feeling—and also excreta. Our sweat, our urine, our shit, the packaging used to contain the food before we ate it—these all go places, and must be dealt with (Hird 2013). As we used to hear in the 1980s, there is no "away" to throw things. In eating, as Haraway argues, "we are most inside the differential relationalities that make us who and what we are and that materialize what we must do if response and regard are to have any meaning personally and politically. There is no way to eat and not kill, no way eat and not become with other mortal beings to whom we are accountable, no way to pretend innocence and transcendence or a final peace" (Haraway 2008, 295). We should understand eating as illuminating our bodies as mere way stations in complex, entwined systems. The eating and excreting body is always entangled, enmeshed, a mess.

Part of the mess that allows us to live is our intense coproduction with constitutive others—the viruses and bacteria that live with and in our bodies. Earlier I mentioned Biss's observation about placentas. She writes: "A rather surprising amount of the human genome is made up of debris from ancient viral infections. . . . The cells that form the outer layer of the placenta for a human fetus bind to each other using a gene that originated, long ago, from a virus. Though many viruses cannot reproduce without use, we ourselves could not reproduce without what we have taken from them" (Biss 2014, 31). Biss's note here is based on popular-science author Carl Zimmer's writing on viruses (Zimmer 2011), but it echoes a growing attention to the multiplicity of our selves, attending to our symbiotic relationships with microbes of all sorts (Dethlefsen, McFall-Ngai, and Relman 2007; McFall-Ngai 2014). The catchphrase that the cells in our body are close to 90 percent nonhuman, that we are "mostly microbe," popularized by research coming out of the Human Microbiome Project, might give some of us ontological whiplash[1]—our bodies are our others, at many scales. As Ed Yong, another popular-science writer, explores even when microbes kill us, frequently they could be (unlike viruses, which need to be in a host to do their work) just accidental murderers. Yong says, "The adaptations that allow bacteria, fungi and other pathogens to cause us harm can easily evolve outside the context of human disease. They are part of a microbial narrative that affects us, and can even kill us, but that isn't *about* us. This concept is known as the coincidental evolution hypothesis or, as the Emory University microbiologist Bruce Levin described it in 2008, the 'shit happens' hypothesis" (Yong 2015). Microbes are neither microbe- nor human-exceptionalist.

In situations where an individual is directly responsible for someone else's death, we have many ways to assess the ethical responsibility involved, and similarly we are able to call for particular ethical norms for helping others—children, for example—to flourish. But in this messy world of enmeshment, things are not so clear. We might be more like microbes in our effects on the world—unintentionally destructive. We presume that viruses and bacteria don't have collectivity or consciousness, and we move forward from the view that we can change our behavior in relation to the world that hosts and nourishes us as we host and nourish nonhuman symbiotes. As individuals who do things like turn on lights or computers, how ought we respond to the ethical conundrums implied in energy usage? How ought we feel about biting a tomato? If we aim in general, through our actions, to *not* cause people's death or sickness, or climate change, or nuclear-reactor meltdown, is there a kind of collective agent with whom we should identify in positioning ourselves in relation to electricity? Theorizations of collective moral responsibility will not, I think, help much; the group "energy user" is too distributed and too variable, and includes too many people with different relationships to energy systems. Understanding the group of people who use electricity as uniformly morally responsible for the harms accruing to energy production as an ethical agent in the relevant sense runs up against multivalent moral complexity. We cannot individually, personally, choose a form of energy production not enmeshed in tremendous harms.

The question of whether we users of electricity are personally at fault for the harms of energy production, of the Fukushima reactor's meltdown, is, I think, the wrong sort of question, asked at the wrong scale. But it does allow us to see something important about the kinds of ethical questions global catastrophes and systemic problems call on us to consider: embodiment produces complex relations with ethical implications. What follows ethically from understanding ourselves to be relationally constituted? We might understand the question of a coconstituted self-and-world as a situation involving politics, ethics, matter, and subject-making. Karen Barad frames our coconstitution as calling for an *"ethico-onto-epistemology*—an appreciation of the intertwining of ethics, knowing, and being." Our knowledge practices arise through our situation as beings in and of the world, and they are mutually implicated in shaping the world. Barad calls this relationship an *intra-action*, and argues that "each intra-action matters, since the possibilities for what the world may become call out in the pause that precedes each breath before a moment comes into being and the world is remade again, because the becoming of the world is a deeply ethical matter" (Barad 2007, 185). We are entangled with the world, and thus our ontology, our knowing relations, and our ethical orientation and practice are all invoked in action.

Our being, following Barad, is entangled—and so how to *be* in relation to our entangled world is at stake. Thus, "ethico-onto-epistemologies." Myra Hird productively attends to the microworlds of bacteria, arguing that attending to life on this scale allows us to perceive our interdependence (in ways consonant with the argument I'll make in chapter 6 about interdependence as a category for disability praxis). Hird writes that "eating well with bacteria requires an ethics absent from most current formulations. By forefronting those organisms on whom eating well literally depends, I invite critical reflection upon the serious limitations we create by eclipsing the much more significant relations all animals enjoy with microorganisms—how our eating (well with) bacteria requires a different relational economy" (Hird 2009, 137). Gail Weiss's call for an embodied ethics, and an ethics of embodiment, which she grounds in an understanding of bodily imperatives, expresses a cognate sense of entanglement. She writes, "Bodily imperatives can be understood as ethical demands that bodies place on other bodies in the course of our daily existence" (Weiss 1999, 22:5). Thus, our electricity use can be understood as arising from our bodily existence in ways that place demands on other people's bodies—perhaps including implicit demands on the bodies of workers in nuclear power plants, or perhaps coal miners heading underground tomorrow.

In the first part of this book, reflecting on the conditions for understanding how we might respond to and remember unjust pasts, I argued that a kind of relational, invested memory practice could—in disparate ways—help us stand in solidarity with people who have resisted and who continue to resist things as diverse as colonial dispossession and medical mis-classification. A key piece of the relation with the constitutive past that I advocated is an acknowledgment of our implication in abhorrent histories, and a memory that holds in view that history is shaped by people. In chapter 3, I started to engage the question of how we might respond to the complex and entangled present signaled by our enmeshment in and coproduction with pesticides and herbicides—along with our stories about them. Here, I am engaging accounts of ethical response to bodily entanglement—a question about how to encounter our constitutive present. Although I take a tremendous amount from theorists such as Barad, Weiss, and Hird, I find that the specifics of how we would understand and act on the specifically ethical call they make are somewhat thin. In these texts, theorists do not tell us how to parse the specifics of the ethical call, or the relational economy toward which we might aim to behave more adequately. Rather, they open the question of what ethical adequacy might be; appreciating their nonauthoritarian theoretical approach, I still hope for something more like a plan. Again engaging Haraway's thinking on eating, I affirm that "because eating and killing cannot be hygienically separated does not mean that just any way of eating and killing is fine, merely a matter of taste and culture. Multispecies human and nonhuman ways of living and dying are at stake in practices of eating" (Haraway 2008, 295). Relationality does not imply relativism, but instead practices of responsibility. In the next two sections, I first deepen the problem and then attempt to resolve at least some of it, arguing for a practice of response even in the face of impossibility.

## Are the Ethics of Embodiment Individual?

In this section, I argue that theorists on the ethics of embodiment extend a focus on individual behaviors and individual responses to their thinking about systems. I will for the most part focus on eating. There is a great deal of philosophical and popular material on the question of whether one ought to refrain from or pursue eating meat. Because meat-eating stands for and crystallizes a wide range of other ethical issues involved in food production and consumption, I will focus on it here. Notice, though, that many of the ethical questions put down to meat-eating are broader: ought we minimize or refrain from the use of fossil fuels to transport things (like food) long distances? Ought we care about the conditions under which sentient beings labor and die for our pleasure or benefit? What weight should our pleasure take in relation to other beings' discomfort or pain? Who counts as a being for the purposes of assessing suffering? Is suffering always bad? Frequently questions about eating practices do not limit themselves to easily assessed ethical areas, and this is one of the virtues of centering food and eating in inquiries about the relations among individuals and systems.

Ethical vegetarians, vegans, locavores, and people who believe that it is good for humans to kill and eat animals share alike an orientation toward how individual people enact ethical assessments of their need for nourishment. This is not to say that writers from all orientations mistake the ethical situation we're in; thinkers who come to vastly different conclusions about how and what to eat can agree that in eating we're engaging with a vast and complex system. Through engaging with food systems, theorists worth their salt know that we traverse vast scales—from microorganisms up to the stratosphere and down to the bottom of the ocean. It is striking, then, that so many thinkers answer the question "How should I eat" with an answer that centers on individual food choices. Even Lierre Keith, author of an antivegetarian call to arms, who emphasizes repeatedly the need to understand eating as a system, and as a system within which we are never free from death, devotes her energies toward convincing vegans and vegetarians to change their individual eating practices on the way to destroying agriculture (Keith 2009). (It is bracing to see that Keith accords so much power to the between 1 percent and 4 percent of the North American eating public she seems to address—current vegetarians and vegans.)

Sherwin's critique of ethical individualism is highlighted in thinking about food and eating because while it is more obvious than in some situations treated by traditional bioethics that no eating choice is truly individual, eating still *feels* personal, intimate, and our own. More interesting is the fact that discussions of the ethics of food frequently appeal to the very global quandaries we face collectively. Appeals for people to go vegetarian, for example, argue that meat production uses more land, more water, more resources per calorie than vegetable production, and that therefore going vegetarian or vegan is an environmental choice more than anything else. And yet, moral choices about food remain individualized.

Consider some canonical vegetarian ethicists' views. Tom Regan argues in *The Case for Animal Rights* that we ought to respect the inherent value of animals and out of that respect make certain systemic changes. Inherent value, on his account, "belongs equally to those who are the experiencing subjects of a life" (Regan 2004, 320): we who have "an individual welfare that has importance to us whatever our usefulness to others" (319). Peter Singer, himself a fraught figure because of his views about disabled people, argues that keeping (and then killing and eating) animals under conditions profitable for modern factory farming expresses manifestly harmful, cruel practices. Since, he argues, "none of these practices cater for anything more than our pleasures of taste, our practice of rearing and killing other animals in order to eat them is a clear instance of the sacrifice of the most important interests of other beings in order to satisfy trivial interests of our own. To avoid speciesism, we must stop this practice, and each of us has a moral obligation to cease supporting this practice" (Singer 2002, 173). Notice that in these cases moral assessment and action is based on an individual actor experiencing life, with its inherent or useful value, and other actors responding ethically to that experience or suffering.

Writers speaking from less conventional ethical positions echo this emphasis on the individual moral actor. Elspeth Probyn is in no way a conventional ethicist, and certainly someone with an awareness of historicity and contingency. Even she walks a path Sherwin identifies, reducing ethical practices of self-making to personal acts and choices. Probyn frames the intimacy of eating as having ethical connotations in part because of the necessary embodiment of eating. Practices of freedom, which are always ethical, have to do with the immediacy and contingency of our bodies. Probyn writes: "Here freedom should be understood not as an abstract term, but as a horizon that is produced *through* practices and activities: more forcefully, it is the body that constitutes the horizon, the body produced and articulated in the ways that it eats, fucks, sleeps, writes. A body lived in the knowledge that it is all we have" (Probyn 1999, 426). Starting from the body in thinking about food practices gives us, Probyn argues, answers to the question of how to live. She writes: "My contention is that the question of how to live today can be best seen at a 'gut' level." Thinking about food and eating gives us a perspective on politics starting from the understanding that "eating is 'a way of placing oneself in relation to others'" (Probyn 1997, 7). I agree with Probyn about the idea that in eating we are placed in relation to others, and that bodies shape our horizon of ethics. But I believe that there is no such entity as "the body," or that the body is never only the body: when we understand eating, or energy use, we understand the otherness we carry within, the interdependence of existence.

Understanding embodiment as central to an ethics of relationality and interdependence without resorting to an individualized and atomized sense of the body as one's horizon of ethical practices of freedom will require more work. Further, notice that accounts of eating focus very heavily on the individual eater who might stand in a slightly more adequate relation to what are in practice megafauna. Animals we can see and touch are framed as the experiencing subjects of a life that advocates for vegetarianism or veganism (or, in fact, even things like a diet calling on us to eat food from within a 100-mile radius) focus on. And yet there is no obvious reason for us to take mammals or fish or even bees as the bright line at which we make an agential ethical cut, bringing them into the fold of our moral regard. The tiny black flies who pollinate blueberries and bite humans avoid death if they can, and worms churned up when the plow comes through to seed vegetable crops seem certainly to be the experiencing subjects of some kind of life. Why should we accord the cow more moral standing than the worm? And, reprising Hird's provocation about the potential ethical standing of bacteria, how would we act appropriately in relation to the bacteria that constitute the conditions of our lives? Here the inclination toward purity enacted through diet breaks against the intractable reality that death and life are entangled, just as our lives are dependent on others.

I have been eating vegan for more than a decade, and so I've had more conversations than I can count about purity and eating. Many don't look like conversations about purity—they happen when I'm ordering food at a restaurant and ask for one salad dressing instead of another, or when I navigate being at someone else's house and eating something. Explicit purity conversations happen, too, and most of mine have been with other vegans, some of whom genuinely feel that through taking up a lifestyle of consuming only plant-based foods and materials they are not participating in cycles of suffering. More nuanced accounts include an awareness of the various layers of suffering inevitable to eating—from the bugs in the fields to the workers who harvest food crops—but there tends to still be a view that even if there is a continuum of suffering, eating vegan puts you firmly on the better end of it. PETA—an organization that in my experience has done more than any other, through a series of video and performance interventions, to convince people that vegetarians and vegans are clueless racists unable to take a feminist stance on body politics—offers the catchphrase: *Animals are not ours to eat, wear, experiment on, use for entertainment, or abuse in any other way* (PETA 2015). I agree; but it is not clear to me that anything is ours to abuse in the relevant sense. And yet, to live, we do use and consume all sorts of other beings. I doubt that humans have or should have any relationship of ownership with plants, ecosystems, or even our own microbiome—and yet, to live, we do definitely have relations of use, and direct or indirect consumption of beings who would prefer not be consumed. In my own eating practice and in theory, I am interested in pursuing forms of noninnocent responsibility that do not rest on the lie that we can step outside relations of entanglement that are also always relations of suffering.

I join a recent current of feminist theorists in attempting to formulate an ethics of entanglement that starts from the view of being always inside relations of suffering, and focusing on eating as a way "in" to understanding entanglement. Kelly Oliver formulates her articulation of our relation to animals with reference to Derrida's generative and contradictory work on purity—its pursuit and its impossibility. Oliver argues that in his "later work on the gift, hospitality and forgiveness, Derrida imports his taste for purity and hyperbole into a hyperbolic ethics that makes impossible yet infinite demands on us." She extends this impossible demand to eating: "Because we must eat something, because decisions about what we eat are based on categorical distinctions among types that do not stand up to scrutiny, and because our motives for eating one thing rather than other[s] have become suspect, the question of how we eat becomes the primary ethical question" (Oliver 2013, 117). Oliver's discussion of the "curdled" borders between states (solid/liquid) and beings (human/animal), though it does not cite Lugones, recalls salient aspects of the metaphysics of impurity I discussed in the Introduction.

Lisa Heldke takes up some of Oliver's discussion of Derrida and the impossible but necessary ethics of eating in a usefully practical register. Heldke stages a contradiction, wondering: "How was I to make sense of the fact that, while I quite resolutely eschewed meat, I was painfully irresolute when it came time to reject the readily-available brands of chocolate that use enslaved children in their production? Why did my pleasure in the taste of chocolate trump my knowledge of the violence that produced it, whereas knowledge of animal suffering helped me decide to forego the pleasures of flesh?" (Heldke 2012, 67–68). Heldke aims for an account that would allow us to recognize the constitutive suffering and violence that we cannot avoid if we are eaters, that can acknowledge relationships with food in more generative ways. She argues for a mode that evades the categorical problems I mentioned above—the bedeviling problem that anywhere we make a cut—"this is to be eaten, this is not"—there will be categorical confusion and constitutive impurity in the eating.

Heldke offers instead the formulation of understanding "foods not as substances, but loci of relations," arguing that "ethical decision making would be better facilitated by an ontological shift in the way we think about food—a shift that emphasizes the relational nature of food-and-us" (70). The substance-based view is compatible with certain purity politics; to define some substances as "to be eaten" and others as "not" and then to succeed at not eating the "nots" could hold out an illusion of purity—which, as Oliver notes, will fall apart on scrutiny. Further, a substance ontology does not serve us when we have conflicting ethical demands. Heldke writes: "For the strict ethical vegetarian, it must always be ethically better to eat vegetables, no matter how they are grown, than to eat animals, however they are raised; vegetarianism, qua vegetarianism, provides no tools for adjudicating among such competing ethical demands. A vegetarian's concern with farmworker exposure to pesticide is separate from and in addition to, her vegetarianism—not an intrinsic layer of it" (81). She follows Raymond Boisvert's turn to an ontology captured in the slogan that "to be is always to be with" (Boisvert 2010, 61). This kind of "withy" approach to food in this example allows us to understand the entangled features of our eating behavior. The relational ontology as applied to food choices mulitplies the forms of violence and flourishing we consider relevant to our dinner plate. And, as Heldke argues, it "also diminishes the degree to which the clean hands of any individual moral agent are the most important result of our reflection" (Heldke 2010,

87). Heldke thus proposes a reorientation that would do away with making ethical decisions based on the categorical work of putatively discrete substances, would instead "sort foods in terms of the relations that produced these particular foods" (88). While I am compelled by this account, it does call for a richer normative engagement with the question of how we determine what relations deserve to flourish. I offer one branch of my solution to this problem in the remainder of this chapter and elaborate the approach in chapter 5, with a discussion of open normativities.

## Embodiment, Implication, and Encountering Suffering

I have been arguing that we should think of the ethics of embodiment as a kind of implication. Our embodiment has certain unstated elements, it carries consequences, and it is an activity and a state of involvement. The ethical implication of embodiment is overdetermined in ways that proliferate embodiment's ethical imperatives—the conclusions about what actions we ought to take, or about how to assess the ethics of embodiment, are thus in certain key ways underdetermined. If there is no way to not cause suffering, how should we decide what to do? Which suffering ought we minimize? One of the important implications here is the sense in which understanding selves as relationally constructed requires an account of embodiment. Relational self-construction is not only narrative, and the consciousness that comes along with subjectivity is at least in part material.

As Heather Paxon has explored, in a move that resonates with Myra Hird's discussion above, eating can become a good site for understanding the material constitution of relationality. Paxon works in line with Latour's investigation of the effects and conceptions of pasteurization, particularly at the moment in the nineteenth century in which microbes became something that could be first understood and then managed. Paxon writes, "While microbes were revealed in laboratories in order to be controlled, hygienists, government officials, and economists laid the groundwork for what they believed to be 'pure' social relations—relations that would not be interrupted by unwanted microbial contamination and therefore could be predicted and rationally ordered" (Paxon 2014, 115). Focusing her attention on making raw cheese, Paxon invokes the idea of *microbiopolitics:* "the creation of categories of microscopic biological agents; the anthropocentric evaluation of such agents; and the elaboration of appropriate human behaviors vis-à-vis microorganisms engaged in infection, inoculation, and digestion" (Paxon

2008, 17). The significance of our microbial others has been highlighted recently, along with the possibility that fecal transplants can address antibiotic-resistant strains of bacteria, or that our gut affects our psychological state, or that parasites spread by cats could make humans more reckless. If biopolitics commands the subjugation of individual bodies to facilitate the governance of populations, microbiopolitics might invite us individuals to pursue a care of the self through tending our intestinal gardens. Paxson says, "Aimed at a variety of moral ends, a post-Pasteurian care of the self goes through the obligatory passage point of caring for the microbe—the good microbe, the *Lactobacilus* or *Penicillium* companion species whose bodies and cultures are coproduced with humans" (40). I cannot deny that I have heard this call—I am a functional potter who makes fermentation crocks and then ferments things in them, and the closest I come to proselytizing usually concerns water kefir. But, again, even being better oriented toward the gut does not give us a simple answer to the question of what it is good to eat.

Any embodied situation is complex and dynamic, imbricated with many webs of connection, carrying ethical implications. Heating our houses, lighting our lamps, eating our dinner—indeed, virtually any embodied situation—when seen in context involves networks of connection so complex that we cannot even conceptually grasp them, let alone make sufficiently nuanced ethical decisions about them to understand ourselves as fully in the right. Managing this constitutive complexity requires us to presort our world, to enact some classification—or we freeze, which is a different sort of acting. The ethics of eating involve at least two different kinds of classificatory work: personal classification and what are usually systemic or state classificatory schemas, which govern things like food safety and the conditions under which food animals are raised. Boundary-making around our ethical choices about food and energy seems to create a crisp understanding of what we ought to do. However, I follow Deborah Bird Rose, as I'll elaborate below, in arguing that it is impossible to have clearly delineated rules about who or what is killable. In contrast, Rose offers an account of ethical relationality that resonates with Sherwin's account. Rose argues that "if we hold fast to relational principles, then we face a conceptualization of ethics based not on rules but action. Relationally, purity is a delusional *as-if*. It is the refuge of those who do not want to face the fact that to live is to be part of it all: clear boundaries become an invitation to act *as-if* there were a place of moral purity. . . . In contrast, the connectivities of life on Earth ensure that we are always called to face ambiguity and to act, to be responsible" (Rose 2011, 142). We act individually, however, in relation to constitutive complexity and boundary maintenance.

Systemically, there is a vast, imbricated set of classificatory practices associated with consumption, and depending on how we are situated in relation to and held by these practices, we will be more or less able to exercise the kind of individual choice most often associated with conventional moral decision-making. So, for example, if people object to practices around food animals, they might choose to buy only free-range eggs or meat, which typically are more expensive than animal-based food grown in factory-farm conditions. We might make the claim that "people should choose free-range eggs" or "hormone-free milk" or "local vegetables." One difficulty here is that food and energy systems are always systems. If we hold ethics to the level of the individual, we restrict ethical choice to those who are most privileged by and within the system. We can't have a theory that assumes that the people who are most "free" in relation to the system are the most ethical. In effect, right now, to hold that it is more ethical to eat local, grass-fed, wild-caught (etc.), is to hold that people who can afford to do these things are more ethical than those who eat battery-caged hens and canned GMO corn. A similar set of problems arises in relation to any call to buy LED lights because they use less electricity, though they are much more expensive, or compact florescent lights because they also use less electricity but are produced using water-poisoning mercury and frequently give people with certain conditions seizures. But even if we could buy purity on any given register with enough money, we ought still to worry about such costly morality. No one wants only the rich to have the capacity to have ethics, since they frequently manifest little or no such behavior.

There are two ways we might respond to the problem of restrictions on ethicality arising from oppression (or differential access to privileged states): we work to make everyone equally free to exercise ethicality in the context of other systems of oppressive classification, or we shift our understanding and practice of morality away from the individual.

On the first point, we would pursue the project of making nongenetically modified (perhaps?), de-commodified seed-saved fruits and vegetables (definitely?), free-range meat raised without the use of low-grade antibiotics or estrogen-mimicking growth hormones, and nutrient-rich organic whole grains as easily and cheaply available as, say, a McDonald's burger and fries.

It would need to be as profitable to grow food without petroleum fertilizers as with, as easy to take the bus as to drive a car, as possible to take a train as a plane, as easy to insulate our houses as to turn the heat up, etc. This would mean that we could then evaluate on a level field the specifically ethical choices farmers and consumers make in our food-growing and eating decisions, our heating and cooling choices. There would be analogous ways to shift the infrastructural conditions for things like taking the bus instead of a car (does the bus run in your neighborhood?), exercising, shopping locally, making ecological energy choices, and so on. To change the conditions for making individual ethical choices in these kinds of systemic ethical circumstances would, I think, constitute a major shift in an intertwined ethical-political system, and a move toward making the individual better able to make ethical decisions in such contexts would address many of the systemic problems we face.

I am more interested in the second proposition, though I have fewer practical conceptions of practices for morality that are not centered on an agent, even an agent better supported in making moral choices by the infrastructure we inhabit. My center of gravity in thinking about forms of ethical practice more adequate to the world is Donna Haraway's conception of response-ability, of "staying with the trouble," "partial recuperation and getting on together." These conceptions help flesh out the approach Heldke advocates.

Haraway theorizes implication as entanglement, as responsibility. She argues that the ethical decisions involved in science experimentation with lab animals require us to articulate ethical stances not based on the instrumental use of others justified by naturalized hierarchies (whereby humans are the masters of the natural world, and thus allowed to make use of it). Nor can we imagine that we can step outside our implication in the suffering of others. Rather, we might craft affective, cognitive, and embodied ethical responses to the complex and unequal multispecies ecologies in which we live. In the kinds of ethical situations we find in science labs, and perhaps more generally,

> entities with fully secured boundaries called possessive individuals (imagined as human or animal) are the wrong units for considering what is going on. That means not that a particular animal does not matter but that mattering is always inside connections that demand and enable response, not bare calculation or ranking. Response, of course, grows with the capacity to respond, that

is, responsibility. Such a capacity can be shaped only in and for multidirectional relationships, in which always more than one responsive entity is in the process of becoming. . . . Response cannot emerge within relationships of self-similarity. (Haraway 2008, 70–71)

Relation, here as elsewhere in Haraway's work, is the smallest unit of analysis, and the capacity to respond coproduces the obligation for response.

I find hope in Haraway's conception of response-ability, the cultivated capacity and orientation to respond. This conception of response as a way to be with suffering offers something profound to an ethics based on embodiment. Our very existence as embodied beings is predicated on the suffering of other beings. Haraway helps me think about how to understand the uncomfortable and impure situation of going on living with this situation. Two points to take up from her work on response. First, taking relationality and coemergence as the smallest possible unit of analysis also encodes difference and contingent separability; response emerges between beings that for the purposes of the action at hand are different. Second, response does not imply parity—quite the opposite! Response does not do away with power. Our embeddedness in systems beyond our ken, and beyond our individual capacity to shift, brings with it differential capacities and differential weights of response. The call Haraway and others make is a call to think nonanthropocentrically about what commitments we might bear to the world—to the water filled with cesium-23 currently pouring out into the Pacific from the reactor at Fukushima, to the fish in that water, to the fishers catching them, or to the cattle in feedlots, the bacteria in their guts, the water systems that feedlot excrement flows into, the children who get sick from *e. coli*-coated lettuce grown using that water—while simultaneously grappling with the possibility that things could be otherwise. I read Haraway's call to stay with the trouble in building responsibility as a call to take seriously the idea that each of us, however situated, could do what we can—recognizing that what we can do, on its own, will never be enough.

Haraway's work here resonates, for me, with Deborah Bird Rose's view on how we might have an ethical relationship with Earth life in the wake of world-shattering events and situations. Rose writes: "I believe that the current extinction crisis is an Earth-shattering disaster, one that cannot be unmade, and in that sense cannot be mended, but yet one toward which we owe an ethical response that includes turning toward others in the hopes of

mending at least some of the damage" (Rose 2011, 5). Rose articulates a relationship of symbiosis and coevolution as one root of this approach of turning
toward others in unresolvable relations of mending. Rose argues that "we are
all participants in relationships that sustain us. Rather than branching lin-
eages, symbiotic processes are better imagined as entangled connectivities,
as interweaving paths and footprints, as waves of life and death" (60). Rose
argues that our response to recognizing the coconstituted nature of our lives
might call up a kind of vulnerable, relational, ethical stance, which she calls
"connectivity ethics." Rose writes that "connectivity ethics are open, uncertain, attentive, participatory, contingent. One is called upon to act, to engage
in the dramas of call-and-response, and to do so on the basis of that which
presents itself in the course of life" (143). Tuning in to the entanglements we
consume through connectivity ethics might open an appreciation for being
connected and coconstituted.

## Distributed Ethics and Opening Freedom to Others

Although I return over and over to Haraway's complex, staying-with-the-
mess approach to constitutive complexity, to Rose's account of connectivity
ethics, and to Barad's account of the entangled ethico-onto-epistemology, I
find either a practical or the philosophical imperative to bring some more
conventional resources to bear on what taking such an approach to the ethics of impurity might be. In this section, I put an account of social cognition
into conversation with Simone de Beauvoir's articulation of what it means to
open freedom to others as an ethically ambiguous but necessary task. I argue
that we must have a distributed or social conception of ethical possibility in
order to make—practically and concretely—ethical responses to our entangled and impure situation.

Distributed or social cognition names a number of essentially epistemic
capacities. The one I'm interested in starts from Edwin Huchins's well-
known example: when a crew is bringing in a large Navy ship, there is no one
human agent who can fulfill the cognitive task of grasping where the boat
is relative to port. Instead, many people take measurements, record position,
transmit that data, and so on, using many different instruments that hold
and calculate information. The instruments are an integral part of the epistemic situation. Similarly, in answering the question "Will this plane fly?"
"knowing" whether a plane will fly is held by a network of epistemic agents
ranging from the engineers to the mechanics who fueled and deiced it to the

pilots who go through the preflight checklist to the flight attendants who make sure passengers are seated in a balanced way. Might we understand the ethics of complex or global systems in this way? On this kind of model, embodied ethical possibilities might be understood to be contingent on multiple guarantors and social conditions in analogous ways to the navigation of a ship coming into port. Hutchins's ethnography of navigation aboard a U.S. Navy ship, *Cognition in the Wild*, is a far richer and more fraught engagement with the work of navigation than I can encompass here, but consider this passage:

> During a long passage, navigation activities may be performed almost continuously for weeks or even months on end. Most of the time the work of navigation is conducted by one person working alone. However, when a ship leaves or enters port, or operates in any other environment where maneuverability is restricted, the computational requirements of the task may exceed the capabilities of any individual; then the navigation duties are carried out by a team. (Hutchins 1995, 20)

As Hutchins's book shows, cognition manifests in a social or distributed way also when there is a crisis (he vividly describes the actions the crew takes after a power failure, to avoid crashing the huge ship). Hutchins argues that "many important human activities are conducted by systems in which multiple actors attempt to form coherent interpretations of some set of phenomena. . . . The complexity of a system may make it impossible for a single individual to integrate all the required information, or that several members of the group may be present because of other task demands, but may be involved in distributed interpretation formation" (240–41). Not many people have taken up Hutchins's work on distributed cognition in a specifically ethical register, though some have worked to include nonhuman actors as holding "joint responsibility" for moral action (Hanson 2009).

I find this ethnographic meditation on a thoroughly impure subject—a Navy transport ship, navigating its imperialist way around the world's waters—good for thinking with. The kind of distributed ethics it calls up for me, by analogy, retains Haraway's commitment to refusing a god's-eye view: each knower and each instrument is in a particular place and doesn't directly know what's happening beyond their area. And yet, for the boat to run, and not run into anything, everyone must do their job well; the instruments must work, the people working with them must understand the theory and the practice of their job—at least well enough to do it, and they must work together. The ship comes into harbor as the manifestation of a distributed, social enactment of individual doings that collectively produces one outcome or another. The moral imperative, taking a *distributed morality* approach, is to understand that we are placed in a particular context with particular limited capacities that are embedded in a big social operation with multiple players. Our obligation, should we choose to accept it, is to do our work as individuals understanding that the meaning of our ethical actions is also political, and thus something that can only be understood in partial and incomplete ways. Political practice will also be only partial and incomplete.

The analogy fails at the point at which we ask where the ship (of nuclear energy use, or of eating) is going, and why. Our collectively shaped ethical world is not a military—not a hierarchical structure; there's no captain steering the way, and certainly no competent navigator. Here I call up Simone de Beauvoir. Her book *The Ethics of Ambiguity* is discussed surprisingly little in scholarship on existentialist ethics, and it is frequently misinterpreted. On my reading, it has much to offer the work of thinking about embodiment and complex or systemic ethical problems, such as those arising in relation to global food, energy, and climate systems. There are many ambiguities implied in Beauvoir's title: the ambiguity of recognizing ourselves as freely willing transcendence in the context of and through our immanent situation, the ambiguity of being a singular individual shaped by our collective group or world membership, the ambiguity of living while dying. The beauty of *The Ethics of Ambiguity* lies in its account of how we can think about ethics with these situated understandings. The book offers, in particular, an extremely useful account of how to understand the conditions for ethical decision-making while taking account of systemic oppression.

For Beauvoir, the question of freedom arises as a necessary covalent with the question of ethics. She writes: "Freedom is the source from which all significations and all values spring. It is the original condition of all justification of existence. The man who seeks to justify his life must want freedom itself absolutely and above everything else . . . to will oneself moral and to will oneself free are one and the same decision" (Beauvoir 1976, 24). So far, so existentialist. And, on first read at least, this conception doesn't move us toward an ethics at the scale of the Fukushima disaster. The aspect of Beauvoir's account that begins this work is through a richer, interdependent, account of freedom.

Although individuals are always self-willing, aiming to unfurl our subjectivities, Beauvoir argues that there is a significant degree to which the meaning of our willing is determined only in relation to others. Things happen to me "by means of others," and I create meaning out of those happenings. When I will, as in the case of responding to a war or occupation, I place myself politically—the wills of others become accordingly "allied or hostile." Beauvoir argues that it is "this interdependence which explains why oppression is possible and why it is hateful. As we have seen, my freedom, in order to fulfill itself, requires that it emerge into an open future; it is other men who open the future to me, it is they who, setting up the world of tomorrow, define my future" (82). Conversely, others can also close down my future. Oppression, on Beauvoir's definition, *is* that operation by which one group of people feeds on the transcendence of others, causing their lives to be measured out in the "pure repetition of mechanical gestures," hopelessly marking time (83). Freedom, which Beauvoir sees as the condition of morality, "wills itself genuinely only by willing itself as an indefinite movement through the freedom of others" (90). To act morally, then, involves holding in view how one's actions open or close down the possibilities for others to unfurl their possibilities; Beauvoir dreams of a future in which "each one would be able to aim positively through his projects at his own future" (81). Since she believes that only people can oppress people, or cause their transcendence to "fall back uselessly on itself," the freedom that constitutes moral activity implies acting toward proliferating freedom. Our freedom is inextricably entangled with and constituted through other beings' freedom.

Two clarifications of Beauvoir's view: it does affirm the importance of individual interests, and it does not rely on an ideal world. Beauvoir understands the centrality of the individual subject of experience as grounding any morality, any move toward freedom. She writes: "In order for this world to have any importance, in order for our undertaking to have a meaning and to be worthy of sacrifices, we must affirm the concrete and particular thickness of this world and the individual reality of our projects and ourselves" (106). This "thickness" of the world means that the world is always experienced from a situated perspective, and a perspective that wills itself toward its own projects. Ethics enters through the necessity to hold in view other people's projects in enacting our own. This *holding in view* will never be completely attained: we will never know all the features present in the moment, and we will never have a clear-enough understanding of the outcomes of our willing. Still, we make choices, nonideal choices. Echoing her earlier work in *Pyrrhus and Cineas* and *Literature and Metaphysics,* Beauvoir argues:

> Just as the scientist, in order to know a phenomenon, does not wait for the light of completed knowledge to break upon it; on the contrary, in illuminating the phenomenon, he helps establish the knowledge: in like manner, the man of action, in order to make a decision, will not wait for perfect knowledge to prove to him the necessity of a certain choice; he must first choose and thus help fashion history. A choice of this kind is no more arbitrary than a hypothesis; it excludes neither reflection nor even method; but it is also free, and it implies risks that must be assumed as such. (123)

Even with method and reflection, then, ethics for Beauvoir remains risky and uncertain. Choosing requires us to make decisions without certainty and in the knowledge that our moral activities change things in the world in ways we cannot predict.

To take up Beauvoir's injunction to unfurl freedom to others, and to pair it with the idea that manifesting freedom will rely on a distributed or social model of ethicality, adds a usefully normative guidance for acting based on relationality and connectivity. I have no settled accounts for where we go from here, only a conviction that we do indeed need to work collectively toward a more collective and relational form of ethics adequate to the global and systemic crises we face. For surely from wherever these crises arise, they produce abiding and urgent moral dilemmas—and surely, it is precisely such situations that such an impure ethics ought to be positioned to address.

To close this chapter, I return to an example that brings together these considerations about the ethics of eating, using energy, and contamination: the cows of Fukushima. Masami Yoshizawa and Naoto Matsumura, formerly farmers, now care for animals left in the wake of the nuclear meltdown that followed on the March 2011 earthquake and tsunami in Japan. Among these animals are cattle too radioactive to eat but which they refuse to kill. These cattle had been declared "walking accident debris," according to a newspaper article about Yoshizawa—"officials from the Ministry of Agriculture ordered them to be rounded up and slaughtered, their bodies buried or burned along with other radioactive waste" (Fackler 2014). The conception of "debris" comes up a lot in response to the disaster at the Fukushima Daiichi reactor. One journalist reflects on going back to his hometown of Hiyoriyama and seeing the cleanup: "The cleanup effort was moving forward at a quick pace, and in a little more than a month, a great deal of the debris had been cleared away, creating an expanding vacant space. We called it debris, but these were things that surrounded us, that supported and sustained our lives: no matter how many times I witnessed it, it was hard to bear watching it all treated as garbage" (Kazumi 2012, 178). Another writer discusses going to visit the devastation wreaked by the tsunami, even before the extent of the nuclear disaster was evident. Ryu Murakami writes that "everywhere you looked were little red flags with names written on them, marking spots where victims' bodies had been discovered. These flags were reminders that the debris wasn't mere wreckage that needed to be cleared away but rather materials, equipment, and tools that had supported and sustained people's lives" (Murakami 2012, 191). How do we respond to the matter and beings in our world that once *supported and sustained* our life but that now are rendered useless or toxic? And what is our relation with the fact of being, necessarily, supported and sustained as an ontological feature of our liveliness?

Yoshizawa says about his care-as-protest work: "The government wants to kill them because it wants to erase what happened here, and lure Japan back to its pre-accident nuclear status quo. I am not going to let them." He is, I think, consciously living in—and calling others to remember—what Joseph Masco, writing about the Cold War and the nuclear imaginary in the United States, characterizes as the "nuclear uncanny." Masco argues that fear of nuclear contamination as "colonized psychic spaces and profoundly shaped individual perspectives of the everyday from the start of the nuclear age, leaving people to wonder if invisible, life-threatening forces intrude upon daily life, bringing cancer, mutation, or death" (Masco 2006, 28). Dislocation or anxiety about perceiving our situation as already contaminated by the effects of nuclear energy and weapons testing hails us to grapple with a world in which our starting point must include the "past effects of the nuclear complex" that "are embedded as a fundamental aspect of the ecosystem" (299). And yet, as I think Yoshizawa argues through his actions, starting from an understanding of our material and ethical implication in the current experience of effects from the past does not imply that we accept as good the present we live. Rather, as I argued in chapters 1 and 2, remembering the past adequately might well involve acting to craft futures that diverge from the path the past has suggested to us. As Povinelli argues, in a different contextual attention to the microbiopolitics of thriving and not thriving, "To care is to embody an argument about what a good life is and how such a good life comes into being. Thus the *arts* of caring for others always emerge from and are a reflection on broader historical material conditions and institutional arrangements" (Povinelli 2011, 160). Although Povinelli is discussing the distribution of staphylococci or streptococci, this approach to thinking about care signals one way that present practice involves a conception of other futures.

Naoto Matsumura, a fifth-generation rice farmer, left Fukushima Prefecture after the earthquake, tsunami, and nuclear meltdown. He narrates his decision to return to the exclusion zone—the area where humans have been evacuated for some undefined amount of time—because his sister-in-law wasn't comfortable housing him and his family, for fear that they were contaminated by radiation, and the shelters were full. But his decision to keep living in the zone seems to arise through his realization that the animals left behind needed to be fed. In a video interview, he says, "That's when I realized that our animals were still waiting to be fed. I had no choice but to stay. I couldn't leave the animals behind—they needed to be fed" (Kosuga, Kovac, and Jousan 2013). Matsumura is opposed to killing the cattle in the zone not because he is vegetarian. He says, "If they're for human consumption, I wouldn't care. That's just how life is. But why slaughter them for no reason? Why bury them? Just because they're here. I'm against that." Matsumura's decision to live in the exclusion zone, according to many newspaper reports about him, means that he is now carrying perhaps the biggest body burden of radiation of any humans alive; he has become a vector, a spatial fix for moving and transforming radiation. He is opposed to slaughtering the cow because it would be done *just because they're here*, in the exclusion zone— just because they were living as food animals in a place that caused them to no longer be of use as food. I understand this opposition as perhaps in line with Haraway's distinction between killing and making killable—a resistance to erasing *what happened here,* in Yoshizawa's phrase, through rendering the animals killable simply through being alive and subject to radiation.

The action Matsumura and Yoshizawa take can be read as a form of fruitless witness—an impossible ethical orientation to an impossible situation, taking the form of loving care that puts the carer at risk. They are suffering alongside the animals they care for; if the nonhuman animals are made killable simply for living in the exclusion zone, are the human animals also walking debris? This implied question is at issue in thinking about the relations between workers and animals in both industrial and nonindustrial animal farming, where the question of suffering matters (Porcher 2011). Matsumara and Yoshizawa are also agitators, not just hanging out in silent towns feeding cows and ostriches and saving dogs that had been tied up after the disaster. In the summer of 2014, they attempted to deliver a bull to the ministry of agriculture in Tokyo; images of the protest show Yoshizawa holding a rope attached to the nose-ring of a bull who manifests unexplained white speckles. He is quoted as saying: "The ministry told us they don't know what is causing the spots. Well, they need to do more research and figure it out. They can't just run away, saying they don't know" (Associated Press 2014). So they are also calling for an approach to knowing that is entangled with the commitment to not erasing what happened in March 2011.

Now, it might look as though I am arguing that in order to take up a relational ontology of responsibility, recognizing that to be is always to be-with, we ought to all move to an exclusion zone and care for our world even though this care would kill us. I do not think that opening freedom to others, in Beauvoir's sense, involves collectively moving to Fukushima Prefecture to eat radioactive mushrooms and bear witness to unexplained white spots forming on radiation-affected cattle. The power-saturated, inseparably ethical *and* political practice of responsibility that Haraway calls for in *staying with the trouble* signals a perpetual attempt to open freedom in a condition in which that freedom is bounded and limited, and thus the condition for distributed collective moral response. And when I say that I do not think we should all move to the exclusion zone, part of what I mean is that of course there is no exclusion zone, or that we are already living in one—we already live in this world thoroughly connected with all of the suffering that individualist practices of purity attempt to manage. In the wake of the Fukushima disaster, there was a widely reported run on potassium iodine, especially on the West Coast of the United States, as people attempted to protect themselves from the thyroid cancer resulting from our bodies taking up radioactive iodine. I embrace the impulse to ward off thyroid cancer. But stopping there is fundamentally an inadequate response to the ethical and political entanglement implied in embodiment—even though it is a good metaphor for the problems with individual purity reactions to collective trouble. Instead, we should act in the present in a way that cares for the harms involved in being alive and that tries to open different futures for all of the beings and relations we are with. I offer two directions for this kind of fraught, generative futurity in the next two chapters.

# PART III

# Shaping
# Unforeseeable Futures

# 5

## Practicing Freedom

### Disability and Gender Transformation

I have been arguing so far that our response to the past constitutes the conditions of possibility for the present, and that understanding ourselves as relationally coconstituted offers us something helpful for both remembering the past and responding to the present. But as we're engaged in the work of feeling the weight of the past and trying to remember it well, and as we work with the complexity and impurity of the present, time flings us on. The future is coming for us, or we are coming for it, and so it matters how we collectively set our course. Remembering the past for the future and deciding how to respond to entangled coconstitution alike invite us to have reasons for choosing one thing and not another. In this chapter I ask, How do we determine what kind of future we want? How, given the fact that we are constituted in relation to a thoroughly oppressive world from which we cannot stand outside as we set our course, can we ever craft worlds radically different from the world we experience now? In chapter 6, I engage speculative fiction and disability futurity as a way to think about the work of imagination in creating new worlds. In this chapter, I argue for what I call *open normativities*: collectively crafted ways of being that shape subjectivities oriented toward widespread flourishing.

Social movement spaces in practice craft new worlds. Sometimes in alliance with movements, feminist theory has been an uneven but generative site for thinking about aiming for futures that don't yet exist, and affirming that some desired future is good and to be worked toward. Too often feminist and queer theory takes a simplistic and reductive approach to normativity, an approach that I see as articulating purity moves. In the first part of this chapter, I trace a thread in current queer theory that equates normativity with oppression, patriarchy, racism, ablism, and more. I put forward a competing lineage for thinking about normativity and delineate the difference among norms, normativity, and normalization. Then I look to a contrasting approach to working with gender norms arising from trans theory and praxis. I am particularly interested in nonindividualistic, nonvoluntarist approaches to institutionally mandated systems of gender classification, and so I examine charges that certain trans theorists are relying on voluntarist conceptions of gender change. "Voluntarist" here refers to political projects that assume individuals can change themselves and their political circumstances through their own force of will, without regard for current realities or history.[1] Finally, I examine the work of transforming norms through creating open normativities. I will argue that normativity is not only not bad, but is necessary to our political work, and I discuss what I mean by "flourishing."

I focus on two cases: the response of the Sylvia Rivera Law Project (SRLP) to the New York City Board of Health's revised guidelines on transgender people's birth certificates, and Sins Invalid, a performance collective aiming to shift standards for beauty, normality, and sexiness through critical disability praxis. SRLP's work on the conditions for changing sex notations on birth certificates was an example of historically contingent political work to craft more expansive and livable norms for gender within the limits of a state-mandated political system. SRLP's response points to the dangers of individualist allegiance to voluntarist gender norms as those norms are enacted by state systems. Sins Invalid's work, in contrast, does not primarily engage with regimes of veridication enacted in state policy; they figure some of the ways to engage with norms and normativity beyond policy engagements. They center artists with disabilities, particularly artists of color and queer and gender nonconforming artists, in performances that directly challenge the categories of the normal and the sexy. Both cases show something important about ongoing sites of contesting policy and norms by creating new, more capacious norms—normativities friendlier to the proliferation of many kinds of embodiments, subjectivities, and ways of being in the world.

## What Is Normativity?

Gender formation is a complex process, situated in history, through which we enact, create, resist, collude with, and change embodied ways of being. Gender is a social problem as much as it is a problem for any of us individually.

If it is true that we are situated in interpenetrating webs of gender, class, and racial formation; that each of these social relations shifts depending on the local experiences of global and transnational power relations; and that all of those categories are themselves intimately linked with social conditions that delimit disability and ability, then thinking about changing gendered social relations is going to continue to be difficult. These changes mark ways we imagine shifting the present toward futures that do not exist but which we bring into being through our work.

Feminists have never been surprised that thinking about and changing the social relation we call gender is difficult, though perhaps we are constantly surprised by the different ways it is challenging. For example, discussions about what's happening when someone changes their gender expression often presuppose that gender enactment (or performance) is something people *do*: we *will* to be perceived in one way or another, and dress or move accordingly. For many theorists, part of the making of gender, or its performance, is the uptake we receive or are refused from others (Butler 1989; Sedgwick and Parker 1995). However, I believe that there has been perhaps too much emphasis in feminist intellectual work on what *individual* people do to perform their gender, resist heteropatriarchy, or collude with a white supremacist capitalist heteropatriarchy. Although such accounts point toward the idea that gender is a relational project, I want to push for a thicker conception of how gender formation is coconstituted.[2] Feminist sociology and some branches of feminist philosophy have made a compelling case for the claim that, as Cressida Heyes puts it, "gender identities must be understood as *relationally* formed . . . gender is not best understood simply as an attribute of individuals, but rather as a set of often hierarchical relations among differently gendered subjects" (Heyes 2007, 39, emphasis in original). An important part of the relational formation of gender involves the role of individual transformations within collective change. To account for this, theorists need better accounts of the relation between individuals and the gendered and racialized systems we instantiate precisely through our agential subjectivities.

In philosophy, computer code, and many social sciences, the term "normative" is generally taken to describe statements that make claims about how things ought to be, or how they in general are. In these fields, to say that something is a normative claim is usually a value-neutral statement about a value-assessing claim. In contrast, in much queer and feminist discourse, "normativity" has become synonymous with "bad," particularly when it is attached to categories such as gender(normative), hetero(normative), or homo(normative). In each of these cases, "normative" indicates a constrictive and restrictive force, delimiting the range of subjectivities one might inhabit in terms of sexuality and gender.[3] In fact, frequently "normative" and "nonnormative" are not defined at all, but the implications of their use are clear.

For example, "queer" is often defined as that which is not normative, while "normative" goes without definition. As the editors of a recent collection focusing on prison abolition argue,

> One of the most notable accomplishments of queer studies has been in show-ing how various regimes of normativity are interconnected and mutually constitutive—how reproductive futurity and heteronormativity are articulated in relation to racialization, (dis)ability, and other socially structuring and insti-tutionally enforced axes of difference—in such a way that much work done under the rubric of queer studies today takes for granted that queerness can be defined as against (and as other to) normativity writ large. Perhaps as a conse-quence of such success, the relationship between queerness and antinormativ-ity can become vaguely tautological—what is queer is antinormative; what is antinormative is queer—and so elastic that useful distinctions between how different normativities get enforced in practice can begin to fade. (Adelsberg, Guenther, and Zeman 2015, 266)

Consider some representative examples. David M. Halperin writes: "Queer is by definition *whatever* is at odds with the normal, the legitimate, the dominant. *There is nothing in particular to which it necessarily refers.* It is an identity without an essence. 'Queer' then, demarcates not a positivity but a positionality vis-à-vis the normative" (Halperin 1995, 62, emphasis in origi-nal). Corie J. Hammers argues that "queer sex and queer sexual subcultures signify non-normative sexual economies, a resistance to heterosexual hege-mony, and the celebration of diversity" (Hammers 2010, 226) and that "'queer' functions as an umbrella term for a wide range of non-normative subjects and sex/gender practices—in short, those subjects which do not conform to the heteronormative sex/gender regime" (232). The editors of a queer studies reader argue that even as work on intersex "complicates our understand-ing of the relationship between sex, gender, and sexuality and the discursive and institutional power brought to bear on maintaining their normative alignment, it raises important questions with respect to race and class that queer studies as a field is only beginning to address" (Corber and Valocchi 2003, 9). Open most any piece of writing about resistance to oppression based in sexuality and gender, and you are likely to find at least one reference to normativity in this mode: the normative is what we resist, and to be queer and feminist is to resist norms.

Framing normativity as always bad is not only rhetorically compelling, it is situated in a context in which oppression does indeed often take the form of forcing people to comply with norms of heterosexuality, whiteness, owning-class practices, and able-bodiedness. However, ceding the terrain of the normative to oppressive forces and defining ourselves *as* nonnormative has two downfalls: it individualizes our resistance, obscuring the agency and power involved in setting norms, and it makes it hard to talk about the normative claims we queers and feminists want to make. Indeed, imagining that we have a choice between normativity and antinormativity elides the work of normalization.[4] In theorizing gender and gender transformation, not to mention all sorts of other social relations, we do actually need the concept of normativity. This concept is more than simply a philosophical term of art, where normativity holds a noncontentious meaning. As Christine M. Korsgaard puts it, ethical standards (for example) are normative in the sense that "they do not merely *describe* a way in which we in fact regulate our conduct. They make *claims* on us; they command, oblige, recommend, or guide. Or at least, when we invoke them, we make claims on one another" (Korsgaard 1996, 8, emphasis in original). Here, then, I understand normativity to mean the process by which people claim that a given way of being is good or beautiful, or to be endorsed. Notice that this conception of normativity is nonrestrictive: there may be many recommended ways of being. Endorsing a way of being is distinct from endorsing the idea that everyone ought to be that way; holding some ways of being open may well close down others. In some such cases, we see open normativities, which I discuss more below.

Georges Canguilhem (1991) inaugurates thinking on normativity as it constrains us, and this aspect of his work has implicitly been taken up in much feminist scholarship on the harms of normativity and normalization. However, we ought also draw from him a lesson on the important spaces of possibility in the work of transforming norms. Mostly, we access Canguilhem via Michel Foucault (see Macherey 2009); Canguilhem was one of his external examiners and mentors, and an interlocutor for thinking about norms. Thus, the lineage of people thinking about norms via Foucault (I focus on Heyes and Judith Butler) are connected to Canguilhem as well. Canguilhem offers two—quite standard—meanings for the term "normal": "1. Normal is that which is such that it ought to be; 2. normal, in the most usual sense of the word, is that which is met with in the majority of cases of a determined kind, or that which constitutes either the average or standard of a measurable characteristic" (Canguilhem 1991, 125). There is, here as elsewhere, important complexity in the term "normal." Often the ostensibly merely descriptive sense, that which is statistically normal, masks the prescriptive sense of that which is how things ought to be (Scheman 1996). Description is rarely, if ever, value-neutral because ascriptions of normality reference norms.

I follow Canguilhem in conceiving the norm as something offering "itself as a possible mode of unifying diversity, resolving a difference, settling a disagreement" (Canguilhem 1991, 240). When a norm is taken up, a normative process is in play: "*Normative*, in philosophy, means every judgment which evaluates or qualifies a fact in relation to a norm, but this mode of judgment is essentially subordinate to that which establishes norms. Normative, in the fullest sense of the word, is that which establishes norms" (Canguilhem 1991, 126–27). Norms structure intelligibility—we assume them in proceeding through life, and in this sense they are polemical or political (Foucault 2003, 50). Note here, though, that in thinking about the social relations produced by gender, one could in theory contest oppressive gendered practices from any of the senses of normal or normative Canguilhem lays out. As we know, both sex and gender (along with norms governing sexuality) are far less than natural or easily measurable as a standard (Fausto-Sterling 2000). Rather, norms expressed through these categories must be constantly monitored, kept up, and managed. Further, gender in particular, is subject to persistent contestation about how it ought to be, across cultures and across time. The degree to which gender transformation is resisted marks, in part, the degree to which new gender norms are being established and worked with.

What we cannot do, however, is live without norms altogether—and thus normativity will always be a part of our experience. This is part of the trouble with framing every norm-setting and contesting activity as repressive. Social norms implicitly underwrite our social worlds, manifesting on affective, embodied, and presuppositional levels. Gender, as Butler argues, is a norm in this "underwriting" sense, and normalization is the process by which particular norms come to be constrained and defined by (currently) a binary system of masculinity and femininity (Butler 1989, 2004).

It is crucial that there is a difference between normativity and normalization: Normativity claims that something is correct, good, to be pursued, acceptable, endorsed, or allowed. Normalization is the disciplinary process that enforces that claim. Foucault's most often cited exposition of normalization treats the formation of disciplinary society as the application of normalizing practices (Foucault 1995, 182–83). Processes of normalization are usually, and I think correctly, understood as delimiting and constraining the terrain of possibilities—in this case, how it is possible to be gendered. The conditions for freedom are thus set by the norms available or created in the context of struggling with the situation in which we live but which we have not chosen and cannot completely control. Normalization should then properly be understood as simultaneously a limiting and enabling part of our exercise of subjectivity. We shape ourselves in relation to norms that are beyond us, and these norms are given to us through other people. As Roderick A. Ferguson has argued, "The queer of color subject can both trace the working of interpellation and inspire other subjects to defy its operation. While canonical formations promise normalcy to the racialized nonwhite subject, the queer of color subject reminds us that such promises are techniques of discipline rather than vehicles toward liberation" (Ferguson 2004, 65). Taking up queer of color critique from various subjectivities, how might we consider sites at which people aim, consciously and intentionally, to change collective norms? How should we think about shifting the grounds of intelligibility and sociality, particularly at points of friction, like racialization, disability, and gender? Worries about the possibilities for shifting normativities tend, with reason, to take the form of charges of voluntarism.

## Gender and Voluntarism

Is attempting to transform or do away with gender norms a voluntarist project? As I mention above, voluntarism names a political position that places emphasis on individual choice and liberty, implicitly assuming that individuals are the locus of change. The concept has different valences depending on context, but here I am sidestepping both its theological roots and the specific Marxian debates that have accrued around it in order to focus on the question of whether transforming social norms is voluntarist in the sense offered here. At first glance, it may not be obvious why one should worry about voluntarism and norms; one of my tasks here will be to affirm the dangers of voluntarism for engaging with oppressive norms. The main such danger is the individualism at the heart of voluntarism, and the supposition that we make change as individuals. Purity politics arise alongside individualism, as I discussed in chapter 4, and here purity about gender maps inadequate models of the relation between anatomy and social relations. However, individuals do have effects on systems. Although individuals cannot, as individuals, transcend oppressive systems, we participate in transforming these systems through shaping norms, often via engagement within fields of interpretive possibilities. To some extent, this view is integral to the relational account of selfhood I assume here: intentional action cannot control interpretive uptake, and thus no expressive action is complete in itself.[5]

Some radical feminists argue that all trans people are ignoring the systemic and power-laden realities of gender either by changing their own sex-gender signification without challenging the harmful norms of gender or by attempting an immanent critique of the gender-binary system simply through refusing to enact one gender or another.[6] In my view, trans people are not necessarily doing either of these things (though some trans people do simply want to change gender signification and be left to get on with their lives), and correcting these two wrong views is one of my aims here. Interestingly, though these views about what is happening are wrong in different ways, I believe they share a common root. Both views assert that people who change gender (individually or through attempting to change the meaning and practice of gender) are voluntarist: they are framed as ignoring the social world of gender oppression while pretending too much individual freedom.[7] One way to understand these sorts of worries is through assessing the workings of normalization, norms, and normativity. Rather than pursuing the comparatively easy task of critiquing trans-hating texts, in this section I instead assess the work of people whose political and theoretical work on gender transformation I respect.

Cressida Heyes's influential piece "Feminist Solidarity after Queer Theory" (2007) critiqued Janice Raymond and Bernice Hausman along trans-feminist lines prevalent in the field before her and elaborated upon since. Most citations to Heyes's piece salute this part of her analysis. Less discussed is the critique she levels at Leslie Feinberg and Kate Bornstein, canonical figures in transgender studies, and it is this critique I take up here. Heyes focuses on Feinberg's germinal text, *Trans Liberation* (1998), highlighting the contrast between hir analysis of the social oppression faced by trans people and hir call for respect of individual freedoms in gender expression. Heyes argues that "in the emerging genre of popular trans feminist polemic (as in much of popular feminist writing) the rhetorical emphasis is squarely on the right of individuals to express their gender as they choose or to engage in free gender play. . . . I also see gender voluntarism as playing an important rhetorical role for transgendered intellectuals" (Heyes 2007, 53). In Feinberg's book, what Heyes frames as gender voluntarism takes the form of an appeal to possessive individual freedom of gender expression, manifest in these quotations from Feinberg: "Every person should have the right to *choose* between pink or blue tinted gender categories, as well as all the other hues of the palette" (Feinberg 1998, 1); "These ideas of what a 'real' woman or man should be straightjacket the freedom of individual self-expression" (3–4); and "There are no rights or wrongs in the ways people express their own gender style. No one's lipstick or flattop is hurting us. . . . Each person has the right to express their gender in any way that feels most comfortable" (53). I think Heyes is right to worry about this rhetorical tendency in popular and scholarly trans writing.

One might think that since the prevalent scholarly view in trans and queer studies is thoroughly grounded in a sophisticated social constructivism, and since voluntarism implicitly relies on the concept of a self-grounding will (contra constructivism), we could simply look beneath surface rhetoric to discover what people actually mean when they say something like "each person has the right to express their gender in any way that feels most comfortable." However, I believe that it is not mere literalism to theoretically assess some of the politically strategic language we use to argue for more expansive freedoms. While arguing for individual rights to expansive expressions of gender and sexuality is politically effective, our rhetoric carries other political (side) effects. Among other things, arguments from individual liberties leave us open to anti-trans screeds that charge trans people and their allies with being interested only in individual liberties and not with collective liberation. Worse, since how we think about things in some ways determines our practices, we might begin to practice harmful voluntarism. A core danger here would be attending more to individual access to the tools of liberation than to the collective transformation; this is dangerous not because people shouldn't have tools for liberation, including hormones, clothing, and surgeries, but because of the distribution of access under social relations of oppression. Since possessive individualism comes freighted with histories of capitalist exploitation, imperialism, and racism, we ought to be particularly careful about invoking it for liberatory ends.[8] Liberalism will not save us.

It is significant that justifications for gender change based in individual liberties and an understanding of the body as one's own property come primarily from European and Western contexts, where possessive individualism reigns. These calls articulate, as well, with a purity politics that posits an uncomplicated relationship between individual anatomy and social standing manifest in gender enactment. Explanations for gender variance and political calls for protections from state and interpersonal violence are often grounded in other social worlds—including Indigenous nations and peoples in North America and Asia who, in particular, ground their political work for gender multiplicity in other logics. In what some call the overdeveloped world, though, it is not only founding texts like *Trans Liberation* that call for freedom of gender expression; rather, this is a widespread trope in trans and genderqueer support spaces, particularly online, and it is on track to being encoded to some extent in state policies (as, for example, policies aiming to add gender identity to the protected category under antidiscrimination law).[9] In North America in particular, the concept of individual rights to free gender expression and change is prevalent, and it is this tendency that Heyes describes as a form of gender voluntarism.

Consider one prominent example of the call for freedom of gender enactment, legal theorist Dean Spade. He founded the Sylvia Rivera Law Project (SRLP), a revolutionary collective project based in New York that provides legal services to low-income trans, intersex, and gender-nonconforming people while simultaneously mounting ambitious programs for law and policy reform on local and national scales. I consider Spade and SRLP among the most significant voices working against gender normalization and its harms, and for this reason conclude this section with an examination of whether gender voluntarism is in play in their work, and if so, where. I take their work as exemplary theory in trans praxis in North America, and as particularly useful for thinking about the institutional effects of norms (Spade 2011).

Spade's short piece calling on others to use trans people's pronouns of choice is instructive. He writes: "I'm hoping that they will feel implicated, that it will make them think about the realness of everyone's gender, that it will make them feel more like they can do whatever they want with their gender, or at least cause a pause where normally one would not exist" (Spade

2004, 97). I appreciate Spade's careful delineation of different ways one might use a pronoun that feels nonintuitive (because the person you're looking at "doesn't look like a guy," or you once knew him as a woman, or you were confused and picked the wrong gendered pronoun), as an expression of tolerance of diversity and difference, or as a transformational and ruptural experience of one's own gender—and, perhaps, of gender more broadly. Notice, though, the slide Spade makes in this quote from thinking about gender to feeling more like one can do whatever one wants with one's gender. This is the crux of the point between seeing oneself situated in and shaped by a system of normalization and taking up a project of shifting or refusing the norms that have shaped one. The difference between feeling implicated and feeling as if one can do whatever one wants with one's gender raises two questions: Is *feeling like you can do whatever you want with your gender* voluntarist? Or does this feeling itself shift the norms that constitute gender?

Susan Stryker and Stephen Whittle, the editors of the first edition of the *Transgender Studies Reader* (2006), say in their brief preface to Spade's article in their volume that Spade examines the "relationship between gender normativity and technologies of gender-related bodily alteration" (314)— another example of the use of the term "normativity" that I discuss above. Technologies of bodily alteration have, indeed, consistently been a flashpoint for theorists of gender transformation on individual and sociocultural scales. Spade characterizes his "basic premise" in this article thus: "That sexual and gender self-determination and the expression of variant gender identities without punishment (and with celebration) should be the goals of any medical, legal, or political examination of or intervention into the gender expression of individuals and groups" (Spade 2006, 317). In this line, consider the self-description of the Sylvia Rivera Law Project: "SRLP works to guarantee that all people are free to self-determine gender identity and expression, regardless of income or race, and without facing harassment, discrimination or violence" (SRLP 2010a). This looks like a kind of voluntarism, or at least individualism—a call emphasizing the freedom to self-determine one's gender could read as ignoring social and political realities. I share the goal of promulgating self-determined gender expression; believe no one should experience harassment, discrimination, or violence because of enactment of gender; and think that voluntarism and possessive individualism are to be avoided in trans, queer, and feminist projects. For these reasons,

I turn next to an attempt to show that these calls for free self-determination are not voluntarist in their orientation toward possible futures.

## Working with and against Norms

Any organization focusing on law and policy to some extent recognizes the importance of collective action, and any organization existing in the real world engages a politics of impurity in the sense that they take certain reform-based actions even when they're aiming for fundamental, revolutionary transformation. SRLP, in self-presentation and by reputation, emphasizes collective and consensus-based process far more than most.[10] Beyond this, they offer theoretical resources for conceptualizing a nonvoluntarist practice of gender. In this section I work to listen to how SRLP theorizes gender. This is perhaps unusual in a scholarly chapter, since I am doing neither sociological research into their institutional structure nor rhetorical analysis of their self-presentation. Rather, I understand the collective as capable of producing theory and implementing it in their praxis.[11]

SRLP's areas of work are simultaneously broad and specific. Holding in mind one of their broader goals, to "participate in the larger movement for racial, social, and economic justice that includes gender liberation and prioritizes the issues of those most affected by the systems of oppression under which we live" (SRLP 2010a), they focus on areas of work that improve conditions for trans and gender-nonconforming people, especially those who are undocumented, living in poverty, and otherwise—as they note—most affected by systems of oppression. In this sense they hold what some call intersectionality as a core optic of analysis and work. Though they aim to ameliorate the effects of systems of oppression, they are not mere reformists. Their first entry under the heading "Core Values/Vision" states: "We can't just work to reform the system. The system itself is the problem" (SRLP 2010b). They answer the question "Why a Collective?" with: "SRLP functions as a multi-racial, inter-generational collective of people committed to a broad understanding of gender self-determination. As a collective, we recognize that it is essential to create structures that model our vision of a more just society. We believe that in the struggle for social justice too often change is perceived as a product and not a process" (ibid.). These two views—that political work must be intersectional and that the oppressive systems are best dismantled through a process-oriented prefiguring of the world—inform their specific work on antidiscrimination, criminal justice, education, health, gender-segregated facilities like homeless shelters and bathrooms, immigration, and identity documents. SRLP coordinates letters-to-prisoners work, produces films on the harms of gender-binary bathrooms, provides direct legal support to trans people in New York, agitates for nationwide changes to law and policy, provides trainings in trans issues, supports community organizing across a range of issues, and more. They interest me because they are effective and because they are not aiming at purity in any register. Here I will focus on their discussions of identity documents and gender. This is a historical rendering about a past campaign, but because classification's consequences continue to carry enormous consequences for people who are made to fall outside the bounds of acceptability, it is still generative to talk about what, and how, SRLP argued for more expansive and livable criteria for identification documentation.

Particularly as state surveillance regimes intensify in the era of U.S.-led wars on terror, identity documents are a site of considerable friction. States closely govern the capacity to change gender identification on passports and birth certificates. Such control affects more than the very small number of people who want to change the sex notations on their documents. Here it is possible to glimpse the depth of the state's commitment to gender norms as a technology for governance; everyone who moves through the classificatory processes that stabilize gender binaries is at the same time experiencing state regimes of norm-enforcement. This enforcement may be mystified and occluded, and it certainly affects people differently depending on their situation, but it is real. Documenting identity is one way the state manages the movement, housing, job prospects, and other material markers of people's lives. In fact, most points of contact with state institutions—and not only within North America—are mediated through gendered forms of identity validation. Looking at the practices around issuing and changing identity documents can reveal significant sites of normalization and also of norm-shifting.

SRLP's critique of a 2006 decision about what surgeries trans people in New York must have in order to change the sex notation on their birth certificate is a good example of their work to promulgate freer gender self-expression.[12] From 2002, they worked with "the New York City Bureau of Vital Statistics to try to get them to change their birth certificate sex designation change policy to not require genital surgery" (SRLP 2010d). In 2006, the New York City Board of Health decided to allow sex designation changes on birth certificates, although as the board's press release notes, the "Health

Code will continue to require proof that the applicant has undergone con-vertive surgery."[13]

As the SRLP response points out, not only is there a wide range in the technologies that trans people are able and interested in taking up in the process of living their gendered lives, the legal definitions of "convertive" surgery vary by place (and, in some countries, by doctor). They write:

> The old policy allowed people to receive new birth certificates only if they provided extensive evidence of very specific, expensive, inaccessible, and often unindicated genital surgeries—vaginoplasty (the creation of a vagina) or phal-loplasty (the creation of a penis). The majority of transgender people do not have one of these two surgeries, particularly transgender men who are esti-mated to have phalloplasty at a rate of less than 10%. Ironically, New York State uses a different narrow set of surgeries as its basis for changing birth certifi-cates: hysterectomy and mastectomy (female-to-male), or penectomy (male-to-female). The two policies beside each other show how arbitrary they are, and how inappropriate a basis for policymaking misunderstandings of a whole population's health care really is. (SRLP 2010c)

People use many practices to enact and transform gender, and SRLP was working—in coalition with a number of other groups—to secure policy recognition for (more) variety in these enactments. Medical evidentiary requirements flatten this complexity, offering in its stead categories (whether "anatomical sex change" or "convertive surgery") simultaneously out of reach of and not desired by many trans people.[14] SRLP instead argues for a form of self-transformation that is utterly reliant on and tangled with world-transformation, and is at the same time critical of a liberal-individualist vol-untarism implicit in the New York City Board of Health's decision and its reliance on genital surgery.

While laudable, SRLP's consistent advocacy for proliferations of gender practices and classifications in situations like the birth certificate struggle could well be voluntarist—just having more freedoms does not do away with possessive individualism. But I believe that the form of self-determination that SRLP invokes can be read as nonvoluntarist in at least three ways. First, any medical intervention is necessarily collaborative, involving self-advocacy, expertise, material resources, and communication. There is no way for indi-viduals to change their secondary sex characteristics by sheer force of will.

This is precisely why some of SRLP's work involves consultations and trainings with medical providers and why doctors, nurses, and pharmacists require training to more adequately meet the needs of trans and genderqueer people. It is also perhaps one reason SRLP does work to help expand trans people's capacities for self-advocacy. Second, the organization is explicitly structured around a commitment to collective and community-based decision-making processes. By grounding the work in specific local struggles, remaining accountable to constituencies, and mixing direct work with policy and law agendas, the organization practices a form of thinking and activism explicitly counter to individualistic practices and aims. Third, the forms of transformation SRLP and others work toward are concerned with a widespread transformation of the world, not merely access to forms of existing, disciplined gender enactment. Rather, they work for a foundational shift in social relations at every level. Recall this part of their mission statement: "SRLP is a collective organization founded on the understanding that gender self-determination is inextricably intertwined with racial, social and economic justice" (SRLP 2010a). To base one's work on these intersections of justice renders the work more than collective; it is to some extent revolutionary. Gender transformations are always social, with social effects.

This final aspect of SRLP's approach points to an orientation that many have characterized as an important part of the queer ethos of early gay liberation struggles. Queer activist-theorist Mattilda reinvokes "the radical potential of queer identity to enable everyone to choose their gender, sexual, and social identities, to embrace a radical outsider perspective, and to challenge everything that's sickening about the dominant cultures around us" (Mattilda 2006, 8). In the United States, a queer critique of what Lisa Duggan terms "homonormativity" echoes this reinvocation, calling for a return to an understanding of liberating sexuality as capable of changing every aspect of the world (Duggan 2003, 50; Puar 2007). For groups like the Gay Liberation Front, a liberated sexuality implied anti-imperialism, anti-capitalism, antiracism, and anti-oppression altogether. Read in an anti-oppression lineage of queer struggle, SRLP is not simply protecting individual freedoms of gender self-expression; they are proliferating gendered possibilities as part of a radical strategy for fundamental social change. Their work resists the force of normalization on individual and social scales.

The proposal voted down by the New York City Board of Health would have shifted the prescriptive force of state normalization to more closely map actual (descriptive) practices of living genders, which also make claims on how we ought to be able to do gender. Gender change and affiliated sex designation would, had the proposed guidelines gone through, not be necessarily tied to very particular genital surgeries but rather would have the potential to be understood based on more collaborative and socially determined criteria for gender enactment. As a first step, this proposal relied on the power of asserting oppressed people's capacities for self-determination, centering those who are usually marginalized. Shifting the criteria for corrected birth certificates from individually grounded so-called convertive surgery to flexibly and relationally grounded markers of gender does more than critique a voluntarist and individualist model of gender definition. It also recognizes that gender is produced through social worlds as much as through fleshy signifiers. Contesting policy decisions that reduce gender to genitals allows us to formulate and understand gender more accurately, and to shape policies more closely attuned to reality. In Canguilhem's terms, SRLP—and other organizations and people pursuing this kind of work—is normative in the sense that they shift the terrain of what is correct, good, to be pursued, or acceptable, endorsed, or allowed. Rather than simply contesting one normative story—here, a narrative that conflates gender with genitals and then asserts that this is a proper and good conflation—they expand the criteria for changing gender status and mark the creation of narratives to account for and produce other modes of doing gender. These new narratives, then, counter some norms while simultaneously setting new norms. They don't swap out one restrictive norm for another; rather, they set norms that expand the space of what can be pursued, endorsed, and so on. This is one aspect of what I call open normativities.

## Open Normativities

As one normativity is contested, new normativities might emerge, creating richer contexts for knowing and being. As I will argue, if normativity can be understood as facilitating a too-easy collapse of complex subjectivity into one or two options, forming new orthodoxies is an important part of the collective work to forge more capacious and diverse ways of being. Shaping new ways of knowing and being with altered criteria for what will count as successfully meeting relevant norms—creating new normativities—opens the possibility for finding our bearings even in the process of working to change the world. However, it may not be enough merely to shape new norms without criteria for assessing them. "Open normativities," then, names those normativities that prioritize flourishing and tend toward proliferation, not merely replacing one norm with another.

"Flourishing" may be the most contentious word in the previous paragraph. I follow Chris Cuomo in thinking that flourishing is, fundamentally, well-being at the individual, species, and community levels (Cuomo 62). Donna Haraway grounds her appeal to an ethics of flourishing in Cuomo's theory of ecological feminism. Concerned with the entanglements between human and nonhuman animals and our shared worlds, Haraway argues: "Multispecies flourishing requires a robust nonanthropomorphic sensibility that is accountable to irreducible differences" (Haraway 2008, 90). So, well-being, ethical entanglements, and irreducible differences. But how to determine what counts as flourishing, and what kinds of flourishing to pursue, is less clear. Haraway is not one to shrink from normative claims; she says one should work "in a way that one judges, without guarantees, to be good, that is, to deserve a future" (106). Elsewhere, she calls for an epistemological and ethical commitment to a "real" world, "one that can be partially shared and friendly to earth-wide projects of finite freedom, adequate material abundance, modest meaning in suffering, and limited happiness" (Haraway 1991, 187). When I use flourishing as a goal for open normativities, I mean it to name the contingent, without-guarantees, partially shared world that recognizes both ethical entanglement and irreducible difference. To judge that something *deserves a future* is to make a normative claim: this, that judgment says, *deserves to continue.* That judgment, following Ladelle McWhorter's rendering of a Foucauldian ethics, is an openness to the possibility of things being otherwise—deviation. McWhorter says, "What is good is that accidents can happen and new things can emerge. It was deviation in development that produced this grove, this landscape, this living planet. What's good is that the world remain ever open to deviation" (McWhorter 1999, 164). McWhorter's normativity organizes itself around the question of pleasure and unexpected formations pleasure might produce. As I'll elaborate more below, we could follow her there.

Calling for open normativities and proliferation, under this conception of flourishing, does not mean that any and all norms are to be pursued or even accepted: not everything deserves a future. Indeed, working to proliferate open normativities will close down many norms. Creating open normativities as a collective and nonvoluntarist endeavor to proliferate flourishing means that norms that flatten complexity and close down flourishing for others are rejected. As Simone de Beauvoir argues, if we take seriously the idea that our freedom consists in willing an open future for ourselves and others, then we open freedoms to one another. It is inconsistent to argue that freedom is taken from us if we are unable to oppress others; our freedom consists in willing freedom for others, not only ourselves (Beauvoir 1976). Notice that flourishing will continue to be an undecided and in-process norm. Norms that proliferate nonreductive flourishing for others are better than norms that harm them or deny them well-being. SRLP's work to open more possibilities for validation of gender change in state identification documents is a good example of this. When state institutions restrict proper identification to either people who have not changed gender or those who have undergone very specific surgeries, they instantiate a norm that closes down the prospects for flourishing for those people who do not want or cannot have those surgeries. In contrast, more varied criteria offer a still-imperfect and contingent set of possibilities that allow more flourishing. If there were people whose idea of well-being consisted of denying trans people state documentation, their norms would be closed down under this normative preference for proliferating flourishing not only for more individuals but for more sorts of individuals, communities, and ways of being.

Under conditions of oppression, norms generally do not proliferate ways of flourishing. Rather, they delimit and constrain the ways of being one can take up, and they contribute to the death and degradation of people who fall outside currently normative bounds—the further out of the normal, the closer to death. Shifting norms is vital for the near-term work of making worlds more livable for people currently imprisoned, deemed killable or unworthy of life, and otherwise subject to diminishment of possibilities. As Nick Mitchell comments, "Regarding the concept of antinormativity, the question for me has to do with whether, and how, antinormativity can found a politics that lives beyond oppositionality. Perhaps it also has to do with the fact that oppositionality, that is, the taking of a stand against the norm, may not exhaust all the political possibilities that become available to us when we are asking about how not only to oppose directly but also to *inhabit* normativity in a way that is corrosive to it" (Ben-Moshe et al. 2015, 271). SRLP's policy and advocacy work directly shifts the effects of norms on people and through those shifts begins to change the norms themselves—the inhabitation can *become corrosive* to forms of normativity that harm us. There are

also ways of directly engaging and changing norms from the subject positions of those most oppressed by current social relations.

Consider, then, Sins Invalid, one of a number of performance collectives
engaging embodiments currently understood as disabled.[15] Their work, as
they describe it, "incubates and celebrates artists with disabilities, centraliz-
ing artists of color and queer and gender-variant artists as communities who
have been historically marginalized. Our performance work explores the
themes of sexuality, embodiment and the disabled body. Conceived and led
by disabled people of color, we develop and present cutting-edge work where
normative paradigms of 'normal' and 'sexy' are challenged, offering instead
a vision of beauty and sexuality inclusive of all individuals and communities" (Sins Invalid 2009a). On first pass, this project is very much in line with
the thread of discourse that equates the normative with the oppressive, using
"normativity" to name the work by which some bodies are rewarded for
meeting standards of racialized, heterosexualized, and able-bodied beauty.
At the same time, this project creates what Sins Invalid identifies as *new
visions of sexuality and beauty*. In effect, creating material practices of such
visions amounts to creating new normativities: collectively shaped and more
enabling standards of success and resistance. Of course, this happens in specific sites: the collective producing the performances, the people who attend
their workshops, the audiences who participate in the happenings they stage.
Still, I would argue that local, new norms are being shaped here.

Shaping inclusive visions of beauty and sexuality is not an individual
project, accomplishable by people on their own. Rather, it is a collective
enactment. Local forms of normativity, then, might contest and dehomoge-
nize other normativities, and indeed might show us how normalization is
always locally constructed. A point of potentially productive bridging emerges
through understanding how socially situated selves might change normalized gender roles. If we see that the social world, and its transformation,
is what matters more than the individual body, which was never individual,
we get another way to think about the inadequacy of charges that changing
norms is voluntarist. The idea that liberal individualist conceptions of selfhood are inadequate to explain the lives of people with disabilities is central
to work in critical disability theory and practice. Further, such conceptions
do not offer much to work toward—they fail normatively, in the prescriptive
sense, because the form of life modeled through such purported independence is neither possible nor desired by many people with disabilities.

In contrast, Sins Invalid bases its work on an ideal of interdependence framed through an understanding of selves as complex wholes always imbedded in social contexts. The group's "Vision" statement reads:

> Sins Invalid recognizes that we will be liberated as whole beings—as disabled/ as queer/as brown/as black/as genderqueer/as female- or male-bodied—as we are far greater whole than partitioned. . . .
>
> Sins Invalid is committed to social and economic justice for all people with disabilities—in lockdowns, in shelters, on the streets, visibly disabled, invisibly disabled, sensory minority, environmentally injured, psychiatric survivors— moving beyond individual legal rights to collective human rights.
>
> Our stories, imbedded in analysis, offer paths from identity politics to unity amongst all oppressed people, laying a foundation for a collective claim of liberation and beauty. (Sins Invalid 2009b)

Telling stories, dancing, singing, and staging interactions that are embedded in analysis is a necessary step toward making "collective claim[s] of liberation and beauty." This vision statement understands the possibility that such a claim can be rooted in what many call intersectionality, or an interlocking oppressions analysis—the idea that it is only as unpartitioned, whole beings that we can approach justice. There is no such thing as pure, single-issue politics: gender, (dis)ability, class, sexuality, racialization, geographies, and more are webbed together such that when we address one node in a web we also tug on all the other strands.[16] Social relations are entangled and intra-implicated.

It is significant that laying a foundation for social and economic justice takes the form of performance. To do justice to the complexity and richness of Sins Invalid's art practice would take a book, and because I do not view them from the stance of a participant-creator I hesitate to talk about what specific performances do, let alone what they mean. However, the form their work takes is central to the possibilities for creating new norms, and it is possible, I hope, to talk about this form without decontextualizing or flattening their creations. They, like SRLP, offer theory as part of their practice. Theories of aesthetics propose that the experience of art work produces a form of understanding irreducible to propositional knowledge. Immanuel Kant's work on art argues that the space of aesthetic judgment is not universal in the way that rationality is (Kant 2000). However, aesthetic judgment is universalizable; our recognition of beauty is collectively produced such that we expect others to agree with us that something is beautiful. Kant frames such agreement as a mode of participating in commonsense—*sensus communis*—forms of recognition. Shaping new standards for beauty is, then, shaping new forms of communal recognition and new collectivities. It is no accident that Sins Invalid makes an "unashamed claim to beauty."[17] The aesthetic realm, accessed through the experience of art, is the space in which judgments of beauty are made. If we follow Kant and others, judgments of beauty in turn tell us who is part of the collective "we" can understand as "us," who has access to dignity and respect. Creating new normativities is always in part an aesthetic project in the sense that it aims to shift the grounds for judgment. It is perhaps most effective, then, to use aesthetic forms to directly alter the conditions of judgment, to claim beauty in the face of invisibility.

Theater dance is a particularly ripe vector for transforming norms of beauty, largely because of a historical tendency to present bodies on stage that conform to what disability performance theorist Owen Smith calls "Apollo's frame," an "exclusive, contained, and homogenous body type." He continues: "Within theatre dance's frame of corporeal reference the failure of the dominant aesthetic to acknowledge, include, and represent heterogeneous corporealities has aided and abetted the configuration of different forms of embodiment as inferior" (Smith 2005, 78). Sins Invalid does more than shift the Apollian frame of embodiment—they make explicitly political interventions in how it is possible to understand disability, racialization, and sexiness. Part of the effect of their performance work is that it is hot—sensual and sexual—at the same time as it can be uncomfortable, confrontational, and abstractly beautiful. Sins Invalid's remarkable variety in types of performance—dance, poetry, staged dialogue, rock-opera—further expands the creation of open and opening claims to beauty as audiences are pulled into shifting configurations of expectation and experience. Much of their work integrates direct conceptual address with dance, music, and song.

Other pieces are more conventional along one axis, highlighting their intervention in other axes, as, for example, when Deaf performer Antoine-Davinci Hunter dances in a form consonant with modern dance but without hearing the music and thereby intervening in a conception of dance that might hold hearing the music to be central to dancing. He and emcee Cara Page stage an intervention into the conception of how Deaf or hard-of-hearing dancers dance. Rather than having some sixth sense, Page's voice tells us—while words appear on a screen—these movers or dancers "take a risk in moving or dancing, often without knowing the sounds around them" (Hunter and Page 2009). Given this, Page challenges the audience to "share in the risk" that Hunter takes in his dance, through rolling a die that will determine which song he dances to. The audience then shares in his risk as he dances a dance that could be read as a standard modern dance piece but that is instead transformed through audience experience of the risk involved. With a modicum of visual literacy of Deaf forms, some audience members might also read the bodily references Hunter makes to, and through, American Sign Language. This piece thus deploys certain aspects of "Apollo's frame" in the viewing of Hunter's body while displacing other aspects of what that frame might usually signal—particularly conventions assuming that dancers hear the music they move with.

Rodney Bell's powerful 2008 aerial dance similarly displaces and reenacts dance modes along a number of lines. Bell descends from the ceiling in his wheelchair to the stage, dancing, turning, and vocalizing as he comes. Thus, one intervention comes at the start, as he uses the wheelchair as an element in a space where wheelchairs don't often appear. Rather than having his chair support him and take him through the world, Bell carries his chair, dances with it, pulls it from gravity. His dance incorporates elements of Kapa Haka, traditional Maori performance modes, especially Waiata-ā-ring, or "action songs."[18] Bell, who is Maori (Ngati Maniapoto), references and enacts these dance traditions in physical forms (how he frames his arms, the trembling of his hands), audibly, and through visual markers that include the physical sign language of the dance, which carries meaning to only some members of the audience, and the tattoos and markings on his face and back. That he is in a wheelchair is only one of the ways he shifts the terrain of expectation and possibility through this dance. His shift in normativities involves a return to traditions strange to many of his audience but a central part of his dance practice. In this way, he interpellates his audience into a norm new to them. Open normativities may not shift into something new in the world. They may, as in this case, reference Indigenous traditions that are new to dominant and oppressive norms.

Sins Invalid's aesthetic interventions happen in a theater, live. They also "happen" in the form of political education workshops, video recordings of performances and video blogs that are accessible online, and through articles by and about the artists and producers of the project. If the unashamed claim to beauty is enacted in the performance space in visceral, somatic, affective, and aesthetic modes, it is simultaneously enacted through the interweaving of conceptual analysis and dialogue within and beyond the space of performance. Thus, claims to liberation and beauty move together to shape collective practices of recognition and desire through technocultures that allow broader participation. The people who participate in the activity of Sins Invalid create new, more open normativities by challenging currently hegemonic paradigms of what it means to be normal, or to be sexy. In other words, they don't simply say or write "these standards are too limited" or "this paradigm shuts us out"—though this is part of the story. Rather, they offer a coproduced experience of beauty and sexiness that pushes at and replaces the limited forms of beauty and collective life dictated under current conditions.

Sexuality is a core point of investigation and transformation, and this is important in part because people with disabilities are so often rendered sexless, childlike, or, conversely, oversexed, perverse, or fetish objects. Sins Invalid stages people having sexual encounters, masturbating, talking about fucking, talking about masturbating, playing with sexualized power relations, and these performances manifest not only the unashamed claim to beauty of their tagline but the experience of people with disabilities as sexual, hot, and full agents of sensuous embodiment. Leah Lakshmi Piepzna-Samarasinha's performance work is part spoken-word, part subtle dance, part theory, highlighting the many layers of identity and identification involved in claiming subjecthood. In one piece, she talks about taking to her bed when she gets sick, and, she says, "fucking myself for hours . . . sometimes I just hover there in that place before coming for hours, and there is no pain, just me being the slut that *kept me alive*" (Piepzna-Samarasinha 2009). She frames pleasure as political, as something that calls to mind all the people fucking themselves, versus being fucked when they don't want to be—as something uncontainable, uncommodifiable, worth loving. In 2006, Leroy Moore moves half-lit across the stage, narrating, "You in my wheelchair/I'm on my knees/ inbetween your legs/ Mmm. . . . I eat./ The question is:/Will she admit/That this disabled Black man is the shit!/And realize/ I am. What she wants" (Moore 2006). Moore trails out the word "wants," evoking the want, the desire. The "you" he addresses, then, is simultaneously the lover of the past and the audience of the present. Other pieces manifest complex inquiries into disability, desire, and agency in more and less conceptual modes.

Frequently, what a given performance means is profoundly undecidable—not everything is a site of uncomplicated positivity.

Both Sins Invalid and the Sylvia Rivera Law Project take up the work of shaping standards for livability beyond currently dominant models. They move beyond critique of ablism, classism, sexism, heteronormativity, racialization, gender binaries, and more, and into a mode of being as becoming. Being as becoming involves active engagement with collective modes of interdependent, agential subjectivity. Agency here shows up in how we navigate the micropractices of power woven through our lives: changing documentation, getting a place to live, having a place at work to use the washroom, being legible and desirable and desiring. These micropractices are sites of friction for people oppressed by dominant forms of life grounded in the ideal of voluntarist individualism. Through challenges to open normativities, the disciplinary force of normalization is loosened; we create and take up new norms and proliferate visions of ways of being that are worth taking up. This loosening returns me to McWhorter's discussion of pleasure as a key to practices of flourishing signaled by open norms. As she argues, in this project, "we cannot know where we are going. To know where we are going would be to have mapped out a developmental program that could and would be subject to normalization" (McWhorter 1999, 181). Instead, pursuing what I am articulating as open norms involves practices of freedom that facilitate more capacities for unforeseen pleasures. As McWhorter writes, "Instead of an increase in docility, then, we might seek out, create, and cultivate disciplinary practices that produce an expansion of behavioral repertoires, practices that increase the range within which we exercise our freedom and within which freedom plays itself out beyond who we currently are. Most likely, these practices will in themselves be intensely pleasurable and will also increase our capacity for pleasures of new sorts" (182). Without knowing precisely where we are going, we can affirm an orientation toward unpredictable practices of capacity-increasing pleasures.

In this chapter, I've attended to how people with disabilities and trans people, particularly people of color and particularly those also experiencing other axes of oppression, encounter the friction of these social relations and transform it into traction for practices of freedom. These things are just as salient to gender-conforming and currently able-bodied lives, though they are less obvious because of the ways such people evade the friction that currently heterodox lives encounter daily. Subjectivity, shaped by gender, race, ability, and more, in this sense is always a coproduction. You only choose it if people around you choose it with you—which does mean that it's chosen, just not in an individual way. Individuals catalyze change, but change only happens collectively. Because gender is already relational, we don't just need the freedom to change our own gendered selves; we need the freedom to change the gendered world. Taking up practices of freedom through shaping open normativities, through claiming beauty in the face of invisibility (or worse), changes social relations and, thus, the world. This nonvoluntarist activity might not look like any freedom associated with the liberal-individual self, though it may require the recognition and dignity affiliated with that subject position. It will, however, be more adequate to our messy, complex, hopeful lives. For those lives, we need practices of open normativities to pursue visions and practices hospitable for worlds to come, to determine what deserves a future.

# 6

## Worlds to Come
### Imagining Speculative Disability Futures

How do we craft a practice for imagining and living a future that does not simply replicate and intensify the present? My thinking here is cued by Octavia Butler's comment in the context of a panel discussion on science fiction: "It's dangerous to assume that whatever we've been doing, we're going to keep doing that. You know: the future is more of the same, only more advanced. . . . It's dangerous to assume that we can actually see the future by only looking at the technological advancements we've made so far" (*Octavia Butler: Science Future, Science Fiction* 2008). While Butler names technological advancements, I think her point holds as well for the idea that it's dangerous to assume that the future is more of the same in terms of the social relations we experience now and project as a possible "then." Imagining and practicing futures that are not "more of the same" is difficult, necessary work. In this chapter, I frame a usable futurity in terms of queer disability prefiguration—living in the present a world we want to create, and crafting that world through our living—as a form of speculative fiction, a practice of world-making creativity.

I am sparked in this chapter by Donna Haraway's lifelong, joyful thinking about SF—speculative feminisms, string figures, scientific facts, speculative fabulations, science fictions, in the cadenced invocation that emerges often in her writing. Likewise, my littermate Sha LaBare offers generous and challenging work on understanding SF as a *mode*, and as I understand him here, as a mode for crafting worlds that don't yet exist in the context of the world that does exist. LaBare offers a formulation of what he calls "the 'sf mode,'" which on his rendering "offers one way of focusing that attention, of imagining and designing alternatives to the world that is, alas, the case" (LaBare 2010, 1). LaBare suggests that we might receive and take up "sf as a mode of aware- ness, interpretation, practice and production" (6). In this world, in LaBare's echo of Samuel Delany, that is, *alas, the case* we need these ways of imagin- ing and designing alternatives. As one of the editors of *Octavia's Brood,* a collection of short stories of visionary social-justice-informed speculative fiction, writes: "The stories we tell can either reflect the society we are a part of or transform it. If we want to bring new worlds into existence, then we need to challenge the narratives that uphold current power dynamics and patterns" (Imarisha and brown 2015, 280). I agree!

Anarcho-syndicalist Buenaventura Durruti famously coined the phrase "a new world in our hearts," a phrase that resonates with the Wobbly motto advocating "building a new world in the shell of the old." Both of these are articulations of prefigurative politics—the practice of collectively acting in the present in a way that enacts the world we aspire to create. It is instructive, though, to consider the longer text of Durruti's statement. He said:

> It is we who built these palaces and cities, here in Spain and in America and everywhere. We, the workers. We can build others to take their place. And bet- ter ones! We are not in the least afraid of ruins. We are going to inherit the earth. There is not the slightest doubt about that. The bourgeoisie might blast and ruin its own world before it leaves the stage of history. We carry a new world here, in our hearts. . . . That world is growing in this minute. (Paz 2007, 478)

Some would say that SF writers agree, particularly about being *not in the least afraid of ruins.* I'm not sure what percentage of SF literature is dys- topian, starting from a "now" of a blasted and ruined world, a fled Earth, an alternate history with alternate forms of oppression, but it is common to find imagined futures in which the bourgeoisie has blasted and ruined its own world, unevenly leaving the stage of history, and we have to somehow get on with life in the ruins. In some way, we can find dystopian fiction simultane- ously extremely depressing in its imagining of how bad we humans might be to ourselves and our worlds; in another way, we might find tremendous heart in the attempt to imagine after the worst-case.

In this chapter, I argue that speculative fantasizing about disability futures can attune us to the possibilities for imagining worlds not identical to the world we're currently in. We can pursue SF *modes,* to follow LaBare's terms, that open practices of what Angela Davis calls *identifying into* a new world, shaping ourselves toward that world such that we call it into being as a pre-figurative practice. I argue that we can do this however we are currently identified in terms of disability. The chapter has four sections. In the first, I examine key strands in disability interventions in identity politics and delin-eate what I see as the profound usefulness of Angela Davis's conception of identifying into politics as a form of prefiguration. In the second, I discuss particular disability, Buddhist, and Indigenous conceptions of interdepen-dence as both descriptive and normative ideals—along the way attempting to track how these very different "sites" of thinking and practice can be in conversation without eliding the specific contexts in with they formulate understandings of interdependence. As I'll emphasize, simply that the same word is used in these different contexts does not indicate that it means the same thing. In the third, I argue that queer SF desire offers us generative practices for imaginative identification grounded in experiences of inter-dependence, looking to Samuel Delany as a guide for how we "manufacture the dreams of possibility, of variation, of what might be done outside and beyond the genre that others have already made a part of our readerly lan-guage" (Delany 1988, 193). The fourth section explores key ways in which Octavia Butler's work imagines disability as a key piece of SF worldings, and then in turn how her work has been taken up by the formation of *Octavia's Brood* as an anchor for imagining the relation between visionary fiction and social movements.

## Nonidentification = Positive Refusals, Dynamic Self-Makings

A central strand in disability studies addresses the question of whether we ought to ground disability politics in the experience of disabled people, in what has been thought of as an "identity politics" mode. The too-simple way to gloss this mode goes like this: If you have a certain identity, you'll have certain politics arising from it. When you oppose oppression based around a given identity category, it is because you experience that oppression. In some versions of the political mobilization of identity politics, epistemic privilege arises from standing on the subordinated side of social relations of oppres-sion. On this view, the people best able to talk about racism are those at whom it is directed; those best able to talk about ablism are those disabled by current social relations. A corollary political effect of identity politics is to consolidate a group identity to which people can belong in "real" ways, and to mobilize politically around that identity. The uptake or refusal of identity politics as a viable or necessary mode for disability activism and theory has been an active site of debate (Mollow 2004). In this section, I look to two ways of rejecting identification and identity politics as a ground of disability work and suggest a third.

Lennard Davis's articulation of dismodernism rejects identity politics even as he formulates a conception of disability as a "neoidentity." Davis writes:

> Rather than ignore the unstable nature of disability, rather than try to fix it, we should amplify that quality to distinguish it from other identity groups that have, as I have indicated, reached the limits of their own projects. Indeed, instability spells the end of many identity groups; in fact it can create a dismodernist approach to disability as a neoidentity. (Davis 2002, 26)

Davis argues that identity politics has been important, but that in pursuing disability work, we should eschew an identity-based politics. He argues that the process of working toward political liberation

> began with the efforts of various identities to escape oppression based on their category of oppression. That struggle is not over and must continue. While there is no race, there is still racism. But dismodernism argues for a commonality of bodies within the notion of difference. It is too easy to say, "We're all disabled." But it is possible to say that we are all disabled by injustice and oppression of various kinds. We are all nonstandard, and it is under that standard that we should be able to found the dismodernist ethic. (31–32)

Thus, somewhat strangely, this argument for a politics not based on identity circles around to an account on which disabled identity applies to everyone nonstandard. Which is everyone. Although this account is generative, I also find it unsatisfactory because it fails to give enough traction for addressing the specificities of oppression and privilege. We are indeed all nonstandard, but how that affects us depends profoundly on a whole complex of social relations of inequality.

I am more compelled by a second way of rejecting simple identity politics as a ground for disability praxis. In their introduction to the recent anthology *Sex and Disability*, Robert McRuer and Anna Mollow articulate one of the problems with pursuing politics based on identity claims. It is the inevitability, despite the intentions of those forging these identities, of exclusions. Taken together, many influential texts in the field of disability studies can be said to have codified a model identity of a disabled person, who has certain crucial characteristics: his or her body manifests visible difference; physical suffering is not a primary aspect of his or her experience; and he or she is not seeking cure or recovery. In these ways, what might be seen as disability studies' construction of a "paradigmatic" disabled person differs from the self-understandings of many people with chronic pain and illness. (McRuer and Mollow, 11–12)

This kind of refusal of a certain mode of identity politics is important to me because I see in it a refusal of purism—a clear delineation between who counts as holding a model disability identity. McRuer and Mollow aspire to a postidentity disability politics, "in which what is interpretable as disability need not be tethered to a disabled identity." Such a politics, they argue, "enables sitings of disability in multiple, often unexpected, locations, rather than solely in the bodies and minds of a few individuals" (13). I like very much their invocation of Roderick A. Ferguson's discussion of 1970s women of color feminism and its "gestural" conception of identity politics, "pointing *away* from the self to the complex array of relations that constituted the social" (12). And yet there is a danger that pointing toward the complex array of relations that constitute us as individuals within a social world ends up presuming or arguing that because we are shaped by the same normalizing forces our various experiences of identity are, in some real way, also the same (as when being Fat or trans are framed as equivalent or equal to being disabled).

I am interested in a form of nonidentification that maintains a thick historical awareness of the significant and constitutive differences between us while simultaneously—or, better, necessarily causally—orienting us toward a collective struggle as a matter of our deepest identities and subjectivities. This approach to understanding identification is consonant with key features of the above accounts of nonidentification. Consider the concept of "identifying into" politics.

When I was a grad student, I had the honor of working with Angela Davis. She frequently argued, in classes and conversations, for a mode of being, an identity politics, which she framed as the grounding of our identities in our politics, instead of taking our politics from our identities. I have been struggling with what this might mean—in theory and practice—for a long time. I take it that from this stance, which I see as part of a broader politic, identity is contingent and situated. It is not essential, pregiven, or natural. If we take our identities from our politics, we collectively craft identities, ways of being, based in the specific political context we encounter and the political commitments that shape our response to those contexts. In a recent speech, Davis talks about the notion of "identifying into." She says:

> We are interested not in race and gender (and class and sexuality and disability) per se, by themselves, but primarily as they have been acknowledged as conditions for hierarchies of power, so that we can transform them into intertwined vectors of struggle for freedom.
>
> When we identify into feminism, we mean new epistemologies, new ways of producing knowledge and transforming social relations.
>
> As scholars and activists, we realize that categories always fall short of the social realities they attempt to represent, and social realities always exceed the categories that attempt to contain them. (Davis 2012, 197)

I read Davis here as offering an understanding of identity politics resonant with speculative futurity. So, to start from the first point: Davis argues that the important thing about social relations of oppression is not that they have some inherent meaning—we are not interested in them *by themselves*—but instead because of what they manifest about *conditions for hierarchies of power*. And that in turn is important to those of us struggling for multifaceted liberation because we aim to transform the conditions for harmful hierarchies of power into *intertwined vectors of struggle for freedom*. On this view, sites of oppression can be or become sites of liberation—but the social relations that determine what makes that difference will be dynamic and shifting. When we think about identity without conceiving of a fixed self that will produce predictable politics, we need to be able to encompass this dynamism in order to track potential vectors of freedom.

Davis is talking specifically about *identifying into* feminism as an uneasy but usable political move. Necessarily, the feminism one identifies into cannot be the same as identifying completely with already existing feminism, because feminism as a body of work—not only the world it aims to transform—is imperfect and frequently a huge problem. And to be explicit: feminism's problem arises most particularly in terms of its normalizing orientation toward the lie that it is possible to "just talk about gender" and concomitant political practices that have sacrificed people of color, Indigenous people, disabled people, and undocumented migrants on the alter of gender parity. But we can identify into feminism in the sense of aiming with and through it toward *new epistemologies, new ways of producing knowledge* and *transforming social relations*. Since social realities always *exceed the categories* that aim to represent them, we work with the flux of changing vocabularies and shifting social practices, leveraging intertwined vectors of freedom.

I suggest that we can think about postidentity disability politics in a similar way. *Identifying into* critical disability praxis doesn't rely on a fixed experience, or a stable identity. We know that the category "disabled" is already so heterogeneous that there has never been a set of defining characteristics capable of encompassing the scope of disabled lives and how to live them. Nor has inhabiting any given disabled identity produced any particular politics. The strand of disability work I follow rejects the idea that what we're looking for is just a better set of diagnostic or definitive criteria. And we know that the social categories practiced at all these sites are more tangled when we hold in mind other vectors of vulnerability and empowerment, oppression and privilege. Further, we know that disability theory and practice can and often has involved people who don't identify as disabled, who worry they're not disabled enough to "count," who understand themselves to be enabled by systems of oppression but whose lives are shaped and entangled with disabled lovers, friends, comrades, or family, and so on.

Identifying into disability praxis means that everyone, however situated, can shape their life's practice in a way that contributes to self-determination and coproduced freedoms. As praxis, this *identifying into* brings together theory, its dynamic stretch to better account for and understand the social world, with practice, the in-the-moment enactment of life. As Robert McRuer argues, "We need a postidentity politics of sorts, but a postidentity politics that allows us to work together, one that acknowledges the complex and contradictory histories of our various movements, drawing on and learning from those histories rather than transcending them" (McRuer 2006, 202). A disability politics praxis is practical: I'm talking about how we engage one another's bodies and minds, how we move through public space, how we talk together, how we have sex, how we plan events. But it's also theoretically informed, and it matters what bigger view we hold. I'm thinking, for example, of Harriet McBryde Johnson's well-known account of debating Peter

Singer about his eugenicist views; she describes asking him to move her arm slightly so that she can continue eating dinner, and the political complexity of engaging with him as a helper of her body, a body he argues should not exist (Johnson 2006). I'm insisting on a praxis as the sign under which we talk about identifying into because it matters both what understanding we hold (our theory) and what we do (our practice). Holding those together shapes a praxis of speculative futures—finding ways to create a world other than the one we're in while keeping our feet in the mud.

## Interdependence Means Fight

Critical disability theory has compellingly made the case that decisions that *seem* to be about personal morality are actually about the structures and conditions for livable and good lives. Over the last dozen years, "interdependence" has become a key concept for theorists working on disability, particularly for activists and scholars looking for ways of understanding disability from perspectives other than either medical *or* strict social construction models. The category of interdependence names a permanently partial, co-produced world and subject, with and through which relational connections are shaped; it names ontological multiplicity and refuses political and ethical individualism. In this section, I put current theories of disability interdependence in conversation with selected Buddhist and Indigenous understandings of interdependence. These accounts of interdependence complement one another, though they come from very different contexts. Together, they articulate the idea that in envisioning futures different from our present, we must be grounded in a responsibility to the past that constitutes our current experience. Certain Buddhist and Indigenous theories also offer two other central conceptions of interdependence: first, the idea that coconstitution is an ontological and not simply a causal relation; second, that coconstitution implies certain practices of responsibility. In thinking about this second point, I'm motivated by the claim, coming primarily from "engaged Buddhist" practitioners, that a correct understanding of interdependence motivates action. One blogger, B. Loewe, puts the claim more succinctly, writing: "Interconnectedness means fight" (Loewe 2015).

I am concerned about my own move to weave these three strands of thinking about interdependence into the broader argument I make in this chapter. It is not the case that simply because people use the same term they are referencing the same thing—indeed, I hope it is clear that the small selection I offer below of thinkers discussing interdependence in their own specific contexts are grounded in particular and nontransferable concerns. In particular, let me underline that I am not trying, here, to give a comprehensive discussion of Indigenous and Buddhist understandings of interdependence. This might be possible, but it would involve telling very complex stories about very diverse and complex societies and philosophical systems. Rather, because I am positioned myself as a practicing Buddhist and someone involved in Indigenous solidarity activist work as a settler aiming for decolonization, I have often thought that disability theorists could fruitfully listen to some of the talk about interdependence from these other quarters, and vice versa. I offer this short section, then, as a small offering toward what I think could fruitfully be a longer conversation.

Harriet McBryde Johnson argues that "choice is illusory in a context of pervasive inequality. Choices are structured by oppression. We shouldn't offer assistance with suicide until we all have the assistance we need to get out of bed in the morning and live a good life" (Johnson 2003, 56). Johnson is talking about assisted suicide and disability, and about the widespread argument that to be disabled is worse than death. Her point applies equally to life "choices" structured by pervasive oppression—which is to say, to lives and how to live them most generally. Given that all of us live in close relation with structures that allow some of us to live, or live more comfortably, through and because of the immiseration of others, (how) does a conception of interdependence help us? Does an understanding of deep connection and coproduction help anyone get out of bed in the morning and live a good life?

A central way of understanding interdependence in disability theory is through looking at how we are reliant on others—people cared for us when we were babies and helpless, we need others when we are sick or unable to do something, and we are situated in dense webs of the conditions that sustain our lives—we rely on others for food, heat, and much more. Paul Longmore has been frequently cited for his claims about interdependence, which are among the first formulations of the mode of talking about interdependence I'm interested in here. I'll quote him at length:

Beyond proclamations of pride, deaf and disabled people have been uncovering or formulating sets of alternative values derived from within the deaf and disabled experiences. Again, these have been collective rather than personal efforts. They involve not so much the statement of personal philosophies of life, as the assertion of group perspectives and values. This is a process of deaf cultural elaboration and of disabled culture-building. For example, some people with disabilities have been affirming the validity of values drawn from their own experience. Those values are markedly different from, and even opposed to, nondisabled majority values. They declare that they prize not self-sufficiency but self-determination, not independence but interdependence, not functional separateness but personal connection, not physical autonomy but human community. This values-formation takes disability as the starting point. It uses the disability experience as the source of values and norms. (Longmore 1995)

To return to the discussion of his work in chapter 3, Lennard Davis argues that in disability work "the ideal is not a hypostatization of the normal (that is, dominant) subject, but aims to create a new category based on the partial, incomplete subject whose realization is not autonomy and independence, but dependency and interdependence" (Davis 2002, 30). All of these theories center an understanding of the subject—every one of us—as complexly reliant, dependent on, and entangled with others.

Conceptions of interdependence in disability theory arise not only in relation to the sense in which individuals are never really autonomous but only relationally autonomous; they are also articulate in terms of group dynamics. Peggy Phelan lauds the refusal of "the ideological imperative of the autonomous self," instead looking toward work that takes "seriously concepts of interconnection, the enmeshed nature of the social body, and the complex work of responding to, in all senses, the richness and awkwardness of extraordinary bodies" (Sandahl and Auslander 2005, 319). This response is, then, a collective issue. Some writers, like Simi Linton, argue that in formulating disability theory, we should take as a key approach the examination of "the complementarity and interdependence of parts to wholes. This involves recognition of disabled and nondisabled people as distinct groups, the relationship of one to the other, and of both to the social structures in which they function" (Linton 1998, 121). Understanding the interdependence of groups can show us something also about the distinction and border that delineates one person or group of people from others while at the same time showing us something about connection.

Interdependence as articulated in many disability theory and practice contexts is, then, a rich and compelling counter to a vision of human potential cashed out in terms of the fictive singular, autonomous agent. Disability theorists of many different stripes agree that interdependence is a key descriptive and normative feature of life, made perceptible in part because people disabled by the world as it is signal how acknowledging our mutual reliance might make the world a more just and livable place. In reading and talking about disability conceptions of interdependence, however, I have found that they often frame interdependence in terms of causal, and in a certain sense exchange, relations; we have been dependent on others, and others depend on us. I have consistently found myself reaching, sometimes to my surprise, for supplemental accounts—and finding them in particular Buddhist and Indigenous theories. As I mention above, I am cautious about bringing these very different archives together; the fact that disparate conversations use the same word definitely does not mean that the terms or stakes of the conversations are the same. And it is possible that my own identification as a Buddhist practitioner and a settler attempting to do Indigenous solidarity work is causing me to perceive generative synergies between these areas and critical disability theory simply because these are the conversations that I engage. Coincidental or not, I see useful contributions to disability theory from these other sites. Both, though in different ways, offer an ontological account of interdependence. That is, rather than interdependence manifesting as a result of anything in particular—social or material relations, or biographical happenings—these approaches understand interdependence as foundational and constitutive of our being. And both—in different ways—make a call to future responsibility based on a recognition of interdependence.

Consider two articulations of interdependence from Buddhist theory, starting with the nineteenth-century theorist Patrul Rinpoche. Though his own lineage is Nyingma, Patrul Rinpoche's text, *The Words of My Perfect Teacher*, is a widely read and recommended introduction to core theories in Tibetan Buddhism. This is in part because he was one of the significant *Rime* practitioners—teachers in Tibetan Buddhism who opposed sectarianism and lineal purity and held and practiced Buddhist texts from multiple traditions. *The Words of My Perfect Teacher* is a commentary on Jigme Lingpa's text, *Heart Essence of the Great Expanse*, in its turn a commentary on the preliminary practices for the *Longchen Nyingitk*, a set of meditative practices. Patrul Rinpoche discusses a traditional Buddhist claim: to live is to suffer. For living beings, there are traditionally catalogued three main kinds of suffering: the suffering of change, the "suffering of suffering," and a category variously translated as "suffering in the making," "conditioned suffering," or "all-pervasive suffering."[1] I am especially interested in this last category. Comprehending conditioned suffering is a more cognitive exercise than understanding the other forms of pain that come along with human existence, and this interests me because it is this form of suffering that is supposed to provoke an ethical response for all beings everywhere. In other words, understanding how suffering is interleaved with and in some way constitutes our existence is central to this account of why one would work to alleviate suffering for others as well as for oneself.

Patrul Rinpoche's discussion focuses on food. He traces the network of relations attending eating foods that might not immediately seem to involve killing, foods that could seem innocent: barley flour and tea. He writes:

> Now, some of us might think that things are going quite well for us at the moment, and we do not seem to be suffering much. In fact, we are totally immersed in the causes of suffering. For our very food and clothing, our homes, the adornments and celebrations that give us pleasure, are all produced with harmful actions. As everything we do is just a concoction of negative actions, it can only lead to suffering. (Patrul Rinpoche, 79)

It is important to note that at least part of suffering supposed to be bound up with the production of our food, pleasures, clothing, and so on is specific to a Tibetan Buddhist worldview: participating in suffering like this is said to lead to rebirth in one of the realms even more suffused with pain than the human realm. In that respect, understanding one's place in a system that immiserates many other beings—that relies directly upon the production of harm and suffering for them—is self-interested, even if the self that one is interested in is a future birth and thus a self one won't actually be. It might not be possible to bracket off the reliance on a story of reincarnation implicit in this ethical system (though North American practitioners of this form of Buddhism do this all the time). Even the view not based on wanting to save oneself from suffering in a future life is based on a belief in reincarnation: one takes the attitude that all beings have at some point in the past been our mother or father—that they have nourished us when we were helpless, cared for us, carried us in their body. This formulation of the conception of interdependence resonates—even with the reincarnation story—with many disability theories of interdependence as mutual care. The central and slightly different idea here, though, is that any thing that exists in this world

is complexly and constitutionally connected with many—and perhaps all—
other things in the world.

Vietnamese Zen teacher Thích Nhất Hạnh's work on interdependence
has been influential in promulgating Buddhist accounts outside traditional
spaces. He takes a nonsectarian Buddhist approach grounded in his own
tradition but drawing on other Mahayana practices and theories, and he
has created an Order of Interbeing, part of the Linji School of Dhyana Buddhism. His conception of "interbeing" offers an articulation of coproduction
or interdependence:

> If you are a poet, you will see clearly that there is a cloud floating in this sheet
> of paper. Without a cloud, there will be no rain; without rain, the trees cannot
> grow; and without trees, we cannot make paper. The cloud is essential for the
> paper to exist. If the cloud is not here, the sheet of paper cannot be here either.
> So we can say that the cloud and the paper inter-are. "Interbeing" is a word that
> is not in the dictionary yet, but if we combine the prefix "inter-" with the verb
> "to be," we have a new verb, inter-be . . . a cloud and the sheet of paper inter-
> are. (Thích, Hạnh, and Levitt 1988, 4–5)

He goes on to describe how the sun, the minerals in the soil, the wheat that
grew to nourish the logger who cut down the tree, and so on, are part of the
paper. This is a similar conception of interdependence; constitutionally, we
are entangled, coproduced beings, and this fact produces an ethical call. We
should care about others because the entanglement of our selves is simultaneously an entanglement with other beings' pain.

As I discussed in chapter 3, our bodily reliance on the environment is a
particularly potent site for a different way of understanding interdependence—
our bodies take up Strontium 90 instead of calcium, just as our teeth take up
fluoride instead of calcium. Pointing to carcinogens in the water and air has
been a way to curb pollution or protest the harms of nuclear weapons testing. This kind of reliance can also be a site for responsibility; because we are
constituted in relation to our world, we also must take responsibility for that
world. Certain Indigenous conceptions of interdependence can be put into
conversation here. As with treating Buddhist theories, I attempt here to be
specific about the context and network of relations involved.[2] This is because
writers often focus on specific thinkers when they're talking about European-
derived theory, but then speak about Indigenous theory in general. For sure,

there are some general things that can be said about Western philosophy, and there are some general things that can be said about Indigenous philosophy. But fields of general agreement could be seen as products of negotiation and conversation, often political and sometimes spiritual, and as necessitating a thorough respect for incommensurability.

Jacob Ostaman, a representative for Kitchenuhmaykoosib Inninuwug, a First Nation in Treaty 9 territory that has resisted mining exploration on its land, says that protecting the land from irresponsible industrial development "is important because this type of development is against the laws of Creation. . . . The watershed is all connected, and we are concerned particularly about the Nuhmaykoos, the lake trout. The lake, the lake trout and the people are all connected and our identity as distinct human beings is tied to the lake and the trout" (Simpson and Ladner 2010, 225). This concept of interdependence holds that we are constituted as beings through a historical placement, as humans, to care for the watershed and the trout. A related conception understands interdependence in and through our relations of responsibility and respect with our world. Kanien'kehá:ka legal scholar Patricia Monture-Angus frames relationality in thinking about the concept of justice beyond punishing crimes: "Justice, for me, is a broader concept intended to capture the idea that we can live at peace and live in balance with our relations. And relation is not a simple concept either. It refers not only to all our human relatives (of all races) but also to the animals, the birds, the water creatures, the thunders, the trees and plants, the earth. It includes all in our universe that has spirit" (Simpson and Ladner 2010, 294). So justice involves understanding what it means to live in balance with all our relations, understanding ourselves as significantly coconstituted with them. And, crucially, the sense of interdependence I am highlighting here takes the form of a practice of responsibility in the present orientated toward relation as a commitment to going on living; a commitment to futures that can nourish relationality for *all that has spirit*.

Within disability studies, as I discuss above, interdependence names a way to refuse to understand individual disabled people as lonely objects for pity or plucky over-comers of adversity, but instead as ordinary complex people embedded in the social and material world. Writer Anne Fingers's discussion of polio highlights some of the social making of a category of disease and disability: "Polio belongs not just to those of us who were paralyzed by it but to our mothers and fathers, our sisters and brothers, our partners and our children; to those who cared for us, to those who brutalized us—not mutually exclusive categories; to those who saw us as palimpsests on which to write their discomfort, their fear, their pity, their admiration, their empathy" (Fingers 2006, 6). Fingers specifies that in writing a memoir of polio, she must talk not only about her experience but also about the "background of social experiences of the disease, which structure the nondisabled as well as the disabled" (8). Thinking in terms of interdependence helps us work from the understanding that our bodies and selves are complex coproductions of our self, other people, the social relations that undergird our world, and the material realities in which we live. Putting disability theory accounts of interdependence into conversation with some Buddhist and Indigenous conceptions gives us traction for understanding coconstitution as ontological, not merely causal. That is, interdependence can be understood as constitutive of our nature as well as arising as part of the causes and conditions of our lives. We might, then, craft practices of responsibility that track how we are differentially situated in relations of coproduction. This final piece opens a way of thinking about the conditions for imagining futures grounded in the interdependent present as a practice of responsibility.

## Queer Desires and Disability Futures

There are many ways of being orientated toward a future—some which unfurl along an expected orientation, some which deviate from the path laid out for us (Ahmed 2006). It is a form of desire. Here, I think about queer desire as a form of deviation, a reorientation, signaling that we want a world that doesn't yet exist, we desire it, and we practice the world we don't have yet in the present. In that practice we bring it into being; queer desire is a speculative fiction. I think about queer desire in terms of prefiguration, which I'll explain in the next section. Thinking about desire can be dangerous; what we want and how we want it comes out of our histories, and overwhelmingly those histories have pushed trauma deep into our bodies, intertwining what we "really really want," to reprise the title of a recent self-help book, with what has hurt and torqued us at the core. Our current desires are shaped, to their roots, by oppressive social relations. In my life, physical and sexual interactions with other people have delineated key sites at which I've experienced gorgeous liberatory potential and crushing *hierarchies of power*, in Davis's words, sometimes confusingly simultaneously. Because I see sexuality in its broadest sense—sexuality as that domain in which we are given or refused particular forms of recognition, sexuality as a social relation, sexuality as a bodily experience of suffusiveness not expressible in words—I think that how we work with and through sexuality is important for political struggle. So I'm interested in working through how hierarchies of power manifest in practices of desire can be transformed, again to recall Davis, into *intertwined vectors of struggle for freedom.* This is not at all simple.

José Esteban Muñoz's generous writing about queerness and the future frames queer desire as an orientation toward a future. He wrote:

> We may never touch queerness, but we can feel it as the warm illumination of a horizon imbued with potentiality. We have never been queer, yet queerness exists for us as an ideality that can be distilled from the past and used to imagine a future. The future is queerness's domain. Queerness is a structuring and educated mode of desiring that allows us to see and feel beyond the quagmire of the present. . . . We must strive, in the face of the here and now's totalizing rendering of reality, to think and feel a *then and there.* . . . Queerness is a longing that propels us onward, beyond romances of the negative and toiling in the present. Queerness is that thing that lets us feel that this world is not enough, that indeed something is missing. . . . Queerness is essentially about the rejection of a here and now and an insistence on potentiality or concrete possibility for another world. (Muñoz 2009, 1)

In this section, I explore what Muñoz thinks of as the *warm illumination of a horizon imbued with possibility* through thinking about queer disability futurity. Let me stay concrete about this, though, by starting from the question of how institutionalized oppression, trauma, and sexuality intertwine. I was thinking about sexuality, disability, and different futures at a poverty town hall focusing on cuts that the province of Ontario was making to a program available to people on Ontario Works or Ontario Disability Support Program: The Community Start-Up Benefit program (CSUB). Under this program, if you needed to get out of an abusive situation, or your apartment had been flooded or had bedbugs, or you needed to buy something like a kitchen table or a bed, you could apply for $1,500 if you have kids or $798 if you're single. Ontario had already cut the program so that people could only apply every twenty-four months instead of every twelve, and in January 2013 it was ended altogether. As anyone who has had contact with state disability "benefits" knows, they are ridiculously low (in Ontario we would have to raise the rates 55 percent just to match inflation to get them to the level they were in 1991). Most of the people at that town hall who were on assistance and houseless would be unable to pay first and last month's rent on an apartment in rapidly gentrifying Ottawa without the CSUB. So cutting this benefit would have direct, very bad, consequences in a lot of people's lives.

It may not be immediately clear that this cut is about sexuality and disability, and it might not be obvious that fighting it could be a form of identifying into queer disability praxis. But consider: Given how often people on ODSP have experienced sexual violation, fighting alongside them for more autonomy and better material support can express an intention to create more possibilities for healing, building resilience in the face of those histories, and for preventing future sexual violence. Without access to the Community Start-Up Benefit, people who experience intimate violence have fewer resources for getting out of their situation—women living in shelters in particular used the CSUB as a first step out. So cutting the CSUB may contribute to the perpetuation of intimate violence. It is also about how sexuality is configured: Ontario Works and ODSP both monitor people's housing situations and cut their monthly rate if they've entered a relationship with someone not on assistance—or if they've been on the family rate and leave their relationship.

But less obviously, poverty itself is about sexuality and disability. Social relations of inequality mean that more queer people, and vastly more disabled people, live on social assistance. When rates are too low to live in a dignified way, when people are institutionalized because that's more convenient for the state than paying for proper assistance, the experience of poverty shapes the possibilities for sex and for making choices about whether or how to live as a sexual person. Institutionalization and imprisonment tightens the weave of constraint.

Amber Hollibaugh writes:

> I know that, for some people, gay rights and gay liberation do not hinge on the particulars of sexual desire. I have heard for the last twenty-five years that we aren't *just* our erotic identities; the current movement is thick with it. But, for many of us, it *does* begin there, does revolve around the ways we organize our erotic choices. And erotic identities are not just behaviors or individual sexual actions; they reflect a much broader fabric that is the weave and crux of

our very personhood, a way of mediating and measuring all that we experience, all that we can interpret through the language of our bodies, our histories, our eyes, our hips, our intelligence, our willful, desiring selves. However we've gotten there, erotic identity is not simply a specific activity or "lifestyle," a set of heels or ties that dress up the quirk. It is as deep and rich, as dangerous, explosive, and unique as each of us dares to be or become. (Hollibaugh 2000, 258)

I follow Hollibaugh in this understanding of erotic identity as more than a lifestyle or a way to *dress up the quirk*; erotic identity as expressive of our selves. In this sense, queer identity as a process of becoming rather than a state of being is always an orientation toward a future that does not yet exist but that is grounded in the past and present we experience.

Understanding ourselves as interdependent might call us to identify into disability praxis as one piece of queer futurity. A key piece of such praxis will be a materially situated, politically radical analysis of how oppressions intermesh—an understanding of how abuse of children connects with poverty and cuts to programs that allow people on programs like Ontario Works and the Ontario Disability Support Program to have better access to minimal standards for dignified lives. Queer disability struggles, resting on a profound view of the situated, partial, and in-process nature of our selves and their expression in complex bodies and desires, can then shape and change this world. And I desperately want us to pursue that transformation. Harriet McBryde Johnson's reflections on hope and interdependence are generative here. Arguing against Peter Singer's utilitarian view that parents ought to be able to select for nondisabled children, she writes:

I can only trust in the fact that, while we struggle, we must also live with our theories and with one another. As a shield from the terrible purity of Singer's vision, I'll look to the corruption that comes from interconnectedness. To justify my hopes that Peter Singer's theoretical world—and its entirely logical extensions—won't become real, I'll invoke the muck and mess and undeniable reality of disabled lives well lived. That's the best I can do right now. (Johnson 2006, 228)

I love this conception of *looking to the corruption that comes from interconnectedness*. Johnson's commitment to starting from the muck and mess is a commitment to the present; against the claim that disabled lives aren't worth living, and so therefore people ought to abort disabled fetuses or kill disabled children, Johnson raises the shield of manifest disabled lives well lived. This shield is also an affirmation of disability futures—because Singer, and others who wrongly believe that disability is worse than death, cannot understand the liveliness of disabled lives, they cannot imagine disability futures with any adequacy at all.

Robert McRuer usefully delineates two ways we can understand the futures at stake here, using the formulation of "the disability to come." This phrase invokes two senses—a frightening one and a welcoming one. McRuer says: "Whether it's the adage of everyone will be disabled if they live long enough, or Harriet McBryde Johnson's report on the 'disability gulag'—that terrible future space that an able-bodied culture has constructed where she, or you, or I might end up—it's clear that we're inescapably haunted by the disability to come. And the disability to come, the one we invoke, has often been frightening" (McRuer 2006, 207). Indeed, often disability activists invoke the horrors of warehousing disabled people, about unlivable conditions in homes and hospitals for the disabled, the elderly, the sick, to try to fight for different conditions. We're saying, "You'll be disabled later; do you want to be treated the way we treat disabled people now?" McRuer is right to frame this as also a way of imagining the future of disability. As he writes: "There are other ways of summoning the future, however. Despite the fact that these frightening futures make it difficult to do so, what might it mean to welcome the disability to come, to desire it? What might it mean to shape worlds capable of welcoming the disability to come? In such terrible times, is it even possible to ask the question that way?" (ibid.). Again, in thinking about prefiguration as part of disability praxis, remaining in conversation with Indigenous thinkers is instructive; as I discussed in chapter 1, Leanne Betasamosake Simpson has offered rich theorization of the notion of resurgence as an orientation toward the future grounded in the past. She argues that the "basic premise of Indigenist and decolonizing theories is that we bring the knowledge of the ancient ones back into contemporary relevance by capturing the revolutionary nature of those teachings" (Simpson 2008, 76). We might welcome the disability to come, echoing Harriet McBryde Johnson, in part because we can invoke the resistant undeniability of lives lived well as a source of resurgent possibility.

It is, I think, not only possible but necessary to ask what it might mean to shape *worlds capable of welcoming the disability to come*. Alison Kafer offers an important understanding of disability futurity, and I want to quote her at length. She writes about desiring crip futures, saying:

> This desire, these imaginings, cannot be separated from the crip pasts behind us or the crip presents surrounding us; indeed, these very pasts and presents are what make articulating a critical crip futurity so essential. To put it bluntly, I, *we*, need to imagine crip futures because disabled people are continually being written out of the future, rendered as the sign of the future no one wants. This erasure is not mere metaphor. Disabled people—particularly those with developmental and psychiatric impairments, those who are poor, gender-deviant, and/or people of color, those who need atypical forms of assistance to survive—have faced sterilization, segregation, and institutionalization; denial of equitable education, health care and social services; violences and abuse; and the withholding of the rights of citizenship. Too many of these practices continue, and each of them has greatly limited, and often literally shortened, the futures of disabled people. It is my loss, our loss, not to take care of, embrace, and desire all of us. We must begin to anticipate presents and to imagine futures that include all of us. We must explore disability in time. (Kafer 2013, 46)

In thinking about this, I follow Kafer in a yearning "for an elsewhere—and, perhaps, an 'elsewhen'—in which disability is understood otherwise: as political, as valuable, as integral" (3). As I'll discuss below, imagining such disability futures can be made easier and more pleasurable through speculative fictions.

Social movement theorists—people situated within and thinking with social movements, rather than theorists about movements—offer the notion of "prefigurative politics"; this formulation is useful for understanding the work of speculative fictions. Harsha Walia defines prefiguration as "the notion that our organizing reflects the society we wish to live in—that the methods we practice, institutions we create, and relationships we facilitate within our movements and communities align with our ideals" (Walia 2013, 11). Chris Dixon frames prefigurative politics as "a commitment to putting vision into practice through struggle . . . the core idea here is that *how* we get ourselves to a transformed society (the means) is importantly related to *what* that transformed society will be (the ends). The means *prefigure* the ends. To engage in prefigurative politics, then, is to intentionally shape our activities to manifest our vision" (Dixon 2014, 84–85). Dixon specifies, though, that it is important to resist understanding prefigurative practices in a general or theoretical way, and in his work he teases apart four different senses of this concept: (1) Lifestylist attempts to live one's values; (2) Working on institutions that can counter existing, unjust institutional forms; (3) Horizontal organizing that builds capacity; and, finally, (4) Being good to each other (85).

Dixon's work engages the question implied in his book's title, *Another Politics: Thinking across Transformative Movements*: If we can't live with this world and its politics, how can we craft another politics? Answering this question will require practical grounding in the daily work of trying to craft another world, which is of course what radical politics aim toward. As Barbara Epstein writes:

> There is always a prefigurative element in radical politics, or at least a pull toward prefigurative politics, because without an effort to live one's values radical claims collapse into hypocrisy. There is also a pull to accommodate to the existing structure so as to be able to operate effectively in it. Each movement finds its own balance between these opposing forces. (Epstein 1991, 122)

In the example I have been considering, I think we could understand transforming the terrain of social assistance payments around access to housing as a kind of critical disability prefigurative practice toward a future in which people have the material conditions for becoming, to reprise Hollibaugh, as "dangerous, explosive, and unique as each of us dares to be or become." Given the proportions of homeless youth who are queer and disabled, who are Indigenous, who are people of color, fighting for access to the basic conditions for dignified and joyful living is multifaceted, intermeshed, prefigurative work. We need, if we're going to open the warm horizon of the disability to come as a place where people can live and flourish, to accommodate the existing structure enough to do things like struggle to raise the rates of social assistance.

My thinking has been sparked by movement practices and accounts of prefiguration as a way to think about how we go about creating another world within the shell of the old. We engage this creation in part through what stories and histories we tell. As Avery Gordon argues: "A history of the present, which could be considered the sociologist's special province, is always a project looking toward the future. To write a history of the present requires stretching toward the horizon of what can't be seen with ordinary clarity yet. And to stretch toward beyond a horizon requires a particular kind of perception where what's transparent and what's in the shadows put each other into crisis" (Gordon 2004, 89). In part, my commitment to the notion of prefiguration comes out of a conviction, which have I explored in earlier work, that this kind of perception and stretching is more and other than propositional, claim-making activity. Political transformation is not an intellectual exercise, but instead is a visceral, emotional, commonsensical refiguration—that when we engage with social movements, we are moved on many levels, only some of them rational and conceptual. In learning about movements of the past, and in my own activist work, I have also seen that it can be difficult to imagine ways the world could be different than it is. This is one reason we turn to history, which teaches us that things used to be very different than they are now; this is also one reason that we turn, sometimes in colonial or orientalist ways, toward "other" cultures, which show that things are very different elsewhere than they are here. Here, though, I move to thinking about how the imagined future can be a resource for prefiguration—what models for the disability to come, as McRuer puts it, can we find in imagining other futures?

In asking this question, notice that it is not possible to ask about what *the* future is—a big part of why we might think about prefiguration: there is never a determinate future, but instead only a present that moves in relation to what we want to move toward. There is not a single pure or perfect future toward which we stretch. As Samuel Delany has argued, speaking of Black SF writers, "We need images of tomorrow; and our people need them more than most . . . only by having clear and vital images of the *many* alternatives, good and bad, of where one *can* go, will we have any control over the way we may actually get there in a reality tomorrow will bring all too quickly" (Delany 1984, 35). The shimmer here between the necessity of imagined tomorrows and control of the too-quickly-arriving tomorrow is the space of the kind of creativity signaled by prefigurative political practice. Delany repeatedly emphasizes the sense in which, as he writes:

> Science fiction is not "about the future." Science fiction *is in dialogue with the present.* We SF writers often say that science fiction prepares people to think about the real future—but that's because it relates to the real present in the particular way it does; and that relation is neither one of prediction nor one of prophecy. It is one of dialogic, contestatory, agonistic creativity. In science

fiction the future is only a writerly convention that allows the SF writer to in-
dulge in a significant distortion of the present that sets up a rich and complex
dialogue with the reader's here and now. (176)

Practices of prefiguration, as engaged by Walia and Dixon, can be understood as ways to relate to the real present with this kind of significant
distortion—opening a space for *dialogic, contestatory, agonistic creativity*
that sets itself against the world as it is. Muñoz frames his work in *Cruising
Utopia* as a call to "think about our lives and times differently, to look beyond
a narrow version of the here and now on which so many around us who are
bent on the normative count. Utopia in this book has been about an insis-
tence on something else, something better, something dawning" (Muñoz
2009, 189). Queer disability movements, holding in view the ways disabled
and queer lives are shaped by poverty and capitalism, and holding in view
the fact of "lives well lived" as Harriet McBryde Johnson frames it, in spite
of the depredations of the racist ableist heteropatriarchal capitalist social
relations, also hold open this space of contestatory, dawning, other worlds.
At the same time, perhaps it is useful to consider one site for producing
other tomorrows.

## Exercises of Speculative Fiction

Octavia E. Butler's work was important to me personally for a long time
before it became politically important to me. As her work becomes a broader
political touchstone for thinking in an SF mode, I have been drawn to think
about what Butler's writing offers for queer disability speculative futures. As
with every attempt to prefigure something, there are parts of Butler's oeuvre
that I find generative, parts we could see as conservative, and parts that
evoke nonteleological SF play. It constellates in story much of what I have
been exploring in theory in this chapter. Butler's work models what it is to
identify into new formations, with a focus on fraught but desired collective
formations of co-identification. As I'll explore in this section, the fraughtness
of identifying into the world to come, in Butler's fiction, traces some of her
enduring questions about what place genetics, "nature," hierarchies, social
formations, and collectivity might have in efforts to shape and live with the
world. Though Butler is sometimes quite heterosexist, her accounts of negotiating with interdependent and comingled alien liveliness also model usable
forms of queer desire. And, finally, Butler consistently offers complex stories

of disability and interdependence. She has also been taken up in an explicitly political imaginary project, currently called *Octavia's Brood*; I argue that this is a generative imagining, and also that a closer attention to the specific disability imaginings Butler offers may be a valuable project for movement work on envisioning another future than the one that seems to be laid out for us.

Although I argue here that Butler's work (and, indeed, much of SF as genre) is organized around an interrogation about what disability could mean, it is rarely the case that disability is obvious or named as the central point of inquiry. Indeed, one of the most interesting things about Butler's fiction is the way things start off as sites of disabilities and later become sites of liberation. All of her books engage the fraught question of how we come together in community, almost always after harm. Such coming together is profoundly ambivalent in Butler's work; it is often forced even as it is enjoyable, and collectivity is never disaggregated from power imbalances. Butler is also consistently concerned with purity and hierarchy in ways manifest in the framing of her narratives as well as by characters themselves.

Disability is frequently figured in standard science fiction literature, usually either because physical manifestations that would be identified as disabilities in the fictive present (the "present past" imagined from the point of view of the future imagined) become or are transformed into physical superabilities. Physical disability is perhaps more imaginable as an impairment inviting a technological fix than is mental disability (though texts such as Elizabeth Moon's *The Speed of Dark*, which imagines a future in which autism is "correctable," do take on bodily difference that manifests in broadly nonphysical terms).[3] Even the hardest SF can be understood as showing that in the future we are all physically reliant on others, on technology, and complexly vulnerable and interdependent. Engagements with disability in SF, when they hold the particular focus of physical disability, are frequently either troubling or boring, and often uphold what McRuer says about Left social movements—that they cannot imagine a disabled world as "possible and desirable" "because in general they are tied to liberationist models that need disability as the raw material against which the imagined future is formed" (McRuer 2006, 71–72). Becoming not-disabled is too often the ideal in SF work engaging disability. Butler is not innocent of this; she unevenly embraces and eradicates disability in her work.

Physical disability manifests in Butler's work primarily through her abiding interest in the problem and promise of heritable traits, and mostly in terms of diseases—and in this way it is (appropriately!) not possible to make a sharp delineation between various experiences of disability depicted in her work. In the *Xenogenesis* trilogy (later remarketed as *Lilith's Brood*), the Oankali are an alien people of travelers and gene traders who enter into gene-and-culture trading partnerships with new entities. In their encounter with humans, they find us after we have destroyed the Earth—a nuclear winter has fallen, and we exist in only pockets of people. They rescue/entrap us, and begin the process of repairing the Earth. We are fascinating to them for two primary reasons; we have what Butler calls "the Contradiction"—first, we have heritable hierarchical tendencies and, simultaneously and conversely, we are intelligent; second, we get cancers. These two destructive features of human being make us "taste" delicious to the gender-neutral super-sexed gene-assemblers among the Oankali, the ooloi.

Donna Haraway, herself positively ooloi-like in her delight at finding new, dangerous understandings and putting them together in heritable, pleasurable, monstrous ways, has engaged Butler's fiction across her writing career. Early on, she framed Butler's work as "preoccupied with forced reproduction, unequal power, the ownership of self by another, the siblingship of humans with aliens, and the failure of siblingship within species. . . . Butler's salvation history is not utopian, but remains deeply furrowed by the contradictions and questions of power within all communication" (Haraway 1989, 378). In a much later piece, Haraway argues that "Butler's entire work as an SF writer is riveted on the problem of destruction and wounded flourishing—not simply survival—in exile, diaspora, abduction, and transportation—the earthly gift-burden of the descendants of slaves, refugees, immigrants, travelers, and of the indigenous too. It is not a burden that stops with settlement" (Grebowicz, Merrick, and Haraway 2013, 140). Butler's engagement with contradictions, power, and wounded flourishing is manifest in how we might see her working with disability.

Many of Butler's key imaginings of wounded flourishing center on the people, mostly women, who have capacities that in some contexts render them disabled and in others open flourishing to them and others. The *Patternist* series imagines a future with dual impurities calling the terrain of the human into question. On the one hand, there is an emerging race (perhaps) of people, no longer quite human, who are telepaths mostly and telekinetics some, bred by their nearly immortal body-stealing progenitor Doro partly as food, who cannot tolerate their own children or each other but feel a confusing biological need to be near their kin. On the other, Butler imagines a race (perhaps) of people, no longer quite human, who have been infected with a virulent alien symbiote brought to Earth. For the telepaths of *Mind of My Mind*, inheriting the possibility of power also gives them what manifests as profound mental illness; they are abused and abusers, until brought into the Pattern by Doro's most successful breeding experiment, Mary. Butler is unstinting in her description of what happens to people ("latents") who are not part of the Pattern. One of the characters goes to a house of latents to collect them and bring them in and finds a horrific scene:

> The baby's starved body was crawling with maggots, but it still showed the marks of its parents' abuse. The head was a ruin. It had been hit with something or slammed into something. The legs were twisted as no infant's legs would have twisted normally. The child had been tortured to death. The man and the woman had fed on each other's insanity until they murdered one child and left the others dying. Rachel had stolen enough latents from prisons and insane asylums to know how often such things happened. Sometimes the best a latent could do was to realize that the mental interference, the madness, was not going to stop, and then to end their own lives before they killed others. (Butler 1978, 171)

In this book, as in others Butler explores, unchosen empathy produces disabling suffering; in the case of latent telepaths, their own suffering manifests as madness figured as harm. Collectivity transforms this kind of suffering into the conditions for flourishing; when people are integrated into the Pattern, mentally linked, they no longer hurt themselves or others. Collectivity does not do away with the experience of sharing with others—in that sense the capacity or quality that is disabling in one context does not disappear— but it is transformed. This transformation is not innocent. Mary, who brings people into collectivity and the possibility for less suffering, feeds off their energy; they do not choose to become part of the Pattern, and many of the telepaths brought in are angry about being forced to join. And, most interesting, in accessing the conditions for flourishing, the Patternists re-situate everyone who is not telepathic as "Mutes," controlling them and using their labor without consent—a category of oppression identified by one of the characters as slavery. Hierarchies of ability and oppression based on ability are, here and elsewhere in Butler's work, fraught and impure.

The *Parable* books, only two of which were finished before Butler's early death, begin from Olamina, a young Black woman with "hyper-empathy syndrome," a result of her mother's drug use—a sharer. Though it is not figured in the same way as telepathy, her work of building a new community and a new religion, Earthseed, is informed by her own response to other people's pain and by "seeds" of the collective in the form of other sharers who help start the community. And in one of Butler's rare short stories, "The Evening, The Morning, and The Night," figures a genetic disease modeled on Huntington's; it is somewhat controlled by diet, but debilitates most sufferers, causing them to disfigure and kill themselves and their loved ones. People who have the disease are presented as warehoused, and suffering until death. In this story as in others, collectivity and biologically cued hierarchy transform what was lived as disability into an altered flourishing; because the disease is carried chromosomally, people with XX chromosomes who have two parents with it are more vulnerable. But, it turns out, they also produce a pheromone that eases the expression of the disease in other carriers—transforming what would be debilitating self-harm into extra focus, leaps of creativity, and the capacity to imagine new technologies. Again, here, what was disability becomes superability in the right, which is to say collective, context.

Butler's work is generative for disability speculation because it is not simple. It does not propose mere reversal as liberatory possibility. When people who have been disabled by a social world's construction and relation of their bodily difference experience or create a transformed world, they do not automatically become paragons of virtue. They remain power-saturated, complex, and uneven. Her work is generative for disability speculation because it offers another world—*many* another worlds—that are better in certain key ways, more livable for more people, but not completely fixed; another world may be on her way, but she's an impure world. At the same time, Butler, for all the hope figured in her work, is uneasily situated as someone we take up as a liberatory thinker—her work offers certain things I worry about even as I find great potential in her writing.

One piece of this is a particular strand of biological determinism and essentialism woven into many of her books; I have wondered if or how Butler would have changed some of her presentation of biology if she had lived to deeply engage work on epigenetics and materialist analyses of entanglement. There is, even in the very queer situations of necessary alien sex, a persistent heterosexism in Butler's work. This manifests as almost constant straight pairings, frequently mandated and biologically imperative because of alien entities, but not always. Men in her books are uncomfortable with sex with other men to a man, and sex between women is apparently a non-issue. Consider two examples: In the *Xenogenesis/Lilith's Brood* trilogy, male and female Humans who partner with the Oankali mate with a male, a female, and an ooloi Oankali. The ooloi are gender-neutral but the site of gene assembly, and sex takes place through them. Linking directly to our nervous system, they web together sexual partners in looping, really hot alien sex that is quite queer. In certain ways! In other ways it is not at all—given the ooloi's capacities for gene mixing, it is not clear that the sex-gender organization of the family is genetically determined, or how to think about the relatively fixed social roles attributed to the various sexes. There are no central characters who identify as queer in the *Xenogenesis* trilogy, no trans characters, no one who is gladly nonreproductive. Physical disability arising from accidents or genetics is correctible by the ooloi; mental disability is, to varying degrees, accepted and worked with in family contexts or, in some cases, "put away" in formerly carnivorous plants for hibernation-style healing over many years. So, as I ardently take up Octavia E. Butler as a foremother of radical speculative imagination, I also hesitate—and this hesitation is perhaps also a fruitful piece of what it means to align ourselves as part of her brood. This is the difference between offering an imperfect, possible world to our imagination as a site for our collective work and laying out something more like a doctrine.

As dialogue with the present and as mode, SF can be an ingredient in prefiguring new worlds. adrienne maree brown, in her "Outro" for *Octavia's Brood: Science Fiction Stories from Social Justice Movements*, the volume she coedited with Walidah Imarisha, writes: "We hold so many worlds inside us. So many futures. It is our radical responsibility to share these worlds, to plant them in the soil of our society as seeds for the type of justice we want and need" (Imarisha and brown 2015, 279). Understanding Butler's work in part as a site of visioning speculative, indeterminate disability futures means nourishing a responsibility to multiple futures, shared. As Imarisha argues in the introduction to the same collection: "Whenever we try to envision a world without war, without violence, without prisons, without capitalism, we are engaging in speculative fiction. All organizing is science fiction. Organizers and activists dedicate their lives to creating and envisioning another world, or many other worlds—so what better venue for organizers to explore their work than science fiction stories?" (3).

Speculative futures can prefigure a practice that welcomes the selves to come. This orientation toward futures to come is grounded in the experience of interdependence, politically organized around the idea of identifying into a world that we create starting from our speculation that it could be otherwise than it is. Shaping our identities out of our politics includes understanding the history that has shaped our field of possibility as a site for identification. The new world we carry in our hearts is always a world grounded in the actually existing present in all its impurity, responsible to the past in all its complexity. Just as we are differentially responsible to the past and present, we are differentially situated in relation to worlds we can identify into—power never disappears. Even so, we can follow Muñoz in reaching toward concrete possibilities—a warm horizon imbued with possibility— prefiguratively practicing open normativities that might produce practices of freedom we cannot predict.

# Conclusion

## The Point, However, Is to *Change* It

Philosophy students reading Karl Marx are either intrigued or irritated by the eleventh thesis on Ludwig Feuerbach: "The philosophers have only *interpreted* the world, in various ways. The point, however, is to *change* it" (Marx 1975, 423). Of course, changing the world necessarily involves interpreting it; adequate ontological work, manifest in the form of purposefully and ethically transforming the material situation of what the world is, requires excellent epistemic work. In the kind of world we're in now, a world of unimaginable complexity and difficulty, excellent epistemic work is hard to come by—it is hard to know everything that matters, and hard to have a solid method for that knowing. I have speculated in this book that the experience of being overwhelmed by any attempt to understand the knottiness and tangle of entanglement is partially responsible for what I have called a purity politics of despair. This approach begins to interpret the world, discovers that there is no easy solution to suffering and implication, and stops at making the more manageable agential cut of personal purity practices. In the introduction, I affirmed John Holloway's reformulation of Marx's eleventh thesis—"We live in an unjust society and we wish it were not so"—and his impulse to always hold the descriptive (despair) and prescriptive (hope) parts of that phrase together (Holloway 2010, 7). For those of us who believe that the world deserves more than interpretation, description, and despair, politics based on purity will remain unlivable.

Purity is never possible in the world, and it is only unevenly possible in concept. And yet the focus on knowing more or better—the epistemic narrowly conceived—expresses a response to purity's impossibility. This matters politically for those of us who want to change the world. In activist spaces over the last ten years, I have seen an upswing in what I would characterize as a commitment to staying at the level of the epistemic as a response to the complexity and impurity of the world: conspiracy theories. Years ago visiting childhood friends in Manhattan, I was shocked (and a little embarrassed by association—my very smart friend was with me, and I worried what she'd think) to discover that one of them was a 9/11 "truther"; he believed that the World Trade towers had been brought down by prelaid charges, that the whole thing was connected to the Illuminati in some way, and other things along these lines. On the way home, talking through the conversation, my friend said that the thing that struck her about the conversation was that—aside from some of the material issues about airline fuel and collapsing buildings—she agreed with a lot of what he'd said; taking an anticapitalist view of the situation of the world leads one to think that there *is* a small group of people causing enormous immiseration for profit, linked together in troubling ways, whose actions are obfuscated even as they are enabled by governmental and extragovernmental policies and practices.

One key difference between a conspiracy theorist and an activist, for lack of a better word, is that the conspiracy theorist holds that the best defense is more and better knowledge (read my website, listen to my explanation, investigate what you know) and the activist holds that the best defense is creating another world. An anti-oppression approach might start on the level of the epistemic, but it always leads toward action in the world, to speculative ontological commitments to different futures. The point is to *change the world*, *this* world, and so the point is complicated, compromised, and impossible to conceptualize, let alone achieve alone. People doing movement work usually get lots of things wrong, which might not be such a problem—if the purpose of the work isn't to be right. Instead, our purpose is to contingently make it be that something that *deserves a future* has one. Almost all the people I know who are doing activist work, effective or not, are trying to move beyond the epistemic and into the ontic—we are attempting to prefigure something.

At the same time, I have been struck by a shift on the left *away* from what could be characterized as righteous politics—collective work toward a future prefigured in present practice. This is a shift toward a *self*-righteous politics startlingly in line with conspiracy theories; what matters is whether you, individually, have the correct language, analysis, and critique. I'm not disparaging posting things on the Internet, but posting things on the Internet should be understood as closer to the "interpreting the world" end of the spectrum than it is to the "change the world" end. Of course, recalling Karen Barad, to interpret the world is to change the world—the "privileging of epistemological issues over ontological ones in the constructivist literature" notwithstanding (Barad, 41). Responding to entanglement and its impurities will benefit from her conception of the entanglement of knowing and being—"Knowing is a direct material engagement, a practice of intra-acting with the world as part of the world in its dynamic material configuring, its ongoing articulation" (379). In this account, interpreting the world and changing it are inseparable—ontoepistemological—and thus they are matters for ethics and for politics.

Global warming and climate change have underlain much of my thinking in this book, perhaps in the sense that Timothy Morton articulates in terms of its nature as a "hyperobject"—sticky, viscous, relational, impossible to not think about, impossible to fully understand, not here but nowhere but here. Hyperobjects are "massively distributed in time and space relative to humans" (Morton 2013, 10). Global warming is one such hyperobject. As Morton writes,

> The enormity of very large finitude hollows out my decisions from the inside. Now every time I so much as change a confounded light bulb, I have to think about global warming. It is the end of the world, because I can see past the lip of the horizon of human worlding. . . . It is helpful to think of global warming as something like an ultra slow motion nuclear bomb. The incremental effects are almost invisible, until an island disappears underwater. (91)

I am sympathetic to key parts of Morton's account of hyperobjects—they are another way to think about the difficulty of orienting ourselves toward constitutive entanglement and living always after the impossibility of separation and purity. That *confounded light bulb*, in Morton's slightly old-fashioned cranky phrase, mixes, muddles, interrupts—the Latin is that that which confounds, *confuses*. In statistics, confounding happens when we cannot eliminate multiple explanations for the relationships we observe between phenomena. And yet, I look for more than the conception of hyperobjects, particularly if it is meant to invoke some form of response from us, and for some way to delineate appropriate different responses to global warming, on the one hand, and a nuclear bomb, on the other. Perhaps for this reason, I return to Anna Tsing's conception of living in disturbance regimes, in blasted landscapes that still can be spaces for hope.

A pair of short stories, both written by Hiromi Kawakami and published in the collection *March Was Made of Yarn: Reflections on the Japanese Earthquake, Tsunami, and Nuclear Meltdown,* have helped me think about living in blasted landscapes. The first version, from 1993, is "Kami-sama," translated as "God Bless You." The "god" in this story is not a Christian god—Kami are more multiple and often more ground-level gods, as Kawakami narrates in her discussion of the story. She writes:

> Many such gods existed in ancient Japan. There were gods who presided over all aspects of greater nature: gods of the mountains, of the ocean and the rivers, of the wind and the rain. There were gods connected to daily life as well: gods of the rice fields, of human habitation, of the hearth, the toilet, and the well. Gods who punished, animal gods. There were demons, too, and giants, goblins, and tree spirits that ranged across Japan, from the archipelago all the way down to Okinawa. (Kawakami 2012, 44)

"God Bless You" is a story about an ordinary day; the narrator receives (and accepts) an invitation to go for a walk from the bear who has moved into apartment 305, just down the hall. The walk to a nearby river is ordinary, and the bear is really a bear; people tease him on the way to the river, he catches fish in very bear-ish fashion. At the end of the story, we see that proximity and intimacy can be negotiated in this slightly strange world; the bear asks the narrator for a hug. The narrator tells us:

> "Would you mind if we hugged?" he finally asked. "Where I come from, that's what we do when we say goodbye to someone we feel close to. If you don't like the idea, of course, then we don't have to."
>
> I consented. The bear took a step forward, spread his arms wide, and embraced my shoulders. Then he pressed his cheek against mine. I could smell the odor of bear. He moved his other cheek to mine and squeezed me firmly again. His body was cooler than I had expected. (53)

The only reference to the kami of the title of the story is a mention of a bear god—the bear who lives next door is not framed or understood as a kami, but just an ordinary, very polite, and old-fashioned bear, who lives next door and maybe goes on a walk with one. This bear practices consent politics in negotiating physical contact. The narrator says: "I tried picturing what the bear god looked like, but it was beyond my imagination" (ibid.). The original version of the story raises questions about how we ought to think about anthropomorphizing animals and what it is to get on with them, as neighbors or gods.

The revised version of the story, "God Bless You, 2011," is exactly the same as the original except that it invites another unpicturable kami into the frame: the god of uranium. In her postscript to the revision of the story, Kawakami asks, "If the god of uranium really exists, then what must he be thinking? Were this a fairy tale of old, what would happen when humans break the laws of nature and turn gods into minions?" (Kawakami 2012, 47). At every point in the story, the ordinary activities of going for a walk, catching fish, coming home are suffused with the nuclear imaginary—the reader experiences every move the narrator makes in relation to their possible radiation exposure levels. When the bear asks for a hug, for example, the language is almost identical to the original:

> "Would you mind if we hugged?" he finally asked. "Where I come from, that's what we do when we say goodbye to someone we feel close to. If you don't like the idea, of course, then we don't have to."
>
> I consented. The fact that bears don't take baths meant that there would probably be more radiation on his body. But it had been my decision from the start to remain in this part of the country, so I could hardly be squeamish.
>
> The bear took a step forward, spread his arms wide, and embraced my shoulders. Then he pressed his cheek against mine. I could smell the odor of bear. He moved his other cheek to mine and squeezed me firmly again. His body was cooler than I had expected. (43)

What does is mean to hug the bear? This is not the ordinary question for thinking about our relations with megafauna others; the story is generative for its everyday, speculative fiction avoidance of the dynamic that Jake Metcalf identifies as intimacy without proximity—our normal relation with bears as companion species (Metcalf 2008). The story refuses also the kind of complex questions raised by a book like the classic novel *Bear*, in which a librarian cataloguing a collection on an island in northern Ontario has a sexual relationship with a chained bear. The intimacy and proximity of "God Bless You," the original story, stages certain questions about purity—who is a person versus who is a human person, about animal odors, and about the kind of respect for bodily boundaries implied in asking for active consent for a hug.

The revised story still stages these questions, but it adds the boundary-crossing, bodily entanglement of radiation exposure. The narrator purposefully does not wear protective clothing, though they do measure and record their exposure in daily microsieverts, shower carefully, and it is not clear if they will eat the cesium-laden bottom feeding salted fish the bear caught at the river. *Hardly being squeamish* is not a practice of letting down all protective practices. Rather, I read the 2011 version of the story, written after the actual earthquake, tsunami, and reactor meltdown but referencing a more general "incident," as an instruction in co-implication. The bodily and social relations we are forced to have in virtue of living in one place and not another are woven together with differential attention to the effects of those places—Becquerel or microsieverts potentially producing burns, cancer, or exhaustion. Kawakami writes about reworking her story:

> I had no intention of standing in the pulpit and preaching against the dangers of nuclear power. Rather, my purpose was to express my amazement at how our daily lives can go on uneventfully day after day and then suddenly be so dramatically changed by external events. The experience left me with a quiet anger that still has not subsided. Yet, in the end, this anger is directed at nothing other than myself. Who built today's Japan if not me—and others like me? Even as we bear this anger, we carry on our mundane lives. Stubbornly, we refuse to give up, to say the hell with it. For when all is said and done, it is always a joy to be alive, however daunting the circumstances. (Kawakami 2012, 47–48)

This quiet anger at *myself* and *others like me*, carrying on our mundane but affected lives, this refusal to give up even in daunting circumstances, this joy, delimits a way to live in the midst of the blasted world. In chapter 4, I discussed what we might understand as the story of the Fukushima meltdown as part of thinking about what Gabrielle Hecht calls "nuclearity," the process by which we come to identify certain things as nuclear, asking what ethical response we might make to our complicity in nuclear disaster and other complex and distributed harms.

To live in an unjust world and wish it were not so is to formulate an impulse to respond. These paired short stories offer a model for response to something to which it is impossible to adequately respond. The last sentences of Morton's book are: "In a strange way, every object is a hyperobject. But we can only think this thought in light of the ecological emergency inside of which we have now woken up. Heidegger said that only a god can save us now. As we find ourselves waking up within a series of gigantic objects, we realize that he forgot to add: *We just don't know what sort of god*" (Morton 2013, 138). Kawakami's stories and reflections offer the possibility of the kami as the right sort of god for us—ordinary, local, powerful, and with whom we can stand in nonidentical and nongenetic relation. This god is multiple, not all-powerful, not vengeful, but not all-loving either; they are not going to save us, but if we stand in the right kind of relation we might help with some collective and contingent salvation. Elizabeth Povinelli reaches for a form of ethical impulse not "dependent on a certain kind of event and eventfulness," but instead in response to mundane, and suffusive, suffering. She asks, "How does one construct an ethics in relation to this kind of dispersed suffering?" (Povinelli 2011, 4). Povinelli is "interested in forms of suffering and dying, enduring and expiring, that are ordinary, chronic, and cruddy rather than catastrophic, crisis-laden, and sublime" (13). The combined ethical and political response I have advocated for in this book refuses the purity politics involved in the catastrophic, crisis-laden sublime—that which signals a before and an after harm, and longs for a return to the state before. Instead, starting from Haraway's sense of response, and her commitment to a contingent real world, we might stay with the trouble of the ordinary. Haraway writes: "I experience becoming worldly as a process of nurturing attachment sites and sticky knots that emerge from the mundane and the ordinary" (Haraway 2008, 296). It may be that the scale and the possibility for response engendered in this space of the ordinary is very different than hyperobjects allow; neither is graspable or pure, but one might allow the kind of joy in daunting circumstances that allow us to work on changing the world.

Global warming is ordinary, chronic, and cruddy—it is more like the radiation emitted in the regular course of a reactor's life changing the bodies of the leaf bugs that Cornelia Hesse-Honegger draws than it is like the experience of a nuclear bomb. But it is also catastrophic, world-shaping, and hard to respond to in its entirety. As I have argued in thinking about distributed ethicality, opening freedom to others will always be a matter of ordinary activity in a world that is emergent in the sense of unfolding, unexpectable, nonlinear results. Global warming is one paradigm case for recognizing our entanglement, becoming overwhelmed, and defaulting to the kind of politics of despair that can result from recognizing that individual purity or actions aiming toward it are not going to solve the collective, complex problems in which we are differentially complicit. When we attempt to turn toward thinking about what's happening to the climate and the world, pretty quickly things get either very depressing or very confusing.

There are a lot of people responding to global warming, with pessimism and with hope, in daunting circumstances. Popular-science writer David Roberts offers this observation on forming social movements around climate:

> Maybe climate is so abstract and nonlinear, spread over such huge geographical and temporal distances, that the intellectual and emotional work required to fully apprehend it is simply out of reach for most ordinary people, living lives in the present, surrounded by people and problems that affect them directly. Maybe there just isn't enough *to* climate, enough emotional calories, to sustain a broad social movement focused directly on it. (Roberts 2015)

He suggests instead that everyone should have a "Climate Thing," a "close-by proxy through which they can express their climate concern in a way that has local effects and tangible rewards." This is a useful conception of the ways we can make of ourselves an attachment site, a sticky knot, for connecting to other people doing work they care about through work we care about. But staying with our own Climate Thing has limited output in setting specifically political goals. One of my favorite interventions in this tendency is a pamphlet called "Organizing Cools the Planet" (Kahn Russell and Moore 2011). This pamphlet begins from an antiracist environmental-justice model of climate justice, centrally recognizing that people experience more of the harm of global warming if they are living in poverty, or in nations that have been colonized—as they write, "climate change certainly doesn't affect everybody equally" (11). Kahn Russell and Moore offer the imperative to "*find your frontline.*" They say, "Figure out the material and systemic impact that climate change has on [you] and [your] community, name it, and get organized around it. Maybe that's where [you] should take action—and maybe not. Everyone has a frontline, but not all frontlines are equally strategic" (14).

And setting and evaluating what will count as strategic, aligning our front-line with collectively determined other frontlines, is political work based on explicit solidarity negotiation. Kahn Russell and Moore offer a quote widely attributed to Murri theorist and artist Lilla Watson, coming out of her work with other Aboriginal activists in the 1970s: "If you have come to help me, then you are wasting your time. But if you have come because your liberation is bound up with mine, then let us work together" (15). Solidarity work in this vein calls on us to lay out practical, concrete methods for assessing and practicing long-haul organizing toward climate justice.

Solidarity and collective strategic work open the space for the kind of distributed ethicality that I discussed in chapter 4, and call for an explicit conception of what it means to imagine a future and organize toward it. Turning toward politics involves turning purity aside—the differential implication and harm of global warming as an object for action means that individual action will never be sufficient to address what needs to be addressed. But this is the case for everything I've engaged in this book—the ongoing present and past of colonialism as a site for resistance, remembering the work and lives of activists of the past as we work in the present, crafting ways to respond to the changes pesticides and herbicides effect on bodies in the world, understanding ethical decisions resulting from our embodied being as distributed and political, and engaging speculative futures that can enact open normativities.

*Against Purity* has been *against*, but in its againstness I hope it has been clear that it is very much *for*—for optimism of the will in these profoundly pessimistic times, for collective determination of how to get on together, for staying with the trouble we're in. Aiming at individual purity can produce a seemingly satisfying self-righteousness in the scant moments we achieve it, but since it is ultimately impossible, aiming for purity will always disappoint. Orienting ourselves toward flourishing, toward the contingent proliferation of ways of being we cannot predict, toward surprise, opens us to the possibility that the world can go on. And sometimes this possibility is more challenging than the idea that the world is over. In the interviews I have been doing recently to gather some of the history of AIDS activism in the Canadian context, I have spoken to many people who have been living with AIDS for longer than twenty years. Many of them say that it was surprisingly hard to live after the arrival of antiretroviral drugs—both materially, since many of them had spent all of their savings, but also in more ephemeral ways encountered in suddenly having to project themselves into a less-bounded future. Frodo and Samwise might not expect to walk out of Mordor, and yet through trying anyhow they have a chance to make it through. To be against purity is to start from an understanding of our implication in this compromised world, to recognize the quite vast injustices informing our everyday lives, and from that understanding to act on our *wish that it were not so*. I believe that this orientation is at the heart of prefigurative, loving, social movement practices whose point is not only to interpret the world, but to change it. We cannot predict what might emerge from individual and collective practices of staying with the trouble, except that it holds the possibility of another world, still imperfect and impure, and another one after that. The possibility of other worlds, hospitable to hosting many worlds, might be beyond our capacity to imagine. Still, such a possibility can only arise because of our imperfect attempts to make it so.

# Acknowledgments

I am grateful for everyone who is caring about the world and working on moving things, bit by bit, away from devastation and toward unpredictable possibilities for life going on in general and in all its particularity. At a moment when it is sometimes hard to see the point of theoretical work, many people have reminded me that understanding the world is a necessary (but insufficient) condition for changing it. One important person was Sue Campbell, a beloved friend and mentor; in the last months of her life she read and responded to several chapters in this book, continuing a practice of critical nourishment that supported and sustained all of my academic work (though in retrospect I do sometimes wish she had hung out with her partner and dog instead of reading drafts). Her consistent injunction to me was to "think like a relational theorist," a complex imperative that I continue to try to work through. One pleasure of such thinking definitely includes thinking of all the people and places entangled in my efforts here to reflect on the ethical and political implications of being implicated and interdependent. And, in the spirit of impurity and imperfection, I will surely forget people in attempting to remember them all.

I thank all the colleagues and friends at the two institutions where I've been fortunate to teach while writing this book, Laurentian University and Carleton University, particularly those who have generously talked with me about this work: Patti Brace, Brett Buchanan, Marie-Eve Carriere-Moisan, Amrita Hari, Danielle Dinovelli-Lang, Stacy Douglas, Aaron Doyle, Patrizia Gentile, Peter Gose, Sheryl Hamilton, Laura Horak, Christine Koggel, Mike Mopas, Jen Ridgely, Megan Rivers-Moore, Janet Siltanen, and Zoe Todd.

Many of these folks have participated in our weekly writing group, in which Jackie Kennelly has been a particularly stalwart presence. Jeff Stewart at Pressed deserves a medal for welcoming our alternately cranky and elated crew to write in his space, and for feeding us. Lara Karaian's generous hosting of several writing retreats with easy access to a frog pond was invaluable; thanks also to Joe Pert and Sidney for welcoming a distracted writer into their home.

Parts of this book have been shared at the College of Charleston Department of Philosophy Colloquium Series, cosponsored by the Coastal Carolina Conservation League; the Radical Imagination Festival in Halifax, Nova Scotia; the Implizites Wissen zwischen Verkörperung und Explikation at FAU Erlangen-Nürnberg; the (Dis)ability?: Queer and Feminist Perspectives Workshop at the University of Alberta; the annual meetings of the Canadian Sociological Association, the Pacific American Philosophical Association, the Canadian Society for Women in Philosophy, and the Canadian Philosophical Association; and a philoSOPHIA conference. I thank participants in these conversations for generative questions and comments.

I love my dispersed but nourishing intellectual community, including Sarah LaChance Adams, Kelly Ball, Alexandre Baril, Kaili Beck, Bettina Bergo, Wilson Bell, Regan Brashear, Alissa Brock, Kami Chisholm, Jim Clifford, Shari Clough, Ryan Conrad, Karen de Vries, Mike Doan, Jane Dryden, Barbara Durward, Kelly Fritsch, Suze Gillian, Ruthie Wilson Gilmore, Adrianna María Garriga-López, Sonya Gray, Lisa Guenther, Lauren Guilmette, Candida Hadley, Max Haiven, Kim Q. Hall, Laura Hall, Eva Hayward, Adam Hefty, Cressida Heyes, Chris Hurl, Bryce Huebner, Lindsay Kelley, Chrissy Kelly, Sharmeen Khan, Alex Khasnabish, Katie King, Rebecca Kukla, Sha LaBare, Mark Norris Lance, Natalie Loveless, Shoshana Magnet, Alexander McClelland, Rachel V. McKinnon, Noel McLellan, Robert McRuer, Jake Metcalf, Sarah Clark Miller, Nick Mitchell, Leroy Moore, Anna Mudde, Robert Nichols, Kate Norlock, Kelly Oliver, Michael Orsini, Mireille Paquet, Danielle Peers, Katie Plaisance, Leslie Robertson, Trevor Sangrey, Jennifer Saul, Susan Sherwin, Sara Smith, Eric Stanley, Joshua St. Pierre, Cato Taylor, Chloe Taylor, Matt Tierney, Kathryn Trevanen, Anika Walke, Harlan Eugene Weaver, Kris Weller, Muhammad Velji, Kalindi Vora, Lesley Wood, and Katie Yates.

Graduate students with whom I've worked at Carleton have been wonderful interlocutors. I've appreciated thinking with Fiona Cheung, Ryan Couling, Kristen Gilchrist, Louisa Hawkins, Abigail Kidd, Janna Klostermann,

Priscillia Lefebvre, Lindsey Mckay, Kevin Partridge, Christine Pich, Sarah Rodimon, Melinda Spry, Benjamin Todd, Kathryn Van Meyl, and Jenelle Williams, as well as others in graduate classes over the last three years. Conversations about their projects have enriched my thinking. My doctoral student Blake MacMillan died suddenly in May 2016, on the cusp of completing a beautiful dissertation on emergence, disability, and the sport imaginary. Conversations with him always surprised and engaged me; he was an important interlocutor as I wrote this book and I grieve his loss.

The social and material contexts in which writing happens matter a lot. At an early stage of this writing I moved to my current home, on unceded and unsurrendered Algonquin land; I thank the multiple historical and current custodians of this place for their ongoing resistance to colonialism, which in the context of Turtle Island, I believe, opens the best chance all of us have for living responsibly toward different futures. I am grateful for financial support from Carleton University, in the form of a start-up research grant and a professional development yearly allowance. And I recognize that I would not have these things were it not for the ongoing work of my union, CUASA, which has negotiated much more livable work worlds than I would have as an individual worker. I acknowledge also that having access to research time and money is itself embedded in a context I abhor, the systemic unequal extraction of labor power from precariously employed contingent faculty and graduate-student instructors and the unjust tuition levied from undergraduate students. May we continue to struggle for the possibility that everyone in the academy—staff, teachers, and students—might have supported time for learning, thinking, and writing. I am grateful to Marlene Brancato, Kim Mitchell, Karen Tucker, Paula Whissell, and Kaitlin Barkley, who keep the Department of Sociology and Anthropology running with grace and good humor; they always make my life much easier.

Doug Armato has been a fabulous editor, seeing potential in this project when it was just beginning, asking the right questions at key points, and shepherding it beautifully through the process of review and publication. I thank him, and with him Erin Warholm-Wohlenhaus and everyone else at the University of Minnesota Press for their care and work to bring out scholarly work that is invested in the world. I am also grateful for the meticulous and generous comments from the anonymous readers of two drafts of the manuscript; this kind of academic labor is incredibly important, unrecognized, and time-intensive. These readers helped the book enormously. Cherene

Holland's copyediting was both precise and encouraging, and I thank her for polishing the text. I thank Muhammad Velji for preparing the index.

Donna Haraway and Anna Tsing co-taught a class ten years ago that I was fortunate to audit; the orientation I take here came from the seed of generative discussions in that class, and I am lucky to have been able to continue to benefit from listening to their thinking and their ongoing conversations from afar in the years since. Angela Davis's philosophical and political mentorship continues to inform, at every step, the way I think about liberation, and I thank her so much.

Many dear friends are woven into this book. Thanks to Idit Agam, Clare Bayard, Dan Berger, Alex Bourne, Sumner Bradley, Marta Brunner, Jessica Carlisle, Daniel Cayley-Daoust, Irina Ceric, Megan Dailey, Barbara Epstein, Owen Gourley, Emily Millay Haddad, Judy Halebsky, Joseph Lapp, Alice MacLachlan, Heidi Mecklenburg, Alexandra Milsom, Peter Murray, Scott Neigh, Michelle O'Brien, Bridget Paule, Rick Paule, Katja Pettinen, Chanda Prescod-Weinstein, Anna Purcell, Maia Ramnath, Ted Rutland, Dan Sawyer, John Sell, Jan Sutherland, Shannon Wilmott, and Amanda Wilson. I am grateful for Jim Maughn's generosity in thinking with me about frogs and other parts of the world, and I look forward to more walks with him and Jessica Breheny, even though we live so far apart. More people than I can name in the Shambhala community, both here in Ottawa and all over the world, have been important friends and comrades on the path of imagining a different world. I thank Chögyam Trungpa, Pema Chödron, and especially Sakyong Mipham for dedicating their lives to being thoroughly unconventional.

I treasure my family, given and chosen. My parents, Hudson Burr Shotwell and Janet Moe Shotwell, my siblings Vivien Shotwell and Gordon Shotwell, Anna Weinstein, Cadence, James Kimmitt Rowe, Trudi Lynn Smith, Gary Kinsman, Patrick Barnholden, Mike Barnholden-Kinsman, Scout Calvert, Nora Madden, and Ursula Sycamore Madden Calvert have all helped me understand what it means to organize a life toward creating worlds in which everyone can live with dignity and joy. I am delighted to be in kin relations with these wonderful writers, thinkers, gardeners, makers, and people it is good to sit with. My mom copyedited the entire final draft of the book with amazing patience, catching entirely different writing tics than she caught in my last book, and helping craft much better sentences. Phone conversations and too-rare time in person with Ada Jaarsma have been a lifeline inseparably intellectual and emotional, and an enactment of the most nourishing form of friendship I know. Ami Harbin read the entire manuscript at a particularly challenging moment and offered both ontological and practical help; I am more grateful than I can say for her steady and sparky brilliance in my life. And finally, I lift up my partner in life and troublemaking, Chris Dixon, whose tremendous heart, luminous mind, fierce commitment to another politics in all its complexity, and irreverent joy inspire me every day.

# Notes

## 1. Remembering for the Future

1. David Spurr's book *The Rhetoric of Empire: Colonial Discourse in Journalism, Travel Writing, and Imperial Administration* compellingly makes the case that classificatory work is central to the rhetorical and discursive practice of colonial power. Spurr focuses on classifications of whole societies, arguing that "the classification of indigenous peoples according to their relative complexity of social organization becomes more systematic and articulated as it directly serves the interests of colonial administration" (Spurr 1993, 68).

2. I have been particularly inspired by the work of the Native Youth Sexual Health Network, http://nativeyouthsexualhealth.com/.

3. For more on these contexts, see Ward Churchill, *Kill the Indian, Save the Man: The Genocidal Impact of American Indian Residential Schools* (San Francisco: City Lights, 2004); A. Dirk Moses, ed., *Genocide and Settler Society: Frontier Violence and Stolen Indigenous Children in Australian History* (New York: Berghahn Books, 2005); Margaret D. Jacobs, *White Mother to a Dark Race: Settler Colonialism, Maternalism, and the Removal of Indigenous Children in the American West and Australia, 1880–1940* (Lincoln: University of Nebraska Press, 2009).

4. I have benefited from Stacy Douglas's important work on museums and the politics of institutionalizing memory (Douglas 2011).

## 2. "Women Don't Get AIDS, They Just Die From It"

1. See Mol 2002; Fleck 2012; Kuriyama 2002.

2. A surveillance case definition, as the CDC puts it, is a "set of uniform criteria used to define a disease for public health surveillance. Case definitions enable public health to classify and count cases consistently across reporting jurisdictions" (CDC 2013). The surveillance definition of AIDS is the way that entities like the CDC count who has AIDS. This counting affects funding decisions, access to disability benefits, and more. Before the definition changed in 1993, it did not include some of the

211

criteria that are now commonsensical. For example, it did not include T4-cell/CD4 counts, tracking white blood cells that help the body fight infections. This meant that in the United States in 1991 a person diagnosed as having HIV could have twenty CD4 cells per microliter of blood (normal values being 500–1200 cells per microliter) and never be diagnosed with AIDS. Thus doctors would not treat them for AIDS, they would not be counted as having AIDS, and they could never receive social and financial support for living with the illness. As I describe above, the case definition of AIDS was an important political situation, and changing it had profound effects.

3. See also Deborah Gould's important book *Moving Politics,* particularly chapter 6, "Solidarity and Its Fracturing."

4. Lisa Diedrich beautifully formulates a Foucauldian approach to the moment I discuss here in her article "Doing Queer Love: Feminism, AIDS, and History" (Diedrich 2007).

5. As Rashad Shabazz eloquently demonstrates, U.S. prisons continue to be a site at which AIDS deaths are distributed along lines of class and race (Shabazz 2012). See also Cohen 1998; Geary 2014.

6. On this, Steven Epstein usefully reflects on Gena Corea's book *The Invisible Epidemic: The Story of Women and AIDS*, focusing on the gender dynamics of women's exclusion from clinical trials and their epidemiological effects (Epstein 1998, 7:288–89).

## 3. Shimmering Presences

1. This phrasing is Eva Hayward's (2014).

2. See also Jasanoff 2004.

3. Karrie Higgins's beautiful memoir-theory work examines the complexity of such coconstitution, evocatively asking how the atmosphere we breathe becomes part of us. "The Bottle City of God," *Cincinnati Review* 11, no. 1 (Summer 2014).

4. There are too many interesting civilian science projects to list, covering a wide array of critters and their ecosystems. Scout Calvert has begun fascinating work on how data-capture can interact with people observing their world, and on "open data" movements to harness this collection; she is thinking an array of projects ranging from monitoring waterways in LA (http://scienceland.wikispaces.com/LARiver), to Beatriz da Costa's project using pigeons carrying sensors for tracking air pollution documented at "PigeonBlog" (https://mutamorphosis.wordpress.com/2008/10/03/pigeonblog/), to projects on health data management. *Scientific American* has a channel devoted to "Citizen Science," http://www.scientificamerican.com/citizen-science/.

5. I thank Sha LaBare for encouraging me to think about this book, and this section of it.

## 4. Consuming Suffering

1. This phrasing is Jake Metcalf's.

## 5. Practicing Freedom

1. I transpose this concept from certain Marxist debates, particularly around the "determinism-voluntarism" line. Antonio Gramsci (voluntarism, 1972) and V. I. Lenin

(determinism, [1902] 1961, available via the Marxists Internet Archive at http://www.marxists.org/archive/) are sometimes understood as two ends of this continuum.

2. In thinking about relational self-formation, I draw especially on feminist theories of relationality (Baier 1985; Held 1993; Babbitt 1996, 2001; Campbell 1998; Bartky 2002; Brison 2002).

3. Key writings on the troubles with hetero- and homonormativity include Warner (2000) and Duggan (2003).

4. As I write, conversations about antinormativity are sweeping the very small section of the queer Internet that cares about these things as Lisa Duggan and Jack Halberstam formulate responses to a special issue of *differences* (26, no. 1 [May 2015]): "Queer Theory without Antinormativity." Edited by Robyn Wiegman and Elizabeth A. Wilson, this issue centers around the idea that, as Wiegman and Wilson write in their introduction, "Antinormativity is antinormative, then, in a way that it presumably does not intend: it turns systemic play (differentiations, comparisons, valuations, attenuations, skirmishes) into unforgiving rules and regulations and so converts the complexity of moving athwart into the much more anodyne notion of moving against. In ways the field has yet to address, queer antinormativity generates and protects the very propriety it claims to despise" (Wiegman and Wilson 2015, 18). Duggan and Halberstam disagree. In this chapter I am not centrally engaging this debate.

5. I thank Sue Campbell for helping me formulate this point.

6. I am thinking, for example, of Raymond (1979), Mantilla (2000), and Jeffreys (2002), though I believe these views are perhaps more prevalent in the ephemera of the radical feminist blogosphere. I have cowritten a chapter examining this phenomenon (Shotwell and Sangrey 2009).

7. In these critiques, there is very little mention of how non-trans or cisgender people's gender enactments themselves support gender oppression by colluding with dominant norms or assuming too much individual freedom.

8. C. B. Macpherson's book *The Political Theory of Possessive Individualism* (1962) was an early critique of the roots and effects of possessive individualism, which he saw as the theory that individuals possess their bodies and skills in ways that owe nothing to society, and that they can therefore sell their capacities on the open market in order to access consumable resources. George Lipsitz's *Possessive Investment in Whiteness* (1998) looks at U.S. white racial formation in these terms, and Gyatri Spivak's article "Three Women's Texts and a Critique of Imperialism" (1985) offered an important early reading of the connection between possessive individualism and imperialism.

9. For the origins of individual-freedom tropes in trans advocacy, see Meyerowitz (2002).

10. SRLP has a truly impressive infrastructure, rare on the left, of both staff workers and collective members. They are remarkably transparent about their practices, as exemplified by their thirty-nine-page Collective Member Handbook, http://srlp.org/files/collective%20handbook%202009.pdf.

11. I follow Chris Dixon and Douglas Lloyd Bevington (2005) in conceiving of this kind of theoretical work as "movement generated theory."

12. Paisley Currah and Lisa Jean Moore (2009) analyze the history and effects of this regulation in their recent article, "'We Won't Know Who You Are'; Contesting Sex Designations in New York City Birth Certificates."

13. New York City Board of Health, "Board of Health Makes NYC Consistent with New York State and Most of the United States by Allowing Sex-Specific Transgender Birth Certificates," press release, December 5, 2006, http://www.nyc.gov/html/doh/html/pr2006/pr115-06.shtml.

14. There is, too, the usual commitment to conventions of legible gender expressions, bolstered by the machine that aims to turn out DSM-IV-appropriate transsexuals: psycho-medico-technics of gender, which here refers to the medical, psychiatric, psychological, endocrinological, surgical, plastic surgical, urological alliance that produces appropriate "converted" men and women.

15. Dance collectives involving disabled dancers include Propeller Dance, in Ontario; the AXIS Dance Company, in California; ILL-Abilities, based in Montreal with members from Canada, the United States, and Chile; Dancing Wheels, in Ohio; Restless Dance Company, in Adelaide, Australia; and Rolling Dancers, in Germany.

16. Though it is notable, especially given this book's earlier worry about the dangers of human exceptionalism, that here as elsewhere the subject of human rights is unevenly situated in relation to critiques of grounding rights in access to humanity. The question of how to pursue disability justice in its entanglement with nonhuman-exceptionalism remains a live one.

17. This is the group's tagline, reading in full, "an unashamed claim to beauty in the face of invisibility." See Sins Invalid's website, http://www.sinsinvalid.org/.

18. See links to this type of dance at http://www.maori.org.nz/waiata/.

## 6. Worlds to Come

1. Patrul Rinpoche goes on to detail the other sufferings: birth, old age, sickness, and death, along with getting things you don't want, not getting things you do want, meeting people you don't like, and not meeting people you do like.

2. I was born on traditional Ute and Arapahoe territory, present-day Colorado, close to one of the sites of a horrific massacre from the "Indian Wars," Sandy Creek. My family moved to K'jipuktuk, Mi'kma'ki (Halifax, Nova Scotia), unceded Mi'Kmaq territory, as part of a Buddhist migration, when I was a teenager. I have lived in Anishnaabeg territories for the last ten years, currently on unceded Algonquin territory. I identify as a settler oriented toward decolonizing possibilities, which means that I understand myself to be in a continuing relation of responsibility for the past I inherit and toward a different future. Central to my identification is the belief that it is possible for me to listen to, learn from, and be in solidarity with Indigenous people without trying to become Indigenous myself. This is an epistemic orientation in that I believe there are many things I cannot and do not need to know about spiritual traditions and lifeways that are not my own.

3. See Allen 2013.

# Bibliography

Adelsberg, Geoffrey, Lisa Guenther, and Scott Zeman. 2015. *Death and Other Penalties: Philosophy in a Time of Mass Incarceration*. New York: Oxford University Press.

Ah-King, Malin, and Eva Hayward. 2014. "Perverting Pollution and Queering Hormone Disruption." *O-Zone: A Journal of Object-Oriented Studies*, no. 1: Object/Ecology, http://o-zone-journal.org/s/01_Toxic-Sexes_FINAL.pdf.

Ahmed, Sarah. 2006. *Queer Phenomenology: Orientations, Objects, Others*. Durham: Duke University Press.

Airton, Liz. 2009. "From Sexuality (Gender) to Gender (Sexuality): The Aims of Anti-homophobia Education." *Sex Education* 9, no. 2:129–39.

Alfred, Taiaiake. 2000. *Wasáse Indigenous Pathways of Action and Freedom*. Toronto: University of Toronto Press.

Alfred, Taiaiake, and Jeff Corntassel. 2005. "Being Indigenous: Resurgences against Contemporary Colonialism." *Government and Opposition* 40, no. 4:597–614. doi:10.1111/j.1477-7053.2005.00166.x.

Allen, Kathryn, ed. 2013. *Disability in Science Fiction: Representations of Technology as Cure*. New York: Palgrave Macmillan.

Aristotle. 2002. *Nicomachean Ethics*. Edited by C. J. Rowe and Sarah Broadie. New York: Oxford University Press.

Associated Press. 2014. "Fukushima Farmers Appeal to Tokyo with Live Bull." *Mail Online*. June 20, http://www.dailymail.co.uk/wires/ap/article-2663401/Fukushima-farmers-appeal-Tokyo-live-bull.html.

Aviv, Rachel. 2014. "A Valuable Reputation." *The New Yorker*. February 3, http://www.newyorker.com/magazine/2014/02/10/a-valuable-reputation.

Babbitt, Susan E. 1996. *Impossible Dreams: Rationality, Integrity, and Moral Imagination*. Boulder, Colo.: Westview Press.

———. 2001. *Artless Integrity: Moral Imagination, Agency, and Stories*. Lanham, Md.: Rowman & Littlefield.

Baier, Annette. 1985. *Postures of the Mind: Essays on Mind and Morals*. Minneapolis: University of Minnesota Press.

Banzhaf, Marion. Interview by Sarah Schulman, interview #070, April 18, 2007, transcript. ACT UP Oral History Project, New York.

Barad, Karen M. 2007. *Meeting the Universe Halfway: Quantum Physics and the Entanglement of Matter and Meaning*. Durham: Duke University Press.

Bartky, Sandra Lee. 2002. *"Sympathy and Solidarity" and Other Essays*. Lanham, Md.: Rowman & Littlefield.

Beauvoir, Simone de. 1968. *The Ethics of Ambiguity*. Trans. Bernard Frechtman. Originally published c. 1948. New York: Citadel.

Ben-Moshe, Liat, Che Gossett, Nick Mitchell, and Eric A. Stanley. 2015. "Critical Theory, Queer Resistance, and the Ends of Capture." In *Death and Other Penalties: Philosophy in a Time of Mass Incarceration*. Edited by Geoffrey Adelsberg, Lisa Guenther, and Scott Zeman, 266–95. New York: Oxford University Press.

Bennett, Jane. 2010. *Vibrant Matter: A Political Ecology of Things*. Durham: Duke University Press.

Bernasconi, Robert. 2000. *The Idea of Race*. Indianapolis: Hackett.

Biss, Eula. 2014. *On Immunity: An Inoculation*. Minneapolis: Graywolf Press.

Boisvert, Raymond. 2010. "Convivialism: A Philosophical Manifesto." *The Pluralist* 5, no. 2:57–68. doi:10.5406/pluralist.5.2.0057.

Bordowitz, Gregg. Interview by Sarah Schulman, interview #004, December 17, 2002, transcript. ACT UP Oral History Project, New York.

Bowker, Geoffrey C., and Susan Leigh Star. 1999. *Sorting Things Out: Classification and Its Consequences*. Cambridge, Mass.: MIT Press.

Brison, Susan. 2002. *Aftermath: Violence and the Remaking of a Self*. Princeton: Princeton University Press.

Butler, Judith. 1989. *Gender Trouble: Feminism and the Subversion of Identity*. New York: Routledge.

———. 2004. *Undoing Gender*. New York: Routledge.

Butler, Octavia E. 1976. *Patternmaster*. Garden City, N.Y.: Doubleday.

———. 1978a. *Mind of My Mind*. New York: Avon Books.

———. 1978b. *Survivor*. Garden City, N.Y.: Doubleday.

———. 1984. *Clay's Ark*. New York: St. Martin's Press.

———. 1987. *Xenogenesis*. [New York?]: Guild America Books.

———. 1998. *Parable of the Talents: A Novel*. New York: Seven Stories Press.

———. 2003. *Kindred*. Boston: Beacon Press.

———. 2005. *Bloodchild and Other Stories*. 2nd ed. New York: Seven Stories Press.

Campbell, Sue. 1998. *Interpreting the Personal: Expression and the Formation of Feelings*. Ithaca: Cornell University Press.

———. 2003. *Relational Remembering: Rethinking the Memory Wars*. Lanham, Md.: Rowman & Littlefield.

———. 2014. *Our Faithfulness to the Past: The Ethics and Politics of Memory*. Oxford: Oxford University Press.

Canguilhem, Georges. 1989. *The Normal and the Pathological*. New York: Zone Books.

Card, Claudia. 1996. *The Unnatural Lottery: Character and Moral Luck*. Philadelphia: Temple University Press.

Carlomusto, Jean. Interview by Sarah Schulman, interview #005, December 19, 2002, transcript. ACT UP Oral History Project, New York.

Castiglia, Christopher, and Christopher Reed. 2011. *If Memory Serves: Gay Men, AIDS, and the Promise of the Queer Past*. Minneapolis: University of Minnesota Press.

CDC (Centers for Disease Control). 2007. "AIDS Surveillance in the United States." N.p., May 18, http://wonder.cdc.gov/wonder/help/aids.html.

———. 2013. "NNDSS Case Definitions Overview," http://www.cdc.gov/nndss/script/casedefDefault.aspx.

Chen, Mel Y. 2012. *Animacies: Biopolitics, Racial Mattering, and Queer Affect*. Durham: Duke University Press.

Churchill, Ward. 2004. *Kill the Indian, Save the Man: The Genocidal Impact of American Indian Residential Schools*. San Francisco: City Lights.

*CNN Report on Measles in Arizona*. 2015, https://www.youtube.com/watch?v=1Y79IFVtWms&feature=youtube_gdata_player.

Cohen, Cathy J. 1999. *The Boundaries of Blackness: AIDS and the Breakdown of Black Politics*. Chicago: University of Chicago Press.

Cohen, Peter F. 1998. *Love and Anger: Essays on AIDS, Activism, and Politics*. New York: Routledge.

Corber, Robert J., and Stephen M. Valocchi. 2003. *Queer Studies: An Interdisciplinary Reader*. Malden, Mass.: Blackwell.

Corcoran, Patricia L., Charles J. Moore, and Kelly Jazvac. 2014. "An Anthropogenic Marker Horizon in the Future Rock Record." *GSA Today*, June 4–8. doi:10.1130/GSAT-G198A.1.

Coulthard, Glen Sean. 2014. *Red Skin, White Masks: Rejecting the Colonial Politics of Recognition*. Minneapolis: University of Minnesota Press.

Cuomo, Chris J. 1998. *Feminism and Ecological Communities: An Ethic of Flourishing*. New York: Routledge.

Crawford, Robert. 1980. "Healthism and the Medicalization of Everyday Life." *International Journal of Health Services: Planning, Administration, Evaluation* 10, no. 3:365–88.

Currah, Paisley, and Lisa Jean Moore. 2009. "'We Won't Know Who You Are': Contesting Sex Designations in New York City Birth Certificates." *Hypatia* 24, no. 3:113–35.

Cvetkovich, Ann. 2003. *An Archive of Feelings: Trauma, Sexuality, and Lesbian Public Cultures*. Durham: Duke University Press.

Daschuk, James. 2013. *Clearing the Plains: Disease, Politics of Starvation, and the Loss of Aboriginal Life*. Regina, Saskatchewan: University of Regina Press.

Davis, Angela Y. 2012. *The Meaning of Freedom*. San Francisco: City Lights.

Davis, Lennard J. 2002. *Bending Over Backwards: Disability, Dismodernism, and Other Difficult Positions*. New York: New York University Press.

Delany, Samuel R. 1984. *Starboard Wine: More Notes on the Language of Science Fiction*. Pleasantville, N.Y.: Dragon Press.

———. 1988. *The Motion of Light in Water: Sex and Science Fiction Writing in the East Village, 1957–1965*. New York: New American Library.

*Democracy Now!* 2014. "Silencing the Scientist: Tyrone Hayes on Being Targeted by Herbicide Firm Syngenta." February 21, http://www.democracynow.org/2014/2/21/silencing_the_scientist_tyrone_hayes_on.

Dethlefsen, Les, Margaret McFall-Ngai, and David A. Relman. 2007. "An Ecological and Evolutionary Perspective on Human–Microbe Mutualism and Disease." *Nature* 449: 811–18. doi:10.1038/nature06245.

Di Chiro, Giovanna. 2010. "Polluted Politics? Confronting Toxic Discourse, Sex Panic, and Eco-Normativity." In *Queer Ecologies: Sex, Nature, Politics, Desire*. Edited by Catriona Mortimer-Sandilands and Bruce Erickson. Bloomington: Indiana University Press.

Diedrich, L. 2007. "Doing Queer Love: Feminism, AIDS, and History." *Theoria* 54, no. 112:25–50.

Dixon, Chris. 2014. *Another Politics: Talking across Today's Transformative Movements*. Berkeley: University of California Press.

Dixon, Chris, and Douglas Lloyd Bevington. 2005. "Movement-Relevant Theory: Rethinking Social Movement Scholarship and Activism." *Social Movement Studies* 4, no. 3:185–208.

Douglas, Mary. 1966. *Purity and Danger: An Analysis of the Concepts of Pollution and Taboo*. London: Routledge & Kegan Paul.

Douglas, Stacy. 2011. "Between Constitutional Mo(nu)ments: Memorialising Past, Present, and Future at the District Six Museum and Constitution Hill." *Law and Critique* 22, no. 2:171–87. doi:10.1007/s10978-011-9083-4.

Dorow, Heidi. Interview by Sarah Schulman, interview #069, April 17, 2007, transcript. ACT UP Oral History Project, New York.

Duggan, Jennifer. 2013. "China's Coal Emissions Responsible for 'Quarter of a Million Premature Deaths.'" *The Guardian*, December 12, sec. Environment. http://www.theguardian.com/environment/2013/dec/12/china-coal-emissions-smog-deaths.

Duggan, Lisa. 2003. *The Twilight of Equality? Neoliberalism, Cultural Politics, and the Attack on Democracy*. Boston: Beacon Press.

Dunbar-Ortiz, Roxanne. 2008. "The Opposite of Truth Is Forgetting: An Interview with Roxanne Dunbar-Ortiz by Chris Dixon." *Upping the Anti* 6 (May): 47–58.

Edelman, Lee. 2004. *No Future: Queer Theory and the Death Drive*. Durham: Duke University Press.

Epstein, Barbara. 1991. *Political Protest and Cultural Revolution: Nonviolent Direct Action in the Seventies and Eighties*. Berkeley: University of California Press.

Epstein, Steven. 1998. *Impure Science: AIDS, Activism, and the Politics of Knowledge*. Berkeley: University of California Press.

Eze, Emmanuel Chukwudi, ed. 1997. *Race and the Enlightenment: A Reader*. Cambridge, Mass.: Blackwell.

Fackler, Martin. 2014. "Defying Japan, Rancher Saves Fukushima's Radioactive Cows." *New York Times*, January 11, http://www.nytimes.com/2014/01/12/world/asia/defying-japan-rancher-saves-fukushimas-radioactive-cows.html.

Fausto-Sterling, Anne. 2000. *Sexing the Body: Gender Politics and the Construction of Sexuality*. New York: Basic Books.

Feinberg, Leslie. c. 1998. *Trans Liberation: Beyond Pink or Blue*. Boston: Beacon Press.

Ferguson, Roderick A. 2004. *Aberrations in Black: Toward a Queer of Color Critique*. Minneapolis: University of Minnesota Press.

Fingers, Anne. 2006. *Elegy for a Disease: A Personal and Cultural History of Polio*. New York: St. Martin's Press.

Fleck, Ludwik. 2012. *Genesis and Development of a Scientific Fact*. Chicago: University of Chicago Press.

Foucault, Michel. 1995. *Discipline and Punish: The Birth of the Prison*. New York: Vintage Books.

———. 2003. *Abnormal*. New York: Picador.

Geary, Adam M. 2014. *Antiblack Racism and the AIDS Epidemic: State Intimacies*. New York: Palgrave Macmillan.

Gilmore, Ruth Wilson. 2007. *Golden Gulag: Prisons, Surplus, Crisis, and Opposition in Globalizing California*. Berkeley: University of California Press.

Gordon, Avery F. 2004. *Keeping Good Time: Reflections on Knowledge, Power, and People*. Boulder, Colo.: Paradigm Publishers.

Gould, Deborah B. 2009. *Moving Politics: Emotion and ACT UP's Fight against AIDS*. Chicago: University of Chicago Press.

Gramsci, Antonio. 1972. *Selections from the Prison Notebooks of Antonio Gramsci*. Edited and translated by Quintin Hoare and Geoffrey Nowell Smith. New York: International Publishers.

Greater Sudbury. 2015. "FrogFind," http://www.greatersudbury.ca/living/environmental-initiatives/biodiversity/citizen-ecological-surveys/frogfind/.

Grebowicz, Margret, Helen Merrick, and Donna J. Haraway. 2013. "Sowing Worlds: A Seed Bag for Terraforming with Earth Others." In *Beyond the Cyborg: Adventures with Donna Haraway*. New York: Columbia University Press.

Guthman, Julie. 2011. *Weighing In: Obesity, Food Justice, and the Limits of Capitalism*. Berkeley: University of California Press.

Hall, Kim Q. 2014. "Toward a Queer Crip Feminist Politics of Food." *philoSOPHIA* 4, no. 2:177–96.

Halperin, David M. 1995. *Saint Foucault: Towards a Gay Hagiography*. New York: Oxford University Press.

Hammers, Corie J. 2010. "Corporeal Silences and Bodies That Speak: The Promises and Limitations of Queer in Lesbian/Queer Sexual Spaces." In *Transgender*

*Identities: Towards a Social Analysis of Gender Diversity*. Edited by Sally Hines and Tam Sanger, 224–40. New York: Routledge.

Hankard, Michael. 2014. *Access, Clocks, Blocks, and Stocks: Resisting Health Canada's Management of Traditional Medicine*. Vernon, B.C.: J. Charlton Publishing.

Hanson, F. Allan. 2009. "Beyond the Skin Bag: On the Moral Responsibility of Extended Agencies." *Ethics and Information Technology* 11, no. 1:91–99. doi:10.1007/s10676-009-9184-z.

Haraway, Donna J. 1989. *Primate Visions: Gender, Race, and Nature in the World of Modern Science*. East Sussex, UK: Psychology Press.

———. 1991. *Simians, Cyborgs, and Women: The Re-invention of Nature*. New York: Routledge & Kegan Paul.

———. 2008. *When Species Meet*. Minneapolis: University of Minnesota Press.

Harvey, Mark, Stephen Quilley, and Huw Beynon. 2003. *Exploring the Tomato: Transformations of Nature, Society, and Economy*. Cheltenham, UK: Edward Elgar Publishing.

Hayes, Tyrone. n.d. "Biography," http://www.atrazinelovers.com/t1.html.

Hayward, Eva. "When Fish and Frogs Change Gender." *Indy Week*, http://www.indyweek.com/indyweek/when-fish-and-frogs-change-gender/Content?oid=2626271.

Held, Virgina. 1993. *Feminist Morality: Transforming Culture, Society, and Politics*. Chicago: University of Chicago Press.

Heldke, Lisa. 2012. "An Alternative Ontology of Food: Beyond Meataphysics." *Radical Philosophy Review* 15, no. 1:67–88.

Heyes, Cressida. 2007. *Self Transformations: Foucault, Ethics, and Normalized Bodies*. New York: Oxford University Press.

Hird, Myra J. 2009. *The Origins of Sociable Life: Evolution after Science Studies*. New York: Palgrave Macmillan.

———. 2013. "Waste, Landfills, and an Environmental Ethic of Vulnerability." *Ethics and the Environment* 18, no. 1:105–24.

Hollibaugh, Amber L. 2000. *My Dangerous Desires: A Queer Girl Dreaming Her Way Home*. Durham: Duke University Press.

Holloway, John. 2010. *Change the World without Taking Power*. London: Pluto Press.

Hunter, Antoine (dancer), and Cara Page (emcee). 2009. Stage dance performance. Sins Invalid, 2009, http://sinsinvalid.org/video%20pages/2009_AntoineHunter_CaraPage.html.

Hutchins, Edwin. 1995. *Cognition in the Wild*. Cambridge, Mass.: MIT Press.

Imarisha, Walidah, and adrienne maree brown, eds. 2015. *Octavia's Brood: Science Fiction Stories from Social Justice Movements*. Oakland, Calif.: AK Press.

Invalid, Sins. 2010. "Our Mission," http://www.sinsinvalid.org/mission.html.

It Starts With Us. 2015. "Background." *Support for Missing and Murdered Indigenous Women and Their Families*, http://www.itstartswithus-mmiw.com/background.

———.a "Why a Community-Led Database?" 2015b. *Support for Missing and Murdered Indigenous Women and Their Families*, http://www.itstartswithus-mmiw.com/partners.

Jacobs, Margaret D. 2009. *White Mother to a Dark Race: Settler Colonialism, Maternalism, and the Removal of Indigenous Children in the American West and Australia, 1880–1940*. Lincoln: University of Nebraska Press.

Jagger, Alison. 1983. *Feminist Politics and Human Nature*. Totowa, N.J.: Rowman & Allanheld.

———. 1992. "Love and Knowledge: Emotion in Feminist Epistemology." In *Women, Knowledge, and Reality: Explorations in Feminist Philosophy*. Edited by Ann Garry and Marilyn Pearsall, 129–55. New York: Routledge.

Jasanoff, Sheila, ed. 2004. *States of Knowledge: The Co-production of Science and Social Order*. International Library of Sociology. New York: Routledge.

Johnson, Harriet McBryde. 2003. "Unspeakable Conversations." *New York Times*, February 16, Magazine, http://www.nytimes.com/2003/02/16/magazine/unspeakable-conversations.html.

———. 2006. *Too Late to Die Young: Nearly True Tales from a Life*. New York: Picador.

Kafer, Alison. 2013. *Feminist, Queer, Crip*. Bloomington: Indiana University Press.

Kahn Russell, Joshua, and Hilary Moore. 2011. "Organizing Cools the Planet." Oakland, Calif.: PM Press, http://www.mediafire.com/?celqaap1g6spwzj.

Kant, Immanuel. 1993. *Grounding for the Metaphysics of Morals; with "On a Supposed Right to Lie because of Philanthropic Concerns."* Translated by James W. Ellington. Indianapolis: Hackett.

———. 2000. *Critique of the Power of Judgment*. Cambridge Edition of the Works of Immanuel Kant. Cambridge: Cambridge University Press.

Kauanui, J. Kēhaulani. 2008. *Hawaiian Blood: Colonialism and the Politics of Sovereignty and Indigeneity*. Durham: Duke University Press.

Kawakami, Hiromi. 2012. "God Bless You, 2011." In *March Was Made of Yarn: Reflections on the Japanese Earthquake, Tsunami, and Nuclear Meltdown*. Translated by Ted Goossen and Motoyuki Shibata. New York: Vintage Books.

Kazumi, Saeki. 2012. "Hiroyama." In *March Was Made of Yarn: Reflections on the Japanese Earthquake, Tsunami, and Nuclear Meltdown*. Translated by Ted Goossen amd Motoyuki Shibata. New York: Vintage Books.

Keith, Lierre. 2009. *The Vegetarian Myth: Food, Justice, and Sustainability*. Crescent City, Calif.: PM Press.

Kier, Bailey. 2010. "Interdependent Ecological Transsex: Notes on Re/production, 'Transgender' Fish, and the Management of Populations, Species, and Resources." *Women & Performance: A Journal of Feminist Theory* 20, no. 3:299–319.

Kinsman, Gary, and Patrizia Gentile. 2010. *The Canadian War on Queers: National Security as Sexual Regulation*. Vancouver: University of British Columbia Press.

Korsgaard, Christine. 1996. *Sources of Normativity*. Cambridge: Cambridge University Press.

Kosuga, Tomo, Ivan Kovac, and Jeffrey Jousan. 2013. "Alone in the Zone | VICE | United States." Translated by Luke Baker. VICE. March 10, http://www.vice.com/video/radioactive-man.

Kuriyama, Shigehisa. 2002. *The Expressiveness of the Body and the Divergence of Greek and Chinese Medicine*. New York: Zone Books.

LaBare, Joshua. 2010. "Farfetchings: On and in the SF Mode." Ph.D. diss., University of California, Santa Cruz.

Law, John, Geir Afdal, Kristin Asdal, Wen-yuan Lin, Ingunn Moser, and Vicky Singleton. 2014. "Modes of Syncretism: Notes on Noncoherence." *Common Knowledge* 20, no. 1:172–92. doi:10.1215/0961754X-2374817.

Lawrence, Bonita. 2004. *"Real" Indians and Others: Mixed-Blood Urban Native Peoples and Indigenous Nationhood*. Vancouver: University of British Columbia Press.

Lenin, Vladimir Ilyich. 1902/1999. "What Is to Be Done?" Marxists Internet Archive, https://www.marxists.org.

Linton, Simi. 1998. *Claiming Disability: Knowledge and Identity*. New York: New York University Press.

Lipsitz, George. 1998. *Possessive Investment in Whiteness: How White People Profit from Identity Politics*. Philadelphia: Temple University Press.

*Living on Earth*. 2011. "Hormone Disruptors Linked to Genital Changes and Sexual Preference." Aired week of January 7. *Living on Earth*, http://loe.org/.

Loewe, B. 2011. "Interconnectedness Means Fight | B Is for Blog." December 16, https://bstandsforb.wordpress.com/2011/12/16/interconnectedness-means-fight/.

Longmore, Paul. 1995. "The Second Phase: From Disability Rights to Disability Culture," http://www.independentliving.org/docs3/longm95.html.

Lourie, Bruce, and Rick Smith. 2014. *Toxin Toxout: Getting Harmful Chemicals out of Our Bodies and Our World*. New York: St. Martin's Press.

Luciano, Dana. 2015. "The Inhuman Anthropocene." *Avidly*, http://avidly.lareviewof books.org/2015/03/22/the-inhuman-anthropocene/.

Lugones, María. 2003. *Pilgrimages/Peregrinajes: Theorizing Coalition against Multiple Oppressions*. Lanham, Md.: Rowman & Littlefield.

Macherey, Pierre. 2009. *De canguilhem à foucault: La force des normes*. Paris: La Fabrique éditions.

Macpherson, C. B. 1962. *The Political Theory of Possessive Individualism: Hobbes to Locke*. London: Oxford University Press.

Marx, Karl. 1975. "Economic and Philosophical Manuscripts." In *Early Writings*. London: Penguin Books.

Masco, Joseph. 2006. *The Nuclear Borderlands: The Manhattan Project in Post–Cold War New Mexico*. Princeton: Princeton University Press.

Mattilda, a.k.a Matt Bernstein Sycamore, ed. 2006. *Nobody Passes: Rejecting the Rules of Gender and Conformity*. Emeryville, Calif.: Seal Press.

McCaughey, Martha. 1996. "Perverting Evolutionary Narratives of Heterosexual Masculinity: Or, Getting Rid of the Heterosexual Bug." *GLQ: A Journal of Lesbian and Gay Studies* 3, nos. 2–3:261–87.

McFall-Ngai, Margaret J. 2014. "The Importance of Microbes in Animal Development: Lessons from the Squid-Vibrio Symbiosis." *Annual Review of Microbiology* 68: 177–94. doi:10.1146/annurev-micro-091313-103654.

McGovern, Terry. Interview by Sarah Schulman, interview #076, May 25, 2007, transcript. ACT UP Oral History Project, New York.

McRuer, Robert. 2006. *Crip Theory: Cultural Signs of Queerness and Disability*. New York: New York University Press.

McRuer, Robert, and Anna Mollow. 2012. *Sex and Disability*. Durham: Duke University Press.

McWhorter, Ladelle. 1999. *Bodies and Pleasures: Foucault and the Politics of Sexual Normalization*. Bloomington: Indiana University Press.

———. 2009. *Racism and Sexual Oppression in Anglo-America: A Genealogy*. Bloomington: Indiana University Press.

———. 2013. "Individuals, Corporate Persons, and Situated Selves." Conference presentation. Eugene, Ore.

Metcalf, Jacob. 2008. "Intimacy without Proximity: Encountering Griz as a Companion Species." *Environmental Philosophy* 5, no. 2:99–128.

Metzl, Jonathan M., and Anna Kirkland, eds. 2010. *Against Health: How Health Became the New Morality*. New York: New York University Press.

Mill, John Stuart. 2001. *Utilitarianism*. Edited by George Sher. Indianapolis: Hackett.

Mills, Charles W. 1998. *Blackness Visible: Essays on Philosophy and Race*. Ithaca: Cornell University Press.

———. 2007. "White Ignorance." In *Race and Epistemologies of Ignorance*. Edited by Shannon Sullivan and Nancy Tuana, 11–38. Albany: State University of New York Press.

Mol, Annemarie. 2002. *The Body Multiple: Ontology in Medical Practice*. Durham: Duke University Press.

Mollow, Anna. 2004. "Identity Politics and Disability Studies: A Critique of Recent Theory," http://hdl.handle.net/2027/spo.act2080.0043.218.

Monture-Angus, Patricia. 1995. *Thunder in My Soul: A Mohawk Woman Speaks*. Halifax: Fernwood.

———. 1999. *Journeying Forward: Dreaming First Nations' Independence*. Halifax: Fernwood.

Moore, Leroy (performer). 2006. Stage performance. Sins Invalid, 2006, http://sinsinvalid.org/video%20pages/2006_trailer.html.

Morton, Timothy. 2013. *Hyperobjects: Philosophy and Ecology after the End of the World*. Minneapolis: University of Minnesota Press.

Moses, A. Dirk, ed. 2005. *Genocide and Settler Society: Frontier Violence and Stolen Indigenous Children in Australian History*. New York: Berghahn Books.

Muñoz, José Esteban. 2009. *Cruising Utopia: The Then and There of Queer Futurity*. New York: New York University Press.

Murakami, Ryu. 2012. "Little Eucalyptus Leaves." In *March Was Made of Yarn: Reflections on the Japanese Earthquake, Tsunami, and Nuclear Meltdown*. Translated by Ted Goossen and Motoyuki Shibata. New York: Vintage Books.

Murphy, Michelle. 2013. "Distributed Reproduction, Chemical Violence, and Latency." *Scholar and Feminist Online* 11.

Myers, Diana Tietjens. 1989. *Self, Society, and Personal Choice*. New York: Routledge.

New York City Board of Health. 2006. "Board of Health Makes NYC Consistent with New York State and Most of the United States by Allowing Sex-Specific Trans-gender Birth Certificates," http://www.nyc.gov/html/doh/html/pr2006/pr115-06.shtml.

*Octavia Butler: Science Future, Science Fiction*. 2008, https://www.youtube.com/watch?v=IgeyVE3NHJM&feature=youtube_gdata_player.

Oliver, Kelly. 2013. *Animal Lessons: How They Teach Us to Be Human*. New York: Columbia University Press.

Omi, Michael, and Howard Winant. 1994. *Racial Formation in the United States: From the 1960s to the 1990s*. New York: Routledge.

Parker, Andrew, and Eve Kosofsky Sedgwick, eds. 1995. *Performativity and Performance: Essays from the English Institute*. New York: Routledge.

Patrul Rinpoche. 1994. *The Words of My Perfect Teacher*. San Francisco: Harper-Collins.

Paxson, Heather. 2008. "Post-Pasteurian Cultures: The Microbiopolitics of Raw-Milk Cheese in the United States." *Cultural Anthropology* 23, no. 1:15–47.

———. 2014. "Microbiopolitics." In *The Multispecies Salon*. Edited by Eben Kirksey. Durham: Duke University Press.

Paz, Abel. 2007. *Durruti in the Spanish Revolution*. Oakland, Calif.: AK Press.

PETA. 2015. "What PETA REALLY Stands For," http://www.peta.org/features/what-peta-really-stands-for/.

Peterson, Melody. 2009. "The Lost Boys of Aamjiwnaang." *@menshealthmag*. November 5, http://www.menshealth.com/health/industrial-pollution-health-hazards.

Philosophy. 2015. "Purity Made Simple | One-Step Facial Cleanser | Philosophy Cleansers," http://www.philosophy.com/facial-cleansers/purity-made-simple,en_US,pd.html?cgid=C111.

Piepzna-Samarasinha, Leah Lakshmi (performer). 2009. Stage performance. Sins Invalid, http://sinsinvalid.org/video%20pages/2009_Leah_Lakshmi3.html.

Porcher, Jocelyne. 2011. "The Relationship between Workers and Animals in the Pork Industry: A Shared Suffering." *Journal of Agricultural and Environmental Ethics* 24, no. 1:3–17.

Povinelli, Elizabeth A. 2011. *Economies of Abandonment: Social Belonging and Endurance in Late Liberalism*. Durham: Duke University Press.

Probyn, Elspeth. 1999. "An Ethos with a Bite: Queer Appetites from Sex to Food." *Sexualities* 2, no. 4:421–31. doi:10.1177/136346099002004003.

Puar, Jasbir. 2007. *Terrorist Assemblages: Homonationalism in Queer Times*. Durham: Duke University Press.

Pure Yoga Ottawa. 2015. "Discover Pure Yoga Ottawa," http://pureyogaottawa.com/#home.

Raffles, Hugh. 2011. *Insectopedia*. New York: Vintage Books.

Ramspacher, Karen. Interview by Sarah Schulman, interview #094, July 13, 2008, transcript. ACT UP Oral History Project, New York.

Rankine, Claudia. 2014. *Citizen: An American Lyric*. Minneapolis: Graywolf Press.

Regan, Paulette. 2010. *Unsettling the Settler Within: Indian Residential Schools, Truth Telling, and Reconciliation in Canada.* Vancouver: University of British Columbia Press.

Regan, Tom. 2004. *The Case for Animal Rights.* Berkeley: University of California Press.

Relyea, Rick A. 2012. "New Effects of Roundup on Amphibians: Predators Reduce Herbicide Mortality; Herbicides Induce Antipredator Morphology." *Ecological Applications* 22, no. 2:634–47. doi:10.1890/11-0189.1.

Roberts, David. 2015. "Everybody Needs a Climate Thing." Grist. April 6, http://grist.org/climate-energy/everybody-needs-a-climate-thing/.

Rose, Deborah Bird. 2011. *Wild Dog Dreaming: Love and Extinction.* Under the Sign of Nature: Explorations in Ecocriticism. Charlottesville: University of Virginia Press.

Sandahl, Carrie, and Philip Auslander. 2005. *Bodies in Commotion: Disability and Performance.* Afterword by Peggy Phelan. Ann Arbor: University of Michigan Press.

Scheman, Naomi. 1996. "Queering the Center by Centering the Queer: Reflections on Transsexuals and Secular Jews." In *Feminists Rethink the Self.* Edited by D. T. Meyers. Boulder, Colo.: Westview Press.

Schmidt, Jeff. 2001. *Disciplined Minds: A Critical Look at Salaried Professionals and the Soul-Battering System That Shapes Their Lives.* Lanham, Md.: Rowman & Littlefield.

Schrader, Astrid. n.d. "Abyssal Intimacies and Temporalities of Care: How (Not) to Care about Deformed Leaf Bugs in the Aftermath of Chernobyl." Manuscript.

Schulman, Sarah. 2003. "Statements." May 12, 2003, http://www.actuporalhistory.org/about/statements.html.

Shabazz, Rashad. 2012. "Mapping Black Bodies for Disease: Prisons, Migration, and Politics of HIV/AIDS." In *Beyond Walls and Cages: Prisons, Borders, and Global Crisis.* Edited by Jenna M. Loyd, Matt Mitchelson, and Andrew Burridge. Athens: University of Georgia Press, http://site.ebrary.com/id/10621793.

Sherwin, Susan. 2009. "Whither Bioethic?: How Feminism Can Help Reorient Bioethics." *International Journal of Feminist Approaches to Bioethics* 1, no. 1:7–27.

Shotwell, Alexis. 2013. "Aspirational Solidarity as Bioethical Norm: The Case of Reproductive Justice." *International Journal of Feminist Approaches to Bioethics* 6, no. 1:103–20. doi:10.2979/intjfemappbio.6.1.103.

Silva, Denise Ferreira da. 2007. *Toward a Global Idea of Race.* Minneapolis: University of Minnesota Press.

Simpson, Leanne. 2008. *Lighting the Eighth Fire: The Liberation, Resurgence, and Protection of Indigenous Nations.* Winnipeg: Arbeiter Ring Publishing.

Simpson, Leanne, and Kiera Ladner. 2010. *This Is an Honour Song: Twenty Years since the Blockades.* Winnipeg: Arbeiter Ring Publishing.

Singer, Peter. 2002. *Animal Liberation.* New York: Ecco Books.

Sins Invalid. 2009a. "About Us: Our Mission." Sins Invalid, San Francisco, http://www.sinsinvalid.org/mission.html.

————. 2009b. "About Us: Our Vision." Sins Invalid, San Francisco. http://www.sin sinvalid.org/vision.html.

Smith, Andrea. 2005. *Conquest: Sexual Violence and American Indian Genocide.* Brooklyn, N.Y.: South End Press.

————. 2007. "Soul Wound: The Legacy of Native American Schools." *Amnesty International Magazine*, March 26.

Smith, Owen. 2005. "Shifting Apollo's Frame: Challenging the Body Aesthetic in Theater Dance." In *Bodies in Commotion: Disability and Performance.* Edited by Carrie Sandahl and Philip Auslander, 73–85. Ann Arbor: University of Michigan Press.

Spade, Dean. 2004. "Once More . . . with Feeling." In *From the Inside Out: Radical Gender Transformation, FTM, and Beyond.* Edited by Morty Diamond. San Francisco: Manic D Press.

————. 2006. "Mutilating Gender." In *The Transgender Studies Reader.* Edited by Susan Stryker and Stephen Whittle, 315–32. New York: Routledge, 2006.

————. 2011. *Normal Life: Administrative Violence, Critical Trans Politics, and the Limits of Law.* Brooklyn, N.Y.: South End Press.

Spelman, Elizabeth. 1989. "Anger and Insubordination." In *Women, Knowledge, and Reality: Explorations in Feminist Philosophy.* Edited by Ann Garry and Marilyn Pearsall, 263–74. New York: Routledge.

Spurr, David. 1993. *The Rhetoric of Empire: Colonial Discourse in Journalism, Travel Writing, and Imperial Administration.* Durham: Duke University Press.

SRLP (Sylvia Rivera Law Project). 2010a. "About." Mission Statement. Sylvia Rivera Law Project, New York, http://srlp.org/about.

————. 2010b. "Collective Structure." Sylvia Rivera Law Project, New York, http://srlp.org/about/collective.

————. 2010c. "The Fight for Fair Access to Birth Certificates Continues." Sylvia Rivera Law Project, New York. http://srlp.org/node/89.

————. 2010d. "New York City Birth Certificate Policy." Sylvia Rivera Law Project, New York, http://srlp.org/new-york-city-birth-certificate-policy.

Steedman, Mercedes, Peter Suschnigg, and Dieter K. Buse. 1995. *Hard Lessons: The Mine Mill Union in the Canadian Labour Movement.* Toronto: Dundurn Press.

Steingraber, Sandra. 2010. *Living Downstream: An Ecologist's Personal Investigation of Cancer and the Environment.* Cambridge, Mass.: Da Capo Press.

Sterritt, Angela. 2010. "Sisters in Spirit Smothered." *The Dominion*, December 13, http://www.dominionpaper.ca/articles/3764.

Stryker, Susan, and Stephen Whittle, eds. 2006. *The Transgender Studies Reader.* New York: Routledge.

Sullivan, Shannon, and Nancy Tuana. 2007. *Race and Epistemologies of Ignorance.* Albany: State University of New York Press.

Sycamore, Mattilda Bernstein. 2006. *Nobody Passes: Rejecting the Rules of Gender and Conformity.* Emeryville, Calif.: Seal Press.

TallBear, Kimberly. 2013. *Native American DNA: Tribal Belonging and the False Promise of Genetic Science*. Minneapolis: University of Minnesota Press.

Terry, Jennifer. 2000. "'Unnatural Acts' in Nature: The Scientific Fascination with Queer Animals." *GLQ: A Journal of Lesbian and Gay Studies* 6, no. 2:151–93.

Thích, Nhất Hạnh, and Peter Levitt. 1988. *The Heart of Understanding: Commentaries on the Prajñaparamita Heart Sutra*. Berkeley: Parallax Press.

Treichler, Paula A. 1999. *How to Have Theory in an Epidemic: Cultural Chronicles of AIDS*. Durham: Duke University Press.

Truth and Reconciliation Commission of Canada. 2012. *Truth and Reconciliation Commission of Canada Interim Report*. Winnipeg, Manitoba.

Tsing, Anna Lowenhaupt. 2013. "Critical Description after Progress: Recognizing Diversity in Damaged Times." Paper presented at the Critical Thinkers in Religion, Law, and Social Theory Conference, University of Ottawa, January 31.

———. 2014. "Blasted Landscapes (and the Gentle Arts of Mushroom Picking)." In *The Multispecies Salon*. Edited by Eben Kirksey. Durham: Duke University Press.

———. 2015. *The Mushroom at the End of the World: On the Possibility of Life in Capitalist Ruins*. Princeton: Princeton University Press.

Tuana, Nancy. 2008. "Viscous Porosity: Witnessing Katrina." In *Material Feminisms*. Edited by Stacy Alaimo and Susan Hekman. Bloomington: Indiana University Press.

Turner, Dale. 2006. *This Is Not a Peace Pipe: Towards a Critical Indigenous Philosophy*. Toronto: University of Toronto Press.

Valaskakis, Gail Guthrie. 2005. *Indian Country: Essays on Contemporary Native Culture*. Aboriginal Studies Series. Waterloo, Ontario: Wilfrid Laurier University Press.

Vazquez-Pacheco, Robert. Interview by Sarah Schulman, interview #002, December 14, 2002, transcript. ACT UP Oral History Project, New York.

Walia, Harsha. 2013. *Undoing Border Imperialism*. Oakland, Calif.: AK Press.

Warner, Michael. 1993. *Fear of a Queer Planet: Queer Politics and Social Theory*. Minneapolis: University of Minnesota Press.

———. 2000. *The Trouble with Normal: Sex, Politics, and the Ethics of Queer Life*. Cambridge, Mass.: Harvard University Press.

Weiss, Gail. 1999. *Body Images: Embodiment as Intercorporeality*. New York: Routledge.

Weheliye, Alexander G. 2014. *Habeas Viscus: Racializing Assemblages, Biopolitics, and Black Feminist Theories of the Human*. Durham: Duke University Press.

Wiegman, Robyn, and Elizabeth A. Wilson. 2015. "Introduction: Antinormativity's Queer Conventions." *Differences* 26, no. 1:1–25. doi:10.1215/10407391-2880582.

Wolfe, Maxine. Interview by Jim Hubbard, interview #043, February 19, 2004, transcript. ACT UP Oral History Project, New York.

Wolfe, Patrick. 2006. "Settler Colonialism and the Elimination of the Native." *Journal of Genocide Research* 8, no. 4:387–409. doi:10.1080/14623520601056240.

Yong, Ed. 2011. "Coincidental Killers." *Aeon Magazine.* June 3, http://aeon.co/maga
   zine/science/bacteria-kill-us-by-accident/.
———. 2015. "When Microbes Kill Us, It's Often by Accident." *Aeon Magazine.*
Young, Iris Marion. 2006. "Responsibility and Global Justice: A Social Connection
   Model." *Social Philosophy and Policy* 23, no. 1:102–30.
Zimmer, Carl. 2011. *A Planet of Viruses.* Chicago: University of Chicago Press.

# Index

**ALEXIS SHOTWELL** is associate professor at Carleton University in Ottawa, Ontario, on unceded and unsurrendered Algonquin territory. She is the author of *Knowing Otherwise: Race, Gender, and Implicit Understanding* and has published in the journals *Signs, Hypatia, International Journal of Feminist Approaches to Bioethics,* and *Sociological Theory,* as well as in various edited collections. She is currently conducting research funded by a Social Science and Humanities Council of Canada five-year Insight Grant on the history of AIDS activism in the Canadian context.